SAPPHIRE FROM THE LAND OF ISRAEL

A New Light on the Weekly Torah Portion

From the Writings of

Rabbi Abraham Isaac HaKohen Kook

Rabbi Chanan Morrison

Sapphire from the Land of Israel

A New Light on the Weekly Torah Portion

From the Writings of Rabbi Abraham Isaac HaKohen Kook

First Edition.

ISBN: 1490909362
ISBN-13: 978-1490909363

"They saw a vision of the God of Israel; and under His feet was like a brick of sapphire, like the essence of a clear sky." (Ex. 24:10)

"I saw a vision: in the sky over the heads of the cherubim, there was something like sapphire stone, like the appearance of a throne, which appeared over them." (Ezekiel 10:1)

CONTENTS

שמות – The Book of Exodus

ויקרא – The Book of Leviticus

במדבר – The Book of Numbers

דברים – The Book of Deuteronomy

9

PREFACE

"Our master [Rav Kook] does not deal with the exegesis or the uncovering of hidden meanings in verses. He rarely takes the verses out of their simple *peshat* meaning. Nonetheless, they are revealed to the reader as tremendous novelties. The innovation here is not in the elucidation of the verse per se, but in the light that he pours over them." (Rabbi Hillel Zeitlin, *Sifran shel Yechidim*, p. 237)

With the exception of an early book of sermons entitled *Midbar Shur*, Rabbi Abraham Isaac HaKohen Kook (1865-1935) did not write any books on Biblical exegesis or *parshanut*. Most of his non-Halachic works are collections of short essays which were selected and organized from Rav Kook's *pinkasim* (notebooks which he used to record his thoughts and insights). The entries in the *pinkasim* usually conclude with one or more quotes from the Bible.

To the casual reader, it might appear that these closing quotes are an afterthought, some sort of literary decoration. Their connection to the topic is often not obvious. But, as Rabbi Zeitlin noted, Rav Kook's writings reveal an innovative *parshanut*; and if the reader makes the effort to uncover the connection between the verses and the topic of the essay, he will be rewarded with a brilliant new understanding of the verse. It then becomes apparent that these quotes are not just a literary device. In fact, they are the *source* which led Rav Kook, after meditating on the verse, to the creative insight he developed in the essay.

The following story appears in Rabbi Simcha Raz's biography of Rav Kook, *Malachim Kivnei Adam*.[1] Rabbi Zalaznik, dean of the Eitz Chaim yeshivah, described the profound impression that an unscheduled visit at Rav Kook's residence in Jerusalem made upon him. I believe that this incident was in fact an eye-witness account of the creative process through which Rav Kook studied Torah texts and captured these brilliant flashes of insight.

> It was a Friday afternoon, a few hours before the Sabbath. Everyone was hurrying home. An urgent telegram arrived from the yeshivah's American office regarding a certain inheritance. It was necessary to respond right away, and the telegram also required the stamp of the Chief Rabbi, Rav Kook. Due to the urgency and importance of the matter, I needed to take care of it personally.
>
> I quickly made my way to Rav Kook's house in order to obtain his authorization and signature. After I arrived at his home, I approached the door to the small room where the Rav would study and write. I did not knock right away, but bent my ear to listen at

---

[1] Rabbi Moshe Lichtman produced an English translation, entitled *Angel Among Men* (Jerusalem: Kol Mevaser, 2003).

the door. Perhaps the rabbi was studying Torah, and it would be improper to interrupt his learning.

I heard sounds of deep emotion from inside the room. I continued to listen at the door. I realized that the Rav was studying a chapter from the Bible with great concentration, and then repeating the verses with greater intensity. Suddenly his voice rose, and he reread the verse with even greater emotion. It was as if the words of the prophet had become revealed to him in some new insight. He progressed to the following verse, and the scene repeated itself. The study session continued on in this fashion.

I grew up in Jerusalem among great scholars and God-fearing *tzaddikim*, holy and righteous men. I observed them study Torah, and I listened to them pray. But I have never witnessed a study of Tanach [Bible] such as that. This was not study, but prayer; and not ordinary prayer, but a true "service of the heart." This is how the holiest *tzaddikim* pray at times of heightened spiritual awareness, when overwhelmed with love and awe of God.

I stood, deeply moved by what I heard, and waited. Even after this study/prayer session was over, I remained standing, chained to my spot, until my inner soul calmed down. Only then did I dare knock lightly on the door. When I entered the room, the Rav's face was still full of emotion; but he greeted me warmly, as was his custom. He listened to my request, and immediately wrote and signed the letter, adding his blessing that God would assist and that the matter would reach a successful conclusion. (*Malachim Kivnei Adam*, p. 252)

* * * *

I had a difficult time deciding on a title for this book. For my first collection of essays on Rav Kook's thought, I based the title, *Gold from the Land of Israel,* on a Midrash which compares *Torat Eretz Yisrael*, the special Torah of the Land of Israel, to precious gold. As this book is also a collection of essays organized according to the weekly Torah reading (the *parashah*), I sought an appropriate title which would indicate that it is a continuation of that previous work.

The Torah briefly describes a prophetic vision that Moses and the elders of Israel experienced at Mount Sinai: an image of God's Heavenly throne, formed from transparent sapphire stone (Ex. 24:10). The Midrash teaches that the two stone tablets (*luchot*) which Moses brought down from Sinai were also hewed from sapphire, with the gemstone's deep blue color evoking the heavens and God's throne. I felt that the metaphor of this beautiful, otherworldly stone from Sinai nicely suited this collection of Torah wisdom, and thus settled on the title, *Sapphire from the Land of Israel.*

I hope this volume will help generate interest in Rav Kook's philosophy and writings, and the reader will be inspired to study them in their original poetic Hebrew.

Chanan Morrison
Mitzpe Yericho, Israel
Av 5773/July 2013
RavKookTorah.org

Common Abbreviations

Gen. – Genesis

Ex. – Exodus

Lev. – Leviticus

Num. – Numbers

Deut. – Deuteronomy

Ps. – Psalms

Ecc. – Ecclesiastes

BREISHIT: THE HIDDEN LIGHT OF CREATION[2]

The *Ohr Ha-Ganuz*

The very first act of Creation, as recorded in the Book of Genesis, was the creation of light. "And God said: There shall be light" (Gen. 1:3). What kind of light was this?

It cannot be the light that we are familiar with, the light emanating from the sun and the stars. These heavenly bodies were created much later, on the fourth day of Creation. The Sages called this primordial light *"Ohr Ha-Ganuz,"* "the Hidden Light." Too pure for the current state of the universe, God concealed it for a future, more deserving world.

What is the nature of this special illumination introduced at the beginning of Creation?

The Sages taught (*Shemot Rabbah* 15:22) that certain topics mentioned cryptically in the Torah were later elucidated by David in the book of Psalms. For example, Psalm 104 speaks poetically of the creation of the heavens:

> [God] wrapped Himself in light like a garment and spread out the heavens like a curtain. (104:3)

---

[2] Adapted from *Midbar Shur*, pp. 95-96.

In this instance, however, it is difficult to claim that the verse in Psalms explains the Torah's account; in fact, it contradicts it. The Torah states that God created light after creating heaven and earth (Gen. 1:1-3). In Psalms, however, the order is reversed: God first created the light, and only afterward the heavens.

Chomer and Tzurah

The philosophers[3] distinguished between *chomer*, matter, and *tzurah*, the form or function of an object. For example, wood is a raw material (*chomer*) that may be used to produce many different functional objects. Once it is designated for use as a table, the wood also has *tzurah*, form, having acquired a particular purpose.

At the very beginning of Creation, there was only *chomer*. God created numerous elements, but they were without *tzurah*. They lacked function and purpose. This state of disorder and dissonance is referred to as darkness – "darkness on the surface of the depths" (Gen. 1:2). The Torah calls this unstable primeval stage *Tohu* and *Bohu*, indicating that it was chaotic and empty of form.

Then God created the *Ohr Ha-Ganuz*. This special light played a critical role in Creation. Just as regular light allows us to see and relate to our surroundings, the Hidden Light enabled the different elements of creation to interact with one another. It dispelled the initial state of darkness, when all objects were isolated and

---

[3] The distinction between form and matter is a fundamental aspect of the religious philosophy of Rabbi Judah Loew ben Bezalel (the "Maharal of Prague," 1520-1609), and is based on Aristotle's theory of hylomorphism.

disconnected from one another.

To use the terminology of the philosophers, the illumination created on the first day of Creation stamped a functional *tzurah* on the material *chomer*. Through this special light, the universe's myriad objects acquired purpose and function and were able to work together towards a common goal.

To Wear Light

The Midrash (*Breishit Rabbah* 3:4) elucidates the verse in Psalms, explaining that "God wrapped Himself in light like a garment and illuminated the splendor of His glory from one end of the world to the other." What does it mean that "God wore light"?

This phrase indicates that the light took on God's qualities of oneness and unity, just as a garment takes on the shape of the one wearing it. When "God wrapped Himself in light," this means that He introduced an underlying unity into all aspects of creation, "from one end of the world to the other."

In summary: the description in Psalms does not contradict the account in Genesis. At first, God created heaven and earth in an isolated state, as *chomer* without form and purpose. This was the unstable state of *Tohu* and *Bohu* described in Genesis, when the diverse elements of creation existed in chaotic darkness, lacking an underlying unity.

Then God said, "There shall be light," creating the special *Ohr Ha-Ganuz*, the Hidden Light with which He bound the matter together with a common purpose. God "wrapped Himself in the light," thereby giving the light His trait of oneness and making it a unifying force. After creating this unifying light, God "spread out the heavens" and stabilized the universe. The continuation of the psalm describes the stability of the world after the creation of light: "He founded the earth on its foundations, so that it will never falter" (104:5).

BREISHIT: CAIN'S OFFERING[4]

God did not turn to Cain and his offering; Cain became enraged and his face fell. (Gen. 4:5)

In the story of the world's first murder, it was God's decision not to accept Cain's offering which triggered Cain's anger and jealousy, ultimately leading to his murder of Abel.

Why did God refuse to accept Cain's offering? What was wrong with it?

The Cainite Philosophy

Rav Kook suggested that the very fact that Cain, soon after this incident, would kill his own brother indicates that terrible evil was already lurking in Cain's soul. The potential to murder existed within Cain's personality at the very hour that he offered his crops to God.

Bringing an offering to God under these circumstances is an abomination. It only serves to amplify the power of evil. The approach exemplified by Cain is one in which a person does not seek to purge himself from evil and immorality; rather, he covers up inner evil with an outward appearance of holiness. This

---

[4] Adapted from *Orot*, pp. 32-34.

approach provides evil with strength and influence within a framework of holiness.

This is the core philosophy of paganism and heresy. They do not aspire to refine human desires and sanctify life. They reject God's great plan to elevate the world through the formation of Israel as a holy people, a source of moral and spiritual inspiration for all humanity.

But in its inner soul, heresy knows that God rejects it and its path. Like Cain, its face falls and rage smolders within. At every opportunity, the violent hand of a murderer is revealed.

Only by Toil

The world must recognize that one cannot gain admission to Paradise by virtue of a pronouncement of faith, while evil and cruelty permeate every chamber of one's heart. The implication of such a theology is that there is no need for introspection, moral reckoning, character refinement, and spiritual growth.

This darkness, however, will not continue forever. Humanity will realize that its energies need to be directed toward purifying the spirit. The method for elevating the nations has been formulated and prepared by God: the establishment of one nation in the world, a kingdom of priests and a holy nation. The Jewish people are a sign that Divine light penetrates the lives of nations.

Then it will become clear that holiness is not some cheap trinket that can be snatched by tainted hands. It is a treasure that is acquired through tenacious toil and self-sacrifice, and through the merit of generations who lovingly upheld this sacred charge. Heresy's mask of hypocrisy will be exposed. Its path of appeasing evil will be recognized as a sham, an ideology that fools the eye and contaminates the soul.

They will no longer harm nor destroy on My holy mountain, for the earth will be full of knowledge of God. (Isaiah 11:9)

BREISHIT: THE TITANS, MEN OF RENOWN[5]

The *Nephilim*

Immediately before the story of Noah and a corrupted world, the Torah makes a passing mention of the *Nephilim*, powerful giants who lived at that time.

> The *Nephilim* were on the earth in those days.... They were the mightiest ones ever, men of renown. (Gen. 6:4)

Who were these titans? Why does the Torah call them *Nephilim*?

The Midrash explains that they were called *Nephilim* because they fell (*naphlu*) and brought about the world's downfall (*nephilah*). These giants were the catalysts for society's great moral collapse.

Studying Foreign Languages

In 1906, fifteen-year-old Tzvi Yehuda Kook, Rav Kook's son, asked his father whether he should devote time to learning other languages. In his response, Rav Kook analyzed the relative

---

[5] Adapted from *Igrot HaRe'iyah* vol. I, pp. 29-30.

importance of expertise in languages and rhetoric:

> We should aspire to help others, both our own people and all of humanity, as much as possible. Certainly, our influence will increase as we gain competence in various languages and speaking styles.... But if perfecting these skills comes at the expense of analytic study, then this will reduce the true intellectual content of one's contribution to the world.

Some people mistake proficiency in many languages for intellectual greatness. This is not the case. Linguistic talent is merely a tool. Genuine perceptiveness and intellectual insight are a function of how well one has established the foundations of one's own inner integrity.

To demonstrate his point, Rav Kook noted that the great *Nephilim* who brought about the world's moral collapse were *"anshei shem."* Usually translated as "men of renown," this phrase literally means "men of names" or "men of words." They were great leaders, skilled in the arts of persuasion and rhetoric. But their talents were an empty shell, devoid of inner content. On the contrary, they used their eloquence for unscrupulous purposes.

It is interesting to contrast the *Nephilim* and their highly developed oratorical skills with the individual responsible for bringing the Torah's teachings to the world, Moses. The highest level of prophecy was transmitted through a man who testified about himself that he was not a man of words, but "heavy of mouth and heavy of tongue" (Ex. 4:10). Moses was not talented in rhetoric and lacked confidence in his communication skills.

Nonetheless, his moral impact on the world is unparalleled in the history of humanity.

Tools of War

In these pre-Messianic times, Rav Kook wrote, when we must wage battle against ideological foes who attack all that is holy to us, we should look to King David for inspiration. David was untrained in the art of war and refused to wear the heavy armor that King Saul presented to him. Rather, he gathered five smooth stones from a stream. The five stones are a metaphor: David utilized the teachings of the Five Books of Moses to wage battle against Goliath and his blasphemy.

We should emulate David and not invest too much time and effort acquiring the tools of ideological warfare. Like the young shepherd who took up a simple slingshot in his fight against Goliath, we should not totally eschew the implements of rhetoric, but realize that David's victory over the blasphemous Philistine was achieved due to the purity of his charge, "in the name of the Lord of hosts, the God of the armies of Israel" (I Samuel 17:45).

Eloquence and elocution are but tools. They may be used for nefarious purposes, like the corrupt *Nephilim*, or for conquering evil, like David. Ultimately, it is not the medium but the message that counts.

NOAH: GATHERING WITHIN THE ARK[6]

Why an Ark?

Why was it necessary for Noah to build an ark to save his family from the Flood's destruction? Could God not have arranged an easier way to rescue him?

The Midrash raises this question, explaining that the 120 years that Noah worked constructing the enormous boat were meant to provide the people of his generation with an opportunity to repent.

Rebuilding the World

Eighteenth-century scholar Rabbi Moshe Chaim Luzzatto offered an alternative explanation to that of the Midrash. He wrote that Noah needed to spend a year living inside the ark in order to prepare the foundations of a new world. Outside the ark, where flood waters swept away the world's evil, nothing could survive. Inside the ark, the inner integrity of the world was reestablished under Noah's direction. The soul of this great *tzaddik* encompassed all the souls of the world. As Noah fed and looked after the animals in his care, he renewed the world on the basis of

---

[6] Adapted from *Mussar Avicha*, pp. 33-39.

goodness and kindness.

A similar preparatory stage of spiritual renewal took place many generations later. Before the revelation of the Zohar, Rabbi Shimon bar Yochai spent thirteen years hiding in a cave. He needed this period of seclusion to purify and prepare himself for the Zohar's inner light (*Adir Bamarom* 7).

The Path of Personal Growth

This same method, Rav Kook wrote, is necessary for our own moral and spiritual growth. Change is difficult. It is not easy to correct old habits and patterns of thought. As human beings, we become accustomed to looking at life in terms of fulfilling our material needs, which can lead us to drift unthinkingly into self-centered pursuit of honor and physical pleasures.

The path to repairing one's deeds and refining one's character has two aspects. The first step is cognitive. We must fully understand each trait and its characteristics, and we must learn the proper time and place for their expression. Therefore our first request in the daily *Amidah* prayer is that God "grant us knowledge, understanding, and insight."

Theoretical knowledge, however, is not enough. After acquiring this wisdom, we must accustom our will to whole-heartedly conform to this new path. We must strive to quiet our heart's desires and distance ourselves from all that leads to a confused state of mind – a state that undermines the very foundations of character-building. We need to acquire a resolute and steadfast outlook and fortify our traits so that we will be able to retain our purity and holiness even when occupied in worldly matters.

A Private Ark

Those who succeed in directing their mind and inner will in this fashion will gain control of all aspects of their lives. Those who have not carefully thought out their path, however, will lack control of their actions and desires. Such individuals need to withdraw the powers of the soul, their strengths and talents, and gather them in, like lines radiating outward that are pulled back to their focal point.

This undertaking is similar to Noah's confinement within the ark. It can be a bitter and heavy burden to constrain the soul's powers in such a way, since the soul naturally seeks independence and freedom. Even confinement in the body is a terrible prison for the soul; all the more so to be constrained in such a fashion.

Converging toward the nucleus of one's mind and inner will is not a pleasant task. One may feel pained and even depressed from the constraints of this path of repair. But after the soul's forces have become accustomed to conducting themselves properly, they may be allowed to return to their natural state. Then all aspects of one's personality will be proper vessels for fulfilling God's will, and one's powers may be released to rule over the body once more, now following the dictates of the intellect.

This path of personal renewal parallels the world's renewal in the time of Noah. The months spent in the ark were a preparatory period of converging and gathering powers under the direction of the *tzaddik*. But when the punishing waters receded and the inhabitable dry land appeared, the ark's inhabitants could be freed from their confinement. So too, as character traits are repaired and perfected, they may be released once again.

Testing the Waters

During the period of confinement, one needs to 'test the waters' – to measure whether one's powers are ready to be set free. This stage corresponds to Noah's sending out the raven and the dove. One tests one's traits in matters that do not involve danger, just as Noah utilized birds – creatures that can fly and thus were not endangered by the flood waters. When Noah realized that the world's repair was not yet complete, he drew them back into the ark.

The Divine command, "Leave the ark!" came only when the land was completely dry. Then it was time to serve God in an unhindered manner, for the active dissemination of Torah and acts of kindness requires an unfettered soul, full of strength and courage.

NOAH: THE BEAUTY OF GREECE[7]

After the Flood, Noah blessed his son Yefeth:

> May God expand Yefeth, and may he dwell in the tents of Shem. (Gen. 9:27)

What does this blessing mean? Why should Yefeth live in Shem's tents?

The Sages noted that Yefeth was the ancestor of ancient Greece. As such, Yefeth's blessing relates to the special accomplishments of the Greeks, especially in the realm of the arts and aesthetics.[8] As the Talmud states in *Megillah* 9b: "May the beauty of Yefeth reside in the tents of Shem."

The blessing links Yefeth and Shem together through the cultures of their descendants, Greece and Israel. Yet the relationship between these two nations was never simple. We know from the story of Chanukah that these two civilizations clashed violently during the Second Temple period. How then can the beauty of Greek culture reside harmoniously in the tents of Israel?

---

[7] Adapted from *Mo'adei HaRe'yah*, pp. 182-184.
[8] The name *Yefeth* is related to the Hebrew word *"yofi,"* meaning "beauty."

Studying Greek Wisdom

On the one hand, the Sages placed no explicit prohibition against studying Greek philosophy. They were content to give general guidance, such as Rabbi Yishmael's instruction to his nephew: "Find an hour that is neither day nor night, and study Greek wisdom at that time" (*Menachot* 99b).

Regarding the education of youth, however, the Sages were more circumspect. They feared that the outward appeal and beauty of Greek wisdom would lure the next generation away from their fathers' faith. Thus they forcefully declared: "Cursed be the one who teaches his son Greek wisdom" (*Baba Kama* 82b). The language of this decree specifically forbids *teaching* Greek wisdom. In other words, it is permitted to study it, but not to teach it. Young students must first acquire a solid basis in Torah, and only then will they be able to discern the difference between the Torah of Israel and the philosophy of Greece.

Style versus Content

We find that the Talmud makes a second distinction regarding Greek culture. "Greek language is one thing, but Greek wisdom is another" (*Baba Kama* 83a). The intent of this statement is to differentiate between style and content.

Greek wisdom, as a philosophy and an outlook on life, profoundly detracts from the sacred and defiles the holy. The Greek language, on the other hand, poses no challenge of ideas and beliefs. Greek is a rich and sophisticated language, and is an appropriate vehicle through which to express our thoughts and ideas. The external language does not influence or harm the inner content.

We have no need to borrow from the content of foreign cultures when our own traditions are so rich and stimulating, ennobling both the individual and society as a whole. But we may adopt from other peoples that which adds external beauty and elegance. Even after the culture clash with Hellenism, the Sages still taught that it is fitting to adopt stylistic enhancements – "May the beauty of Yefeth reside in the tents of Shem."

This approach is not limited to ancient Greece, but is true for all foreign cultures. It is not inappropriate for us to utilize the innovations and talents of other nations. After all, the focus of the Jewish people is primarily on inner matters, on ethical and spiritual advancement. Even for the construction of the holy Temple, we find that King Solomon turned to Hiram, the king of Tyre, for his workers' expertise in cutting down and preparing the wood, "for we have none among us who knows how to hew timber like the Zidonians" (I Kings 5:20). Solomon used artisans from other nations to chop the wood and quarry the large stones for the Temple. But after these external preparations, it was the Jewish people who secured the Sanctuary's inner holiness.

LECH LECHA: GREAT LIKE THE STARS[9]

Stars and Sand

When Abraham complained to God that he was childless, God promised that his children would be as numerous as the stars in the sky:

> God took him outside and said, "Look at the sky, and count the stars if you can! So will be your descendants." (Gen. 15:5)

On another occasion, God promised Abraham that his children would be like "the sand on the seashore" (Gen. 22:17). Why are the Jewish people compared to both stars and grains of sand?

Greatness at Mount Sinai

The Sages took note that God's promise uses the uncommon word "כֹּה" – "So [כֹּה] will be your descendants." They explained that this word alludes to the Jewish people's future greatness at Mount Sinai, where the word "כֹּה" also appears: "So [כֹּה] shall you

---

[9] Adapted from *Midbar Shur*, pp. 110-121.

say to the House of Jacob" (Ex. 19:3). What does the state of the Jewish people at Mount Sinai have to do with being likened to stars?

In general, we need to understand the metaphor of the star. The psalmist wrote that God gave each star a name (Ps. 147:4). Why do stars need names?

Personal and Collective Missions

What is in a name? A name reflects an entity's inner essence. It defines the nature of its existence and indicates its fundamental purpose. Stars are wonderful, powerful creations. Each star has a unique function for which it was created, and each star has a unique name corresponding to its special purpose.

The comparison of Abraham's descendants to stars indicates the importance and greatness of every individual member of the Jewish people. Every soul is a universe unto itself, as the Sages wrote: "One who saves a single soul of Israel, it is as if he has saved an entire world" (*Sanhedrin* 37a).

But the Jewish people also have a collective mission, as indicated by their comparison to sand. A single grain of sand is of no particular consequence; but together, these grains of sand form a border against the ocean, establishing dry land and enabling life to exist. Israel's collective purpose is to bring about the world's spiritual advance, as it says, "This people I have created for Me [so that] they will proclaim My praise" (Isaiah 43:21).

It is logical for God to first establish the collective mission of the Jewish people, and only afterwards adjoin their individual goals. Thus, upon leaving Egypt, Israel was formed into a people with a unique collective purpose. This collective mission is an integral part of their very essence, regardless of any individual merits. The collective aspect of the Jewish people was valid even though the Israelites lacked personal merits and good deeds when they left Egypt, as it says, "I have made you [Israel] numerous like the plants of the field, and you have increased and grown... yet you were naked and bare" (Ezekiel 16:7).

Like the Stars

The prominence of the stars, on the other hand, is indicative of the special mission of each individual. This metaphor refers to the potential for greatness that each member of the Jewish people acquired at Mount Sinai.

These special goals are a function of each individual's efforts, deeds, and Torah study. This level is based on the revelation of Torah and mitzvot at Mount Sinai. The Midrash teaches that when Israel promised to obey the laws of the Torah, the angels tied two crowns to the head of every Jew. These spiritual crowns reflected the greatness of each individual; every Jew was a prince, bearing his own unique crown of holiness.

LECH LECHA: THE INNER WILL OF THE UNIVERSE[10]

Abraham, the Sages noted, was the first person in history to address God as "My Master" (Gen. 15:8). What makes this event so noteworthy?

Completing the Master's Work

We must first understand the essence of the servant-master relationship. The servant fulfills the wishes of his master by completing the master's work. The servant is an extension of his master, his *shaliach* or agent. When the servant acts, it is as if the master has acted.

Before Abraham, people acknowledged the existence of a Prime Mover, an infinite Being Who created the universe. But they could not fathom how a truly perfect Being would be concerned with an imperfect and lowly world such as ours. Why would God, transcendent beyond all things, be involved in the smallest details of the workings of the universe?

They failed to recognize that an integral aspect of creation – its inner core – is that the universe aspires to perfect itself. This underlying aspiration for perfection and the world's gradual moral

---

[10] Adapted from *Ein Eyah* vol. I, p. 33 on *Berachot* 7b (I:77).

progression is by plan and purpose; thus Divine providence governs all moral paths in the world, even the smallest and least significant.

The central conduit for the universe's pursuit of perfection is mankind's efforts to elevate its deeds, traits, and thoughts. We have free will to choose good or evil. And that which leads us to choose good over evil is God's will stamped in creation, resulting in the universe's inner aspiration to perfection.

By declaring God as his Master, Abraham publicly proclaimed that God governs the world and desires its moral perfection. God wills that we should be His agents in bringing about the world's gradual advancement. As we work toward our own personal spiritual growth, we promote the work of our Master – the spiritual elevation of the entire universe.

VAYEIRA: PREPARING FOR THE AKEIDAH[11]

The Torah records a peculiar exchange that took place immediately prior to the *Akeidah*, the Binding of Isaac. Before commanding Abraham to offer up his beloved son Isaac, God called out to Abraham, "Abraham!"

And Abraham responded, "Here I am" (Gen. 22:1).

Why did God call out to Abraham by name? And what was Abraham's response, "Here I am"? Did Abraham think that God did not know where he was? What was the purpose of this brief exchange?

Personal Aspirations

Truly great individuals, who devote their lives working for the benefit the community – or the nation, or all of humanity – may identify with the needs of the community to such an extent that they neglect their own private lives and aspirations. For example, after the Sin of the Golden Calf, God made Moses a remarkable offer. God suggested that the Jewish people be replaced by Moses' descendants. Moses, however, immediately rejected this opportunity for self-advancement at the expense of the people. "Please forgive their sin," Moses responded. "And if not, then

---

[11] Adapted from *Olat Re'iyah* vol. I, p. 85.

erase me from Your book which You have written" (Ex. 32:32).

Abraham and Sarah concentrated all of their energies in promoting belief in one God. They "made souls in Haran," converting people to monotheism. They set up an *eshel*, a rest station in Beersheba, to spread their message to travelers. They ran a seminary with hundreds of students, and they opened up their home to all. Abraham pleaded for the sake of the wicked people of Sodom, even at the risk of displeasing God. With all of this communal activity, how much time and energy did Abraham and Sarah have left to attend to their own personal needs?

A name is a reflection of one's individual nature and personality. When God calls a person by name, this Divine summons highlights one's individual essence. In order for the trial of the *Akeidah* to be a true test of Abraham's free choice, it was necessary for Abraham to be fully cognizant of his own private needs and aspirations. God called out "Abraham!" – and Abraham immediately became profoundly aware of his innermost desires and goals.

"Hineini"

Abraham responded to God's call, saying, "*Hineini*" – "I am here." I am here, inside myself. I have concentrated myself inwards, to fully experience all of my private needs, wants, and aspirations – including the deep-felt desire, answered miraculously in old age, of fathering a son. A son worthy of continuing the unique spiritual path his father had forged.

Fully aware of his own personal aspirations, Abraham was ready for the test of the *Akeidah*.

VAYEIRA: THE JOURNEY TO MOUNT MORIAH[12]

> On the third day Abraham lifted his eyes, and saw the
> place from afar. (Gen. 22:4)

Following God's command, Abraham traveled toward Mount
Moriah for three days. What happened during this long journey,
the prelude to the *Akeidah*? What was Abraham – a loving father,
soon to offer up his only son to God – thinking about? What were
his feelings and emotions?

In general, the Torah's narrative style is terse. The text focuses
on actions, rarely describing inner thoughts and emotions.
Nevertheless, a careful reading of the text reveals much about the
manner in which Abraham undertook this trial.

The Greatest Challenge of the *Akeidah*

God did not initially tell Abraham where the *Akeidah* would take
place. The Divine command was deliberately vague. "Bring him
there as an offering, on one of the mountains that I will tell you"
(Gen. 22:2). According to Rav Kook, this minor detail in fact
comprises the most challenging and most remarkable aspect of the
test.

---

12 Adapted from *Olat Re'iyah* vol. I, pp. 86–87.

It would not be sufficient for Abraham merely to carry out the technical aspects of the *Akeidah*. If Abraham had gone through the outward motions – preparing the wood and the knife, bringing the fire and his son – and yet was troubled by inner fears and doubts, he would have failed the test.

Abraham needed to be prepared to receive an additional prophecy. Only after three days would God reveal to him the exact location of the *Akeidah*. And that was the catch. Only one who is at peace with himself, filled with joy and happiness, is a fitting vessel for prophecy. In order to complete the test, Abraham would need incredible reserves of courage and spiritual fortitude so that he would be able to receive prophecy.[13] If Abraham was disturbed by misgivings and doubts, if his faith was shaken, he would not merit receiving God's instructions as to where to offer up Isaac. Without rock-solid faith and inner joy in his mission, Abraham would never make it to Mount Moriah.

Energetic yet Serene

In fact, the text hints at Abraham's remarkable inner strength and calm determination as he readied himself to fulfill God's command.

"Abraham woke up early in the morning." Abraham had been called to sacrifice his beloved son – how could he sleep? A man of lesser faith would doubtlessly have been unable to sleep, troubled over what was expected of him. But no feelings of depression or anxiety disturbed the sleep of this *tzaddik*. He awoke at his usual

---

[13] A prophet cannot attain prophecy "when sad or depressed, but only when in a state of joy" (Maimonides, *Yesodei HaTorah* 7:4).

hour, eager to perform God's will with the swiftness of a deer and the strength of a lion.

"He saddled his donkey." Abraham's every move was deliberate and precise. His first priority was to arrange the fastest and most-assured means of transportation to fulfill his mission. Only afterwards did he attend to other, less essential preparations for the journey.

"He split wood for the offering." Abraham could have waited until later to find wood, or he could have brought the wood and only later split it into smaller pieces. But a profound love of God, beyond ordinary measure, burned so fiercely in his heart that he made sure to carefully prepare every detail beforehand.

"And he rose" – not bowed and beaten, but proud and tall, full of strength and vitality – "and traveled to the place that God had told him." All of Abraham's actions were focused on reaching the sought-after destination and fulfilling God's word. Everything else, whether of a personal or social nature, became inconsequential compared to his soul's intense yearning to carry out the Divine command.

"On the third day." What happened during those three days of traveling? The Torah does not say. The experiences of that spiritual journey cannot be expressed in words. Those lofty events cannot be described by the limited scope of human language.

"Abraham lifted his eyes and *saw* the place from afar." What was to be an orally transmitted prophecy – "on one of the mountains that I will *tell* you" – was in fact a prophetic vision. Abraham's soul experienced a spiritual elevation so great that his senses became united. The senses of hearing and sight, together with his faculty of prophetic insight, were combined as one.

"Abraham lifted his eyes," and his physical eyes became receptors for prophetic vision.

Abraham had passed the most extraordinary aspect of the trial. He had reached Mount Moriah, where the *Akeidah* would take place.

VAYEIRA: ABRAHAM'S RETURN FROM THE AKEIDAH[14]

The *Akeidah*, the Binding of Isaac, was over. Abraham had passed this extraordinary test. He descended from the heights of Mount Moriah – physically and spiritually. The Torah concludes the narrative with a description of Abraham's return to the world:

> Abraham returned to his young men; and they rose
> and went together to Beersheba. And Abraham lived
> in Beersheba. (Gen. 22:19)

Why does the Torah mention that Abraham rejoined the young men he had left behind with the donkey? And why the emphasis on his return to Beersheba and his settling there?

Rejoining the World

The powerful experience of the *Akeidah* could have caused Abraham to disengage from the world and its mundane ways. The extraordinary spiritual encounter on Mount Moriah might have led him to forgo the battle against ignorance and idolatry in the world and withdraw to live a secluded life dedicated to his private service

---

[14] Adapted from *Olat Re'iyah* vol. I, pp. 96-97.

of God.

However, this did not happen. Every word in the text emphasizes the extent of Abraham's return to society after the *Akeidah*.

"Abraham returned to his young men." Abraham did not relinquish his mission of influencing and educating others. Before ascending Mount Moriah, Abraham had instructed the young men to stay behind. They were not ready for this supreme spiritual ascent. They needed to stay with the donkey – in Hebrew, the *chamor* – for they were not ready to sever all ties with their "*chomer*," their materialistic life.

But now Abraham returned to them. He descended to their level in order to enlighten and elevate them.

"They rose and went together to Beersheba." They rose – with elevated spirits, in an atmosphere of purity and holiness. And the most remarkable aspect of Abraham's return was that, despite everything that had taken place at the heights of Mount Moriah, Abraham and the young men were able to proceed *together* – united in purpose and plan of action – to Beersheba.

Beersheba

What is the significance of their journey to Beersheba?

The name "Beersheba" has two meanings. It means "Well of Oath" and "Well of Seven." An oath is a pledge to take action. When we take an oath, we vow that our vision will not remain just a theoretical ideal; we promise to translate our beliefs into action.

The number *seven* signifies completion of the natural world. It took seven days to finish creating the universe. Beersheba is thus not just a location. It is a metaphor for Abraham's commitment to apply his convictions and ideals in practice.

"Abraham lived in Beersheba." Abraham stayed in Beersheba, continuing his outreach activities there. His name Abraham – meaning "father of many nations" – was particularly appropriate in Beersheba. There he set up his *eshel*, an inn that brought wayfarers to recognize God's providence and to "call in the name of God, the Eternal Lord" (Gen. 21:33).

Where was Isaac?

While the Torah describes Abraham's return, it is mysteriously silent about Isaac. What happened to Isaac after the *Akeidah*?

Concealed behind Abraham's public works was a hidden ray of light. This light was Isaac's unique trait of *mesirut nefesh*, the quality of total devotion and self-sacrifice that he had demonstrated at the *Akeidah*.

While Abraham's activities were directed towards all peoples, Isaac passed on this legacy of *mesirut nefesh* to his descendants, a spiritual gift to the Jewish people for all generations.

CHAYEI SARAH: GUARDING THE INNER CHILD[15]

The Torah counts the years of Sarah's long life: "A hundred years and twenty years and seven years; these were the years of Sarah's life" (Gen. 23:1). Noting the verse's wordiness, the Sages commented that throughout all the years of her life – whether at age seven, twenty, or a hundred – Sarah retained the same goodness, the same purity, and the same youthful innocence.

Despite her long years of barrenness, despite twice being kidnapped as she accompanied her husband Abraham on his many journeys, Sarah did not become hard and cynical. Their son was named Isaac – יִצְחָק, "he will laugh" – due to Abraham's feelings of wonderment and Sarah's amazed laughter. "God had given me laughter; all who hear will rejoice for me" (Gen. 21:6).

How to Educate

From the inspiring example of Sarah's purity and faith, we can learn an important lesson about education.

The nation's future depends upon how we educate the next

---

[15] Adapted from *Ma'amerei HaRe'iyah* vol. II, pp. 230-231, from a lecture that Rav Kook delivered at the opening of a Talmud Torah school in Rehovot in 1905.

generation. How should we tend to the vineyard of the House of Israel so that the saplings will prosper and grow, anchoring fast roots below and producing pleasant fruit above? How can we make sure that our children will develop into complete Jewish adults, their values firmly rooted in their heritage, living lives that are "pleasing to God and to man"?

We must take care to avoid slavish imitation of the educational methods of other nations. Our educational approach must suit the special nature and unique characteristics of our nation.

Two Views of Childhood

The question of education revolves around an even more basic question. What is childhood? Is it just a preparatory stage leading to adulthood, or does it have intrinsic value in and of itself?

If life is all about working and earning a livelihood, then a child is simply a lump of clay to be formed into a tool to serve in the nation's workforce. Childhood is but a preparation for adulthood, when one becomes a productive member of society, a cog in the great machine of the nation's economy.

But there is another view of life, an idealistic outlook which values the qualities of purity and innocence. Such a viewpoint sees childhood as a stage of life that has value in its own right. The Sages recognized the special contribution of children to the world. "The world endures only for the sake of the breath of school children," for their Torah is learned in purity, undefiled by sin (*Shabbat* 119b).

When children are educated properly, we may discern within their pristine souls untold measures of holiness and purity. But this is only true if the grace and beauty of these delicate flowers is not crushed by the spirit-numbing reality of the factory floor and the cynical manipulations of greedy corporations.

Childhood is good and holy, but it is too weak and vulnerable to withstand the powerful forces of society. It is our duty to preserve the simplicity of childhood, to carefully allow our children to mature without losing their innate innocence. This will enable them to acquire the physical strength and spiritual resilience that they lack, while retaining the innocent exuberance of childhood.

My Anointed Ones

"'Do not harm *meshichai*, My anointed ones' – this refers to school children" (*Shabbat* 119b). Why are children called "God's anointed ones"? Anointing is not a one-time event, but an initiation ceremony which influences the years to come. Thus a king is anointed, and throughout the years of his reign he is the *melech ha-mashiach*, the anointed king.

The same is true with childhood. When it has not been debased by the pressures of an exploitative society, childhood is our anointing, our initiation, so that we may enjoy its pure fruits throughout our lives.

This is the beautiful example that Sarah provides. She lived a life of holiness and pure faith, retaining her childlike wonder and purity throughout the many vicissitudes of her long life. "All her years were equal in goodness" (Rashi).

CHAYEI SARAH: THE TORAH OF THE PATRIARCHS[16]

Even the Sages were puzzled why the Torah describes with such detail the story of Abraham's servant and the search for a wife for Isaac. Why are so many verses devoted to the servant's encounter with Rebecca at the well, as well as his subsequent report of this event to Rebecca's family? The Torah is so parsimonious with its words – important laws are often derived from a single letter. Why such verbosity here?

Due to this textual anomaly, the Sages made a bold claim: "The conversation of the Patriarch's servants is superior to the Torah of their descendants" (*Breishit Rabbah* 60). What does this mean? Is their everyday discourse really more important than the Torah and its laws?

The Lofty Torah of the Patriarchs

In fact, the "conversations" of the *Avot* (Patriarchs) were also a form of Torah. This Torah was more elevated than the later Torah of their descendants, as it reflected the extraordinary holiness and nobility of these spiritual giants. If so, why did the Sages refer to it as mere "conversations"?

---

[16] Adapted from *Orot*, pp. 66-67.

A conversation is natural, unaffected speech. The Torah of the *Avot* was like a conversation, flowing naturally from the inner sanctity of their goals and aspirations. Holy ideals permeated the day-to-day lives of Abraham, Isaac, and Jacob to such a degree that these ideals were manifest even in the everyday discourse of their servants.

The Torah of their descendants, on the other hand, lacks this natural spontaneity. It is a thought-out religion based on willed-holiness, a compendium of detailed rules and regulations calculated to govern all aspects of life. This is especially true for the development of Torah law during the long years of exile, when Torah was limited to governing the religious life of the individual.

Torah of Redemption

With our national return to *Eretz Yisrael*, we also return to the Torah of *Eretz Yisrael*. The generation of national rebirth has no patience for the feeble lights of Judaism as it exists in the exile. The people seek lofty ideals and great deeds. They aspire to build a model society, to correct injustice, and restore the Jewish people to a state of autonomy and independence. There is an inner Divine spirit driving their brazenness, as they reject the paltry lights of exilic Judaism, lights that glow faintly, like candles in the brilliant midday sun.

What will satisfy the spiritual needs of the generation of rebirth? They will gain new life from the comprehensive Torah of the Patriarchs. The daily *Amidah* prayer makes this connection between the *Avot* and the era of redemption: "[God] remembers the Patriarchs' acts of kindness, and lovingly brings the redeemer to their descendants." It is the "Patriarchs' acts of kindness" and their vibrant, natural Torah that will redeem their descendants in the final generation. The Messianic light will shine forth, and out of the darkness of heresy and denial, a supernal light will emanate from the lofty Torah of the *Avot*, a Torah of authenticity and greatness which will redeem the generation.

The lofty *tzaddikim* must recognize this secret. Their task is to combine these two Torahs, that of the *Avot* with that of their descendants. Then they will reveal a Torah crowned with honor and strength, beauty and splendor.

TOLDOT: JACOB RESCUED ABRAHAM[17]

According to an intriguing Midrash (*Tanchuma Toldot* 4), Abraham would not have made it out of his hometown of Ur Casdim alive were it not for the intervention of his grandson Jacob. King Nimrod ordered Abraham to be thrown into a fiery furnace because of Abraham's rejection of idolatry. But Jacob came to the rescue, as it says:

> So said God to the House of Jacob who redeemed Abraham: Jacob will not be ashamed, nor will his face become pale. (Isaiah 29:22)[18]

Even given the poetic license of Midrashic literature, Jacob could not have literally rescued his grandfather in an incident that took place before Jacob was born. Rather, the Sages wanted to teach us that Abraham was saved due to some special merit or quality his grandson Jacob possessed. What was this quality?

---

[17] Adapted from *Midbar Shur*, pp. 289-292.

[18] The simple reading of the verse interprets the phrase "who redeemed Abraham" to refer back to God, not to Jacob.

Two Paths of Change

There are two paths of spiritual growth that one may take. The first path is one of sudden, radical change, usually the result of some external catalyst.

One example of such a transformation may be found in the story of King Saul. The prophet Samuel informed Saul that he would meet a band of prophets playing musical instruments. This encounter, the prophet told Saul, will be a turning point in your life. "The spirit of God will suddenly come over you, and you will prophesize with them. *And you will be transformed into a different person*" (I Samuel 10:6).

The second path is one of slow, deliberate growth. We attain this gradual change through our own toil; it does not require an external stimulus and thus is always accessible.

But why are there two different paths of change available to us? If God provided us with two paths, then clearly both are needed. We should first prepare ourselves and advance as much as possible through our own efforts. After we have attained the highest level that we are capable of reaching, we may then benefit from unexpected inspiration from the inner recesses of our soul.

Abraham was a spiritual revolutionary, initiating a revolt against the idolatry of his generation. Abraham is the archetype of radical change. The defining moments of his life were dramatic events of astonishing dedication and self-sacrifice, such as his *brit milah* (circumcision) at an advanced age, and the *Akeidah*, the Binding of Isaac. In the merit of Abraham's far-reaching spiritual accomplishments, his descendants inherited those soul-qualities which foster sudden transformation.

Future generations, however, cannot rely solely on Abraham's style of radical change. As a normative path for all times, we need the method of gradual spiritual growth. The model for this type of change is Jacob. Unlike his grandfather, Jacob never underwent sudden transformations of personality or direction. Rather, the Torah characterizes him as "a quiet, scholarly man, dwelling in tents" (Gen. 25:27). Jacob's place was in the tents of Torah. He worked on himself step by step, growing through perseverance and diligence in Torah study.

Two Names for Jerusalem

The Midrash teaches that the name "Jerusalem" is a combination of two names, indicating that the holy city possesses qualities respresented by both names. Abraham called the city "*Yireh*," while Malki-Tzedek called it "*Shalem*." Not wanting to offend either of these righteous men, God combined both names together, naming the city "*Yerushalayim*" – "Jerusalem" (*Breishit Rabbah* 56:10).

What does the name "*Yireh*" mean? The holy city, particularly the Temple, had a profound impact on all who experienced its unique sanctity. This profound spiritual encounter is described as a form of sublime perception – "Your eyes will see your Teacher" (Isaiah 30:20). This elevated vision inspired visitors to reach beyond their ordinary spiritual capabilities. Due to the spiritual transformation effected by perceiving Jerusalem's holiness, Abraham named the city "*Yireh*" – "he will see."

Malki-Tzedek, on the other hand, referred to the city's qualities which assist those who seek to perfect themselves in a gradual fashion. Jerusalem is a place of Torah and ethical teachings, "For Torah shall go forth from Zion" (Isaiah 2:3). Therefore, Malki-Tzedek named the city "*Shalem*" (perfection), referring to this incremental approach towards achieving spiritual perfection.

Jacob to the Rescue

Returning to our original question: how did Jacob rescue his grandfather from Nimrod's fiery furnace? In what way will Jacob "not be ashamed"?

The Kabbalists explain that the goal of humanity – the reason why the soul is lowered into this world – is so that we may perfect ourselves through our own efforts. This way, we will not need to partake of "*nehama dekisufa*" (the "bread of shame"), a metaphor for benefiting from that which we did not earn.

While this explanation fits the path of gradual change, it would appear that the path of radical transformation is an external gift that we do not deserve. Is this not the undesired "*nehama dekisufa*" that we should avoid?

Not necessarily. If we are able to take this unexpected gift and use it to attain even greater levels of spiritual growth through our own efforts, then there is no shame in accepting it. We can compare this to a father who gave his son a large sum of money. If the son simply lives off the money until it is finished, then the father's gift is "*nehama dekisufa*," an embarrassment for the son, reflecting no credit upon him. If, however, the son uses the money to start a new business, and through his efforts doubles and triples the original investment, then the son has certainly pleased his father and brought honor to himself.

This is exactly the way that Jacob 'rescued' his grandfather Abraham. Left on his own, the most natural path for Abraham – whose revolutionary soul called for sudden, drastic change – would have been to achieve complete and absolute self-sacrifice in Nimrod's fiery furnace. It was Jacob's trait of gradual change that saved Abraham from the fate of martyrdom. Abraham adopted the path of measured spiritual change which his grandson Jacob exemplified. Abraham left the furnace, and over the years worked diligently to attain the spiritual elevation that he had relinquished inside Nimrod's furnace.

Why bother with the slower path? "Jacob will not be ashamed." By growing slowly through our own efforts, the spiritual gifts of radical change are no longer an embarrassing "*nehama dekisufa*," but an honorable gift which we have utilized to the fullest.

TOLDOT: ABRAHAM KEPT MITZVOT[19]

Why are practical mitzvot so central to Judaism? Why is it not enough just to believe in the Torah's central tenets and teachings?

When famine struck, Isaac considered leaving the Land of Israel. But God commanded him to remain in Israel. God allayed Isaac's fears, promising him:

> I will make your descendants as numerous as the stars of the sky, and grant them all these lands.... Because Abraham obeyed My voice; and he kept My charge, My commandments, My decrees, and My laws. (Gen. 26:4-5)

Abraham kept God's commandments?

Indeed, the Sages interpreted this verse literally. They wrote that the Patriarchs fulfilled the precepts of the Torah, even before their revelation at Sinai centuries later.

Fifth-century scholar Rav Ashi made an even more audacious claim. He asserted that Abraham even observed the mitzvah of *eiruv tavshilin* – a rabbinically ordained ritual which enables one to prepare food and lights for the Sabbath when a holiday falls out

---

[19] Adapted from *Igrot HaRe'iyah* vol. I, p. 135 (1908); vol. III, p. 92 (1917).

on a Friday (*Yoma* 28b).[20]

Observing *Eiruv Tavshilin*

A certain scholar once commented to Rav Kook that Rav Ashi's statement clearly cannot be taken at face value. How could Abraham know what the rabbinical courts would decree a thousand years in the future? The Sages must have intended to convey a subtler message: Abraham's philosophical mastery of the Torah was so complete, his grasp of the Torah's theoretical underpinnings so comprehensive, that it encompassed even the underlying rationales for future decrees.

Rav Kook, however, was not pleased with this explanation. In his response, Rav Kook emphasized that the Torah's theoretical foundations cannot be safeguarded without practical mitzvot. It is impossible to truly internalize the Torah's philosophical teachings without concrete actions.

This is the fundamental weakness of religions that rely on faith alone. Without an emphasis on deeds, such religions retreat to the realm of the philosophical and the abstract. They abandon the material world, leaving it unredeemed. The Torah's focus on detailed mitzvot, on the other hand, reflects its extensive involvement with the physical world.

Levels of Holiness

Rav Kook elucidated this Talmudic tradition in a slightly different

---

[20] Ordinarily, it is forbidden to cook on a holiday if the meal is intended to be served after the holiday is over.

vein. While Abraham did not literally perform the ritual of *eiruv tavshilin* as we do today, he was able to apply the essential concept of this ceremony to his day-to-day life. This was not just some abstract theory, but practical knowledge which guided his actions.

What is the essence of *eiruv tavshilin*? The Sages explained in *Beitzah* 15b that this ceremony helps one fulfill the Biblical injunction to "Remember the Sabbath to keep it holy." Due to the fact that there is a holiday preceding the Sabbath, the Sabbath could be forgotten or neglected. In what way might one forget the sanctity of Shabbat?

The holiness of Shabbat is greater than the holiness of the holidays. But when Shabbat immediately follows a holiday, one might mistakenly equate the two and forget that there are different laws governing them. This could lead one to desecrate the Sabbath by performing activities that are permitted on holidays, such as cooking.

Just as we need to distinguish between the holy and the profane, so too we need to distinguish between different degrees of holiness. This is the underlying purpose of *eiruv tavshilin*: to remind us of the higher sanctity of the Sabbath.

Abraham, who kept the entire Torah, also made this fine distinction – in his life and actions. Abraham differentiated not only between the sacred and the profane, but also *bein kodesh le-kodesh*, between different levels of holiness.

VAYEITZEI: PRAYER BEFORE SLEEP[21]

After leaving his family in Beersheba, Jacob reached Beth El at nightfall. Before lying down to sleep, Jacob prayed there.

> He entreated at the place and stayed overnight, for it suddenly became night. (Gen. 28:11)

The Sages taught that it was in Beth El that Jacob established the third daily prayer – *Ma'ariv*, the evening service.[22] While less obligatory than the morning and afternoon prayers, *Ma'ariv* has its own special benefits. The Talmudic sage Abba Benjamin testified that he took great pains every day of his life to recite the evening prayer before going to sleep (*Berachot* 5b). What is so special about this prayer?

Refining Desires and the Imagination

When we are asleep, our cognitive and rational functions are suspended, and the body's involuntary processes take over. Only

[21] Adapted from *Ein Eyah* vol. I, p. 19.

[22] The Talmud in *Berachot* 26b quotes a tradition that the three Patriarchs instituted the three daily prayers. Abraham established the morning prayer (*Shacharit*), and Isaac the afternoon prayer (*Minchah*).

our powers of imagination remain active, guiding our dreams as we sleep. Without the control and regulation of our intellectual faculties, a measure of impurity descends on the body during the night. We remove this impurity by washing our hands when we rise in the morning.

Holy individuals may experience sublime visions in their sleep, like Jacob, who dreamt of angels ascending and descending a Heaven-bound ladder as he slept in Beth El. However, it is only the soul that experiences these visions. The body is detached from the soul during sleep and is not influenced by the soul's uplifting experiences.

We have two tools for spiritual growth: Torah study and prayer. Abba Benjamin's statement on the importance of the *Ma'ariv* prayer helps clarify how each tool ennobles a different facet of the human soul.

When we study Torah, we refine and elevate our intellectual powers. The function of prayer, on the other hand, is to uplift our faculty of *ratzon*, our will or primal desires. Through prayer and introspection, we refine our will and powers of imagination. As we articulate our inner needs and aspirations in prayer, our desires are elevated toward holier, more spiritual goals.

Our imaginative faculties are closer to our physical side than the intellect is. Thus they function even as we sleep, in our dreams. Since it is through prayer that we can most effectively direct those faculties still active during sleep, it is logical that prayer before sleep will have the strongest impact on this aspect of life. For this reason, Abba Benjamin stressed the importance of his nighttime prayer.

VAYEITZEI: THE RIVALRY BETWEEN RACHEL AND LEAH[23]

Jacob did not have an easy life. He loved Rachel, but was tricked into marrying her sister Leah. And when he finally married Rachel, his home suffered from rivalry between the two sisters.

This strife was not limited to Jacob's household. It continued on in future generations: in the struggle between Rachel's son Joseph and Leah's sons; and in the conflict between King Saul, a descendant of Rachel, and David, a descendant of Leah. Why did Jacob need to endure so many obstacles when setting up his family – complications that would have such a long-term impact on future generations of the Jewish people?

The Present versus the Future

We live in a divided reality. We continuously deliberate: how much should we live for the moment, and how much should we work for the future? We must constantly balance between the here-and-now and the yet-to-come. This dilemma exists across all levels of life: individual, familial, communal, and national.

God's original design for the world was that the entire tree, even the bark, would taste as sweet as its fruit (Gen. 1:11). In

---

[23] Adapted from *Ein Eyah* vol. IV on *Shabbat* 55 (5:46), pp. 44-46.

other words, even during the intermediate stages of working toward a goal, we should be able to sense and enjoy the final fruits of our labor. When the world is functioning properly, the present is revealed in all of its glory and serves as a suitable guide toward a loftier future. In such a perfect world, our current desires and wishes do not impinge upon our future aspirations.

But the physical universe is fundamentally flawed. The earth failed to produce trees that taste like their fruit. We endure constant conflict between the present and the future, the temporal and the eternal. As individuals and as a nation, we often need to disregard the sensibilities of the present since they will not lead us toward our destined path.

Rachel and Leah

Jacob's marriage to two sisters, and the ongoing rivalry between them, is a metaphor for this duality in our lives.

Like all things in our world, Jacob's home suffered from a lack of clarity. Jacob should have been able to establish his family on the basis of an uplifted present, blessed with integrity and goodness. He should have been able to marry and set up his home without making calculations with an eye to the future. The natural purity and simple emotions of his holy soul should have sufficed.

Rachel, whom Jacob immediately loved for the beautiful qualities of her soul, is a metaphor for the simple and natural love we feel for the revealed present. Jacob felt that Rachel's external beauty was also in harmony with the unknown realm of the distant future.

But God's counsel decreed that the future destiny of the

people of Israel belonged not to Rachel, but to Leah.[24] Leah would be the principal matriarch of the Jewish people. Yet this future was so profoundly hidden, that its current state – in Leah – was hidden from Jacob.

This concealed quality of Leah is embedded in the very foundations of the Jewish people. Because of the legacy of Leah, we can raise our sights afar, skipping over the present circumstances, in order to aspire toward a lofty future. Just as Jacob found himself unexpectedly wed to Leah, so too, the path of the Jewish people throughout history does not always proceed in an orderly fashion. The future often projects its way into the present so that the present time may be elevated and sanctified.

Two Kings and Two Messiahs

The rivalry between Rachel and Leah, the conflict between the beautiful present and the visionary future, also found expression in the monarchy of Israel. The temporary reign of Saul, a descendant of Rachel, struggled with the eternal dynasty of David, a descendant of Leah.[25] Even in the Messianic Era, the divide

---

[24] Six of the twelve tribes of Israel, including those designated for spiritual and political leadership (Levi and Judah), were born to Leah.

[25] Saul, who is described as "the most handsome young man in Israel, head and shoulders above the people" (I Sam. 16:2), was a natural choice for king. And yet God chose to appoint David – a simple shepherd boy whose leadership qualities even his own father failed to see – as the true king of the Jewish people. As God explained to the perplexed prophet Samuel: "Look not upon his appearance, or the height of his stature, for I have rejected him. For it is not as man sees [that which is visible] to the eyes; the Lord sees into the heart" (I Sam.

between Rachel and Leah will continue, with two Messianic leaders: the precursive redeemer, Mashiach ben Joseph, a descendant of Rachel, and the final redeemer, Mashiach ben David, a descendant of Leah.[26]

Nonetheless, we aspire for the simpler state in which the present is uplifting, and by means of its light, the future acquires its greatness. For this reason, Rachel was always honored as Jacob's primary wife. Even Leah's descendants in Bethlehem conceded: "Like Rachel and Leah who both built the house of Israel" (Ruth 4:11), honoring Rachel before Leah.

16:7).

[26] For further explanation regarding the two leaders of the Messianic Era, see "*Vayishlach*: 'I Have an Ox and a Donkey.'"

VAYISHLACH: PILLARS AND SANCTUARIES[27]

After twenty years of hard labor working for his treacherous uncle, Jacob returned safely to the Land of Israel. Jacob was successful in appeasing his brother Esau, and finally made it back to Beth El.

Beth El was the place where, as he set out to leave the Land of Israel, Jacob dreamt of a ladder reaching to the Heavens, of angels and God's promise to watch over him. Now Jacob fulfilled his twenty-year-old promise and erected a *matzeivah*, a pillar in God's Name, in Beth El.

From the Torah's account, it appears perfectly acceptable for Jacob to erect a pillar. Later on, however, the Torah specifically prohibits all pillars of worship, even if they are used to worship God: "Do not erect a sacred pillar, which the Eternal your God hates" (Deut. 16:22).

What about Jacob's pillar? The Sages explained that serving God through pillars "was beloved in the time of the Patriarchs, but abhorred in the time of their descendants" (*Sifri Shoftim* 146).

Why did the status of pillars change?

The Mountain, the Field, and the House

---

[27] Adapted from *Igrot HaRe'iyah* vol. III, pp. 10-12 (letter 546).

To answer this question, we need to examine the difference between a **pillar** and a **sanctuary**. A pillar is a large single stone, a focal point of Divine service, around which all may gather. A sanctuary, on the other hand, is a house of worship, a building in which worshippers gather.

Why does it matter whether the worshippers gather around or inside?

The prophet Isaiah envisioned a future time when many nations will say, "Let us go up to God's mountain, to the house of the God of Jacob" (2:3). Why will they be attracted to the God of *Jacob*, as opposed to the God of Abraham or the God of Isaac?

The Sages noted that the unique spiritual service of each of the *Avot* (Patriarchs) was expressed by the different spatial contexts in which they connected to God:

- Abraham – served God on the *mountain* of Moriah during the *Akeidah,* the Binding of Isaac.
- Isaac – reached his own spiritual heights in the *field* where he meditated (Gen. 24:63).
- Jacob – promised that the location of his lofty dream would become a *house* of God (Gen. 28:22).

The Sages interpreted Isaiah's prophecy as follows: The nations will seek neither the "mountain of Abraham" nor the "field of Isaac," but rather the "house of Jacob" (*Pesachim* 88). What does this mean?

When Abraham began introducing the concept of one God into the world, he did not lecture about detailed, organized forms of worship. Abraham did not instruct his followers to observe the

613 mitzvot that govern all aspects of life. Rather, he taught the overall concept of one Creator. The "mountain of Abraham" and the "field of Isaac" are a metaphor for this spiritual message, which, like a mountain or an open field, is accessible to all.

This is also the type of service that is associated with a *pillar* – a central point around which all may gather.

Jacob, on the other hand, vowed that he would establish a *house* of worship. While pillars were an acceptable way to worship God in the time of the *Avot*, Jacob envisioned a future era when the Jewish people would be ready for a higher form of Divine service. The open, accessible service of Abraham would prepare the way for an all-encompassing and detailed service of Torah and mitzvot. The metaphor for Jacob's service is a *house*, with walls that enclose and surround the worshippers, binding them to a specific form of worship.

A second aspect of a house is that it serves to differentiate between those who are inside of it and those who are not. Once the Jewish people merited access to this loftier service and entered the elevated sanctuary, it was no longer appropriate for them to relate to God through the abstract service represented by pillars.

Isaiah prophesied that, in the future, the nations will recognize the beauty and depth of a service of God that encompasses both the spiritual and physical realms. They will recognize the importance of good deeds, mitzvot, and Halachic discipline. Then they will declare: simple faith in God and abstract theology are not enough. Let us enter into the sanctuary, into "the House of the God of Jacob."

VAYISHLACH: "I HAVE AN OX AND A DONKEY"[28]

Upon his return to *Eretz Yisrael*, Jacob sent a message to his brother Esau: "I have an ox and a donkey" (Gen. 31:6). Why was it necessary to tell Esau about this ox and donkey?

According to the Midrash (*Breishit Rabbah* 75), Jacob was not speaking about the material possessions he had amassed, but about something of far greater significance. The ox refers to Mashiach ben Joseph, the precursive Messianic leader descended from Joseph. The ox is a symbol of the tribe of Joseph; both Jacob and Moses used the imagery of an ox when blessing Joseph (Gen. 49:6; Deut. 33:17).

And the donkey? That is a reference to Mashiach ben David, the ultimate Messianic king descended from David, who will arrive as "a pauper riding on a donkey" (Zechariah 9:9).

Why do we need two Messianic leaders? And why are they represented specifically by these two animals?

Two Forces

---

[28] Adapted from *Shemuot HaRe'iyah* (*VaYishlach* 5691), quoted in *Peninei HaRe'iyah*, pp. 68-72. "Eulogy in Jerusalem" from *Ma'amarei HaRe'iyah*, pp. 94-99.

In a remarkable eulogy entitled "The Eulogy in Jerusalem," delivered after Theodore Herzl's death in 1904, Rav Kook explained this concept of two Messiahs. The eulogy beautifully articulates his views on the secular Zionist movement and the tragic rift between the religious and secular sectors of the Jewish people.

God created us with both body and soul. We have forces that maintain and strengthen the body, and forces that protect and develop the soul. The ideal is to have a robust body together with a strong and healthy soul. The soul, with its remarkable faculties, is meant to utilize the body to fulfill God's will in this world.

The Jewish people function in an analogous fashion to the body and soul. There are forces within the nation that correspond to the body, working to meet its material and physical needs. These forces prepare a firm basis for Israel's holy mission. And there are forces in the nation that work directly toward developing Israel's special spiritual qualities.

Efforts to promote public security and welfare are common to all nations, just as all creatures have bodily and physical functions. But the higher aspect of furthering our spiritual aspirations on the national level is unique to the Jewish people – "It is a nation dwelling alone, not counted among the other nations" (Num. 23:9).

Joseph and Judah

These two tasks were divided between two tribes, Joseph and Judah. Joseph looked after the material needs of the Israelites in Egypt. The Sages taught that Joseph spoke seventy languages, thus indicating that his task was a universal one, common to all nations. He protected the Jewish people in Egypt, and is described as "the opposing force to Esau" (*Breishit Rabbah*), defending the nation against those who attack the Jewish people.

Judah, on the other hand, was responsible for cultivating the special holiness of the Jewish people. "Judah became His holy nation" (Ps. 114:2). Ultimately, both of these aspects were to be combined in the Davidic monarchy. David was a warrior who fought the enemies of Israel and brought peace to the nation. But he was also the "sweet singer of Israel," the psalmist who would rise at midnight to compose holy poems praising God.

The Split

When Jeroboam led the northern tribes of Joseph to split from the southern kingdom of Judah, he introduced a tragic divide between these two forces, the material and the spiritual. The Midrash says that God grabbed Jeroboam by the coat and told him: "If you repent, I and you and [David] the son of Jesse will walk together in the Garden of Eden." Together, you and the Davidic monarch will nurture the Jewish people and enable them to accomplish their Divine mission.

Jeroboam's reply, however, was: "Who will lead?" God answered, "The son of Jesse will lead." Jeroboam refused to recognize the pre-eminence of the nation's spiritual mission. Throughout history, we have witnessed the ongoing conflict between these two forces: secular movements that work towards improving the nation's material lot, and religious ones that promote its spiritual nature exclusively.

The redemption of the Jewish people can only be attained when both of these forces are functioning. Those who work towards strengthening the nation's spiritual aspects are preparing for Mashiach ben David, who personifies the ultimate goal of the nation. This spiritual goal, however, cannot be attained without the necessary material foundations. All efforts to better the material conditions of the nation are part of Mashiach ben Joseph's mission.

The Fall of Mashiach ben Joseph

The Talmud in *Sukkah* 52a teaches that Mashiach ben Joseph will be killed, and that a "great eulogy in Jerusalem" (Zechariah 12:13) will be delivered at his death. What is the significance of this piercing eulogy, when the nation will mourn the loss of Mashiach ben Joseph "as one mourns for an only child"?

Due to the rift within the Jewish people, these two forces clash. Those who promote the nation's material aspects belittle the importance of Torah and mitzvot. And those who stress the special nature of Israel reject all changes and attempts to better its material standing. This leads to rebellion against religion on one side, and anemic stagnation on the other.

With the fall of Mashiach ben Joseph, all will realize that these are not opposing movements, but forces that should work together so that material progress will form a basis for developing the unique character of the nation. This is the significance of the "great eulogy in Jerusalem." All sectors of the nation will mourn this loss, all will recognize that it is a tragic mistake for these forces to be divided and estranged from one another.

The Ox and the Donkey

What about Jacob's message to Esau? Why did he use these two animals, the ox and the donkey, to allude to the two Messianic leaders?

The ox is used to plow the ground, preparing the area to be planted. This corresponds to the mission of Mashiach ben Joseph – to defend the nation from enemies and prepare the way for the revelation of Mashiach ben David. We also see this in the fact that the Tabernacle, a preparation for the Temple, was established in Shiloh, in the territory of Joseph, while the Temple itself was built in the inheritance of Judah.

The donkey, on the other hand, is used to carry produce from the field. This corresponds to the mission of Mashiach ben David, who brings the final fruit of redemption.

A Hint to Esau

Jacob's message to his brother, "I have an ox and a donkey," alluded to the future Messianic Era, a time when he will no longer fear Esau's enmity. We find a second hint later on. After the two brothers meet, Jacob promises that he will visit Esau on Mount Seir. The Sages wrote:

> We searched throughout the text of the Torah, but we never found that Jacob visited Esau on Mount Seir. It could not be that Jacob was deceiving him. So when will Jacob go to him? This will take place in the future

era, as it says, "Saviors will ascend Mount Zion to judge the mountain of Esau" (Obadiah 1:21). (*Breishit Rabbah* 78:14)

VAYISHLACH: THE PROHIBITION OF GID HA-NASHEH[29]

Jacob was limping, but he had survived the nighttime struggle at Penuel. Nervously awaiting a confrontation with his estranged brother Esau, Jacob was attacked by a mysterious opponent. With the approach of dawn, the stranger dislocated Jacob's thigh.

> Therefore the Israelites do not eat the displaced nerve
> (*gid ha-nasheh*) on the hip joint to this very day, because
> he touched Jacob's thigh on the displaced nerve.
> (Gen. 32:33)

What is the significance of this prohibition? Do we refrain from eating the sciatic nerve only to commemorate a mysterious wrestling match that took place thousands of years ago?

A Vision of Violence

At first glance, the prohibition of *gid ha-nasheh* appears to be yet another limitation that the Torah places on eating meat. While the Torah permits the consumption of meat, it instituted a number of restrictions, such as which animals may be eaten, how they are to

---

[29] Adapted from *Oztrot HaRe'iyah* vol. II, p. 507.

be slaughtered, how their blood should be handled, and so on. These regulations indicate that we may not deal with animals as we wish, without regard for their welfare. On the contrary, we have moral obligations and responsibilities towards animals.

The prohibition of *gid ha-nasheh*, however, is meant to project a broader ethical aspiration, beyond the issue of how we should treat animals.

According to tradition, the stranger who fought Jacob that night was the guardian angel of Esau. Jacob's opponent symbolized the lifestyle of the hunter, a man of violence and conquest whose prophetic blessing was that he would live by his sword. This nighttime struggle was not a private experience, a personal event in Jacob's life. It was a vision for all times. It epitomizes our constant battle against belligerent foes who claim the right to subjugate others by virtue of their physical strength and military prowess.

This struggle appeared to Jacob in its most unadorned fashion, without any pretense of gallantry and shining swords to mask its visceral violence and naked aggression. For the truth is that all wars, no matter how 'civilized,' are nothing more than a brutal struggle to subdue and conquer.

If there is one area in which the human race is continually advancing, it is the art of war. Methods and tools of combat constantly grow ever more sophisticated. We have progressed from primitive spears and swords to guns and canons, and onwards to modern warfare with armored tanks, fighter jets, and nuclear bombs. And yet the essence of war remains the same: one-on-one combat between two opponents. All warfare boils down to the violent struggle to overcome and subdue, where victory is achieved by felling one's adversary.

Protesting Aggression

By not eating the *gid ha-nasheh*, we demonstrate our revulsion at unprovoked aggression and violence. Just as Jacob fought Esau's angel that night, we also oppose the cynical belief in 'the right of might.' There is no legal or moral right to terrorize and subjugate those who are weaker.

While nationalism provides many benefits, in its extreme form it can descend into imperialism and fascism. As Rav Kook wrote in *Olat Re'iyah* (vol. I, p. 234):

> Nationalism is a lofty emotion in its natural, pristine state. But if it is not directed towards the highest goal – the aspiration of universal happiness and perfection – it will end up crossing the boundaries of morality.

We may need a strong army to defend ourselves, and we may need to slaughter animals to provide for our physical needs. But by refraining from eating the *gid ha-nasheh*, we demonstrate that our goal is not to subjugate others, whether man or beast. Even as we eat the meat of animals, we avoid the sciatic nerve that allows the body to stand upright. This is a moral sensitivity which should govern every form of interpersonal interaction, enabling all to benefit from a Divine-spirited and harmonious existence.

VAYISHLACH: THE SERVICE OF PILLARS AND ALTARS[30]

Returning to Beth El

Having survived the confrontation with Esau and his private militia, the mysterious nighttime struggle at Penuel, the abduction of his daughter Dinah, and the battle against the city of Shechem – Jacob finally made his way back to Beth El. Twenty years earlier, Jacob had stayed overnight in Beth El, dreaming of angels and Divine protection as he fled from his brother Esau. Now he would fulfill his decades-old promise to worship God in that holy place.

In preparation for this spiritual journey, Jacob instructed his family:

> "Remove the foreign gods that are in your midst. Purify yourselves and change your clothes. Then we will rise and ascend to Beth El. There I will construct an altar to God, Who answered me in my hour of trouble, and Who accompanied me in the path that I took." (Gen. 35:2-3)

---

[30] Adapted from *Midbar Shur*, pp. 74-75.

The first time Jacob had come to Beth El, he erected a *matzeivah*, a pillar with which to worship God. Now, Jacob built a *mizbei'ach*, an altar. What is the difference between worshipping God with a pillar or with an altar?

The Torah later prohibits erecting a *matzeivah*, even if it is to be used to worship God (Deut. 16:22). The Sages explained that the *matzeivah* "was beloved in the time of the Patriarchs, but abhorred in the time of their descendants" (*Sifri Shoftim* 146).

What brought about this change in status?

Service of the *Klal*

The difference between a *matzeivah* and a *mizbei'ach* is primarily a physical one. A *matzeivah* is a single large stone, while a *mizbei'ach* is an altar constructed from many stones. The switch from pillar to altar indicates a paradigm shift that took place in the way God was to be served in the time of the Patriarchs and in the time of their descendants.

Each of the three *Avot* – Abraham, Isaac, and Jacob – had his own unique way of serving God. Abraham served God with his overriding traits of love, kindness, and hospitality. Isaac served God with awe and submission, traits he acquired at the *Akeidah*. And Jacob, the "scholarly man who dwelled in tents [of Torah]," served God through Torah study.

In the time of the Patriarchs, each of the *Avot* was the leading light of his generation. His special trait dominated the era; his path of serving God was the appropriate path for that time. This period was aptly represented by the metaphor of the *matzeivah*: a single stone, a single way of serving God.

When Jacob returned to the Land of Israel, however, the situation had changed. He arrived at Beth El with twelve sons, the twelve tribes of Israel. No longer was there a single spiritual path for the generation. This was the start of a new era: the service of the *klal*, the collective, in which each individual fills a particular role in order to reach a common national goal. Each of Jacob's sons developed his own way of serving God, based on a unique combination of the spiritual paths of the three *Avot*.

To fully function, the Jewish nation requires a variety of talents and fields of expertise. Spiritual leadership, in the form of teachers of Torah and *kohanim*, came from the tribe of Levi. Kings and national leaders arose from Judah. Issachar excelled in producing scholars and judges. Other tribes specialized in commerce, agriculture, and national defense.

The altar Jacob built from many stones upon his return to Beth El embodied the new paradigm of serving God. This was no longer a time of a single, uniform service of God. There were now many paths to serve God, which joined together in one altar, as all aspired toward the common goal of Divine service.

"Change Your Clothes"

With these divergent paths to serve God, however, a new problem arose. Each group may come to believe that its path is the most important and belittle the efforts of others. As they prepared to worship God with the multiple-stone *mizbei'ach* at Beth El, Jacob realized that it was necessary to take special measures to unite his family.

Jacob therefore instructed his family, "Remove the foreign

gods in your midst." The Sages taught that the evil inclination is a "foreign god" (*Shabbat* 105b). Jacob pleaded that they remove the evil inclination which convinces us that others are 'foreign.' He wanted his family to recognize that, on the inside, the disparate members of the Jewish people are united in purpose and soul. For this reason, the Torah refers to Jacob's family as "seventy soul" (Ex. 1:5), in the singular, emphasizing that the souls of Israel are united at their source.

It is only the externals – our deeds and actions – that separate us. Therefore Jacob requested that his family purify themselves by changing their clothes, by removing the superficial exterior which conceals our true inner unity.

Then, Jacob announced, we will be ready to ascend to Beth El and worship God together. There we will serve God using a *mizbei'ach*, composed of many stones and many paths – but all working together toward the same ultimate goal of serving God.

VAYEISHEV: THE REALITY OF DREAMS[31]

Joseph, the ambitious protagonist of the final four readings of Genesis, was the "master of dreams." In addition to his own two dreams of future greatness, Joseph was called upon to interpret four more dreams: the dreams of the royal baker and steward, and Pharaoh's double dream about the seven-year famine.

All six dreams bore prophetic messages. "A dream," the Sages taught, "is a sixtieth of prophecy" (*Berachot* 57b). And yet, Joseph's dreams contained inaccuracies. Joseph dreamt that the sun and moon would bow down to him – i.e., even his father and mother would acknowledge his greatness. But, as his father quickly pointed out, Joseph's mother had passed away long before!

Nevertheless, "Jacob waited to see the results" (Gen. 37:11). He knew that this impossibility did not invalidate the rest of the dream. As the Sages noted in *Berachot* 55a: "Even if most of a dream comes true, not all of it will come to pass."

Why do dreams include extraneous elements and inaccurate details?

Rav Kook explained that this is due to the very nature of dreams. All dreams originate from our imaginative and emotional faculties. As a result, they are subject to exaggeration and nonsensical elements. Even prophetic dreams may contain details

---

[31] Adapted from *Ein Eyah* vol. I, p. 267.

that do not correspond to reality.

This is because the truth contained in a prophetic dream relates to the general reality of what *should* happen. It may be that due to circumstances, certain details in fact occurred differently. This does not mean that the dream is false. Rather, the dream's message relates to what potentially could or should have occurred.

Joseph dreamt of his parents bowing down before him. In reality, Joseph's mother had died many years before. Yet the fundamental message of the dream was true, for had Rachel still been alive, she too would have bowed down before her son, viceroy of Egypt.

VAYEISHEV: TAMAR'S SACRIFICE[32]

Perhaps the most astonishing aspect of the story of Judah and his daughter-in-law Tamar took place after Judah was informed that the young widow had behaved loosely and was pregnant. Judah meted out a harsh punishment for her promiscuity: "Take her out and have her burned" (Gen. 38:24).

Confronted with such a severe sentence, Tamar could have easily pointed an accusing finger at Judah. After all, it was Judah who had made her pregnant, not knowing the true identity of the 'prostitute' he had met on the road to Timna. Incredibly, Tamar chose to be silent. Only as she was led out to be executed did Tamar remark enigmatically, "I am pregnant by the man who is the owner of these articles" (Gen. 38:25). When Judah heard that cryptic message, he immediately realized that her pregnancy was not the result of promiscuity, but a form of *yibum* (levirate marriage), which Tamar had only been able to consummate through deception.

Why didn't Tamar save her life by openly identifying her father-in-law – and judge – as the person responsible?

The Talmud derives an amazing lesson from Tamar's selfless act:

---

[32] Adapted from *Ein Eyah* vol. II, p. 191.

It is better to throw oneself into a fiery furnace than
to shame another person in public. (*Berachot* 43b)

This remarkable statement raises two questions. First of all, is
honor really such an important thing? Did the Sages not teach
(*Avot* 4:21) that the pursuit of honor and fame is an undesirable
trait that can "drive one from the world"?

Secondly, there are only three crimes – murder, idolatry, and
illicit relations – so grievous that it is preferable to die rather than
transgress them. Why was Tamar willing to die rather than
embarrass her father-in-law?

Superficial Honor versus Inner Worth

To answer the first question, we must distinguish between two
types of honor. The first is an illusory honor based on external
acquisitions – wealth, position, fame, and so on. Pursuing this type
of honor is certainly a negative trait, a mindset which can cause
one to lose his way and squander his time on inconsequential
matters.

There is, however, a nobler form of honor. This honor is based
on our awareness of our true inner worth as human beings created
in God's image. Recognition of our innate dignity, and an aversion
to ignominy, has the opposite effect to the pursuit of superficial
honor. This awareness is the very foundation of morality. It
enables one to value the nobility of a life rooted in ethical and
spiritual ideals.

In an essay describing our generation's need to deepen its
appreciation of the spiritual side of the universe, through the study

of the Torah's esoteric teachings, Rav Kook noted a decline in humanity's awareness of inner values:

> As the world advances in its superficial culture, it simultaneously declines in its inner worth. This deterioration is due to the phenomenon that, with the advance of society's external values, the eye is increasingly captivated by superficialities and learns to belittle inner awareness. Due to this process, humanity's true worth continually dwindles. The world's redemption is dependent upon the revival of our inner perceptions. (*Orot HaKodesh* vol. I, p. 96)

Human life has value only when it is accompanied by recognition of one's inner worth and dignity. It is preferable to forfeit life in this world rather than publicly shame another person, permanently disgracing him and ruining his honor. Such a public defaming will bring about the loss of all value in living, a slow and degrading demise.

In practice, however, it seems that one should not take such a drastic step. With time, a life lived fully can heal and restore lost honor. Nonetheless, those with a noble and sensitive soul should feel that their own will to live is weakened if their own survival must come at the expense of another's public disgrace and humiliation.

For this reason, the Sages did not write, "One is *required* to throw oneself into a fiery furnace," but rather, "It is *better*." This is how one should feel, even if in practice it does not come to that.

MIKEITZ: JOSEPH AND JUDAH[33]

The strife among Jacob's sons centered on two conflicting viewpoints vis à vis the sanctity of the Jewish people. Judah felt that we need to act according to the current reality and that, given the present situation, the Jewish people need to maintain a separate existence from other nations in order to safeguard their unique heritage. Joseph, on the other hand, believed that we should focus on the final goal. We need to take into account the hidden potential of the future era, when "nations will walk by your light" (Isaiah 60:3). Thus, according to Joseph, even nowadays we are responsible for the spiritual elevation of all peoples.

So which outlook is correct – Judah's pragmatic nationalism or Joseph's visionary universalism?

The Present versus the Future

The dispute between Judah and Joseph is in fact a reflection of a fundamental split in the world. The rift between the present reality and the future potential is rooted in the very foundations of the universe. On the second day of Creation, God formed the *rakia*, the firmament separating the waters below from the waters above (Gen. 1:7; see *Chagigah* 15a). This separation signifies a rupture

---

[33] Adapted from *Shemuot HaRe'iyah* 10, *Mikeitz* 5690 (1929).

between the present (as represented by the "lower waters" of this world) and the future (the "higher waters" of the heavens). The inability to reveal the future potential in the present is a fundamental defect of our world; unlike the other days of Creation, the Torah does not describe the second day, when this breach occurred, as being "good."

Joseph and the Letter 'ה'

According to the Midrash (*Sotah* 36b), the angel Gabriel taught Joseph seventy languages. Gabriel also added the Hebrew letter *hey* (ה) from God's Name to Joseph's name, calling him "Yehosef" (Ps. 81:6). What is the significance of this extra letter?

The Sages wrote that God created this world with the letter *hey*, and the World to Come with the letter *yud* (י) (*Breishit Rabbah* 12:9). In Joseph's view, each nation is measured according to its future spiritual potential, according to how it will fit in the final plan of *kiddush ha-Shem*, the sanctification of God's Name and revelation of His rule in the world. The particular role of each nation is indicated by its unique language. Without the letter *hey*, however, Joseph could not properly grasp the language of each nation, i.e., he could not ascertain the nature of their role in the future world. With the addition of the letter *hey* to his name – the letter used to create this world – Joseph gained the ability to understand the universe as it exists *now*. Joseph was then able to comprehend the languages of all peoples and assess their spiritual potential.

Joseph was able to discern the world's potential for *kiddush ha-Shem* with the help of a single letter. He used the *hey*, a letter which

92

is closed from three sides, as this future potential is currently almost completely hidden. Judah, on the other hand, looked at the world's spiritual state as it is revealed now. "Joseph, who sanctified God's Name in private, merited one letter of God's Name. Judah, who sanctified God's Name in public, merited that his entire name was called after God's Name" (*Sotah* 36b).

Two Types of *Tzaddikim*

According to the Zohar, Benjamin complemented his brother Joseph. "Rachel gave birth to two *tzaddikim*, Joseph and Benjamin. Joseph was a 'higher *tzaddik*,' while his brother Benjamin was a 'lower *tzaddik*'" (*Vayeitzei* 153b). What are these two types of saintly *tzaddikim*?

The "higher *tzaddik*" is a conduit for the *shefa* (the Divine influence), drawing it down from above, while the "lower *tzaddik*" passes the *shefa* to the physical world below. Benjamin's role, as the "lower *tzaddik*," was to imbue our world with holiness. His whole life, Benjamin was concerned that the Temple should be built in the portion of *Eretz Yisrael* that his tribe would inherit. Why was that so vital to Benjamin?

The Temple is "a house of prayer for all peoples," allowing all to share in its holiness. "Had the nations known how important the Temple was for them, they would have surrounded it with forts in order to guard over it" (*Tanhuma Bamidbar* 3). The Temple has a fundamental role in Joseph's universal outlook.

The Monarchy and the Temple

The dialectic between Judah and Joseph finds expression in two institutions: the monarchy and the Temple. The monarchy, whose role was to protect the national sanctity of the Jewish people, was established in Judah's inheritance, in Hebron and Jerusalem. The Temple, whose role was to elevate all of humanity, was built on Benjamin's land. Yet the Temple was partially located on a strip of land that extends from Judah's portion into Benjamin's portion. This strip represents the synthesis of Judah and Joseph, the integration of the national and universal viewpoints.

Mikeitz, the name of the Torah reading, means "at the end." The *Midrash Tanchuma* explains that God established an end for all things. Just as Joseph's imprisonment ended in *Mikeitz*, so too, the conflict between Judah and Joseph will be resolved after a constructive period of development and change. The fundamental dissonance in the world will be repaired, and the rift between the present and the potential, between the lower and higher waters of creation, will be healed.

MIKEITZ: WAITING FOR THE DREAM[34]

It took a long time, but Joseph's dreams eventually came to pass.

How long did it take? Joseph became viceroy of Egypt at age thirty, and nine years later (after seven years of plenty and two years of famine), his brothers came to buy food. So Joseph's dreams that his brothers would one day bow down before him and recognize his greatness were fulfilled when he was 39 years old. Since he had dreamt those dreams of future greatness at age 17, we see that his dreams took 22 years to come true!

> Rabbi Levy taught: One should wait as long as 22 years for a good dream to come true. This we learn from Joseph. (*Berachot* 54a)

What is special about the number 22? In what way is it connected to the fulfillment of dreams?

Rav Kook noted that the Hebrew alphabet contains 22 letters. Through myriad combinations and permutations of these 22 letters, we are able to express all of our thoughts and ideas. If we were to lack even one letter, however, we would be unable to formulate certain words and ideas.

The ancient mystical work *Sefer Yetzirah* offers an intriguing

---

[34] Adapted from *Ein Eyah* vol. II, p. 268.

insight into the functioning of the universe. Just as hundreds of thousands of words are formed from a small set of letters, so too, the vast array of forces that govern our world are in fact the result of a relatively small number of fundamental causes. If 22 letters are needed to express any idea, then 22 years are needed for the universe's elemental forces to bring about any desired effect. Thus it is reasonable that we should allow a dream as long as 22 years to be realized.

Rabbi Levy is also teaching a second lesson: nothing is completely without value. One should not be hasty to disregard a dream. In every vision, there resides some element of truth, some grain of wisdom. It may take 22 years to be revealed, or perhaps its potential may never be realized in our world; but it always contains some kernel of truth.

VAYIGASH: THE HAZARDS OF LEADERSHIP[35]

Joseph Dies First

The text implies that Joseph was the first of Jacob's twelve sons to die. "Joseph died, and [then] his brothers and all that generation" (Ex. 1:6). Why was Joseph's life shorter than that of his brothers?

The Sages suggested that Joseph's early demise was due to his position of public office. When one assumes a position of authority, "one's days and years are shortened" (*Berachot* 55a). Yet this hardly seems fair. Why should those who dedicate their lives to public service be penalized by having a shorter life?

Joseph's Mistake

Working for the public good is certainly laudable. However, there are certain hazards inherent in such a path. Precisely because one is busy attending to important communal affairs, one may neglect one's own personal needs. A communal leader may come to view his own needs – whether material, spiritual, or moral – as insignificant.

We may observe this phenomenon in Joseph. As viceroy, Joseph was busy supervising the national and economic affairs of

---

[35] Adapted from *Ein Eyah* vol. II on *Berachot* IX: 25.

Egypt. He saw his position of public office as the vehicle through which God's covenant of *Bein HaBetarim* – which foretold the exile of Abraham's descendants in a foreign land – would be realized.

When Joseph heard his father referred to as "your servant," he did not object to this display of disrespect toward his father. Joseph was occupied with the overall objective; he did not want it to be compromised due to his obligation to show his father respect.

Joseph's error is not uncommon. This is a universal lesson for all leaders: they should not allow any goal or aspiration, no matter how lofty, to lead them to disregard lesser obligations.

The King's *Sefer Torah*

We find a similar idea in the special laws pertaining to a Jewish king. The Torah instructs the king to write his own *sefer Torah* and keep it with him at all times. In this way, "his heart will not be raised above his brothers, and he will not stray from the Law to the right or to the left" (Deut. 17:20). The Torah specifically cautions the monarch that, despite his involvement in critical national affairs, his public service should not lead him to neglect his private obligations. He is obligated to observe the law in his personal life, like every other citizen.

The Torah promises that a king who heeds this warning will be blessed with a long reign. Unlike those who fail the tests of public office, such a king will not live a life of "shortened days and years."

Life is not just major goals and aspirations. All of us, even those serving in high public office, must conduct ourselves appropriately in all facets of life. Those who maintain their integrity in their personal lives will be blessed with success in their most important and loftiest goals.

VAYIGASH: THE REUNION OF JOSEPH AND JUDAH'[36]

We all have limited amounts of time and energy and must learn how to apportion these resources wisely. In particular, we need to find a balance between activities that are directed inwardly, for our own personal development, and those directed outwardly, for the benefit of others. As Hillel taught, "If I am not for myself, who will be for me? And if I am only for myself, then what am I?" (*Avot* 1:14). Both areas are crucial. The difficulty lies in deciding how much of our time and resources should be dedicated to inner growth, and how much for reaching out to others.

The nation as a whole also needs to juggle these two competing spheres. The search for the correct balance was played out in the dispute between Joseph and his brothers. Their struggle corresponded to two different paths within the Jewish people – one stressing the nation's own spiritual development, and the other emphasizing Israel's universal responsibility and influence.

Eidut and Torah

The Jewish people are crowned with two qualities, *Eidut* (testimony) and Torah, as it says: "[God] established testimony in

---

[36] Adapted from *Shemuot HaRe'iyah*, vol. 10 (1930).

Jacob; He set down Torah in Israel" (Ps. 78:5). What are these two qualities?

The essence of *Eidut* is to accurately report facts as they occurred. Nothing may be added or altered when giving testimony. Torah study, on the other hand, involves *chiddush* – creative and innovative thought.

This dichotomy of *Eidut* and Torah is the root of the conflict between Jacob's sons. Joseph stressed the concept of *Eidut*, as it says, "a testimony [*eidut*] for Joseph" (Ps. 81:6). The aspect of *Eidut* reflects Joseph's desire to interact with the nations and expose them to the authentic message of monotheism and morality.

On the other hand, the other brothers – and especially Judah, their leader – emphasized the Torah and the special holiness of the Jewish people. They sought to develop and cultivate the unique heritage of Israel. Thus it was Judah whom Jacob picked to establish an academy of Torah study in Goshen. Furthermore, the Midrash credits Judah with burning the wagons that Pharaoh sent to bring Jacob's family to Egypt. Judah ordered that the wagons be destroyed when he saw that they were engraved with idolatrous symbols *(Breishit Rabbah* 94:3). This act, introducing the law of destroying idols with fire,[37] demonstrated Judah's focus on the aspects of purity and innovation in Torah.

The Message of *Shema*

Joseph and Judah, and their paths of *Eidut* and Torah, were united

---

[37] Later codified in Deut. 7:25 – "You must burn their idolatrous statues in fire."

when Jacob brought his family down to Joseph in Egypt. The Sages noted a peculiar incident that took place during the family reunion. The Torah relates that Joseph cried on his father's neck, but is silent regarding Jacob's actions at this emotional meeting. What was Jacob doing? According to the Midrash, he was busy reciting the *Shema*. What was the significance of the *Shema* at that particular time?

The *Shema's* message is, of course, one of unity. "Listen, Israel: God is our Lord; God is one" (Deut. 6:4). These two phrases refer to two levels (or stages) of God's unity in the world. The first level is "God is our Lord." This is God's unity as it is currently revealed in the world, a world created according to the blueprint of Torah, and through which we can recognize the greatness of the Creator. The second, higher level is "God is one." This is God's unity as it will be revealed in the future, a unity that will encompass the entire universe. "After all has ceased to be, the One Revered will reign alone" (from the *Adon Olam* hymn).

Judah represents the first level of God's unity, a unity manifested through the Torah and the special role of the Jewish people. Joseph, on the other hand, sought to sanctify God's Name among the nations and bring knowledge of one Creator to the entire world. He represents the second level, the universal unity of God. Jacob's recitation of the *Shema* thus encapsulated the combined visions of both Judah and Joseph.

The Scales of the Leviathan

The two paths within Jacob's family – Judah's path of particularity and Joseph's path of universality – split when Joseph was sold as a slave. The brothers' reconciliation and the unification of these two paths took place in *Vayigash*, when Judah drew near to his brother Joseph (Gen. 44:18).

The Midrash (*Breishit Rabbah* 93:2) chose a curious verse to describe the coming together of Joseph and his brothers. The word *vayigash* ("and he drew near") also appears in Job's description of the scales of the giant Leviathan: "One is so near (*yigshu*) to the other, that no air can enter between them" (Job 41:8). What do the Leviathan's scales have to do with the reunification of Jacob's family?

According to the Sages, this fearsome sea creature belongs in a category of its own. All living creatures have both males and females, except the Leviathan (*Baba Batra* 74b). In other words, while all other creatures reflect a quality of duality and fracture that exists in our imperfect world, the Leviathan retains something of the universe's original unity. Thus the Talmud describes the Leviathan as being *akalton* – twisting around and encompassing the entire world (Rashi ad loc). The Zohar (2:179a) teaches that "its tail is placed in its mouth." In other words, this wondrous creature has neither beginning nor end. Undetected, it surrounds and unites the entire world. This hidden unity will be revealed in the future, when the righteous *tzaddikim* will feast on the Leviathan (*Baba Batra* 74b).

The future will reveal the underlying oneness of the universe, the ideal balance of Torah and *Eidut*, of Judah and Joseph, of our inwardly and outwardly directed efforts, of the particular and the universal. The two paths will be united like the scales of the Leviathan, magnificently arranged "one so near to the other that no air can enter between them

VAYECHI: REVEALING THE END OF DAYS[38]

> Jacob called for his sons. He said: "Gather together, and I will tell you what will happen at the End of Days." (Gen. 49:1)

In fact, Jacob never revealed to his sons when the final redemption would take place. According to the Midrash, this secret – the time of redemption – was hidden from Jacob. The Midrash uses the following parable to explain what transpired between Jacob and his sons at Jacob's death bed.

The Parable of the Devoted Servant

> This is like the case of a devoted servant whom the king trusted with all that he possessed. When the servant realized his end was near, he assembled his sons in order to set them free and inform them where their will and deed were located.
>
> The king, however, discovered [this plan] and stood over his servant. When the servant saw the king, he backtracked from what he had planned to tell his sons. He began to entreat his sons, "Please, remain servants of the king! Honor him just as I have honored him all of my days."

---

[38] Adapted from *Midbar Shur*, pp. 273-280.

So, too, Jacob gathered his sons to reveal to them the End of Days. But the Holy One revealed Himself to Jacob. "You summoned your sons, but not Me?"... When Jacob saw God, he began to entreat his sons, "Please, honor the Holy One just as my fathers and I have honored Him."

The Holy One then informed [Jacob]: "'It honors God to conceal the matter' (Proverbs 25:2). This attribute does not belong to you." (*Midrash Tanchuma VaYechi* 8)

This Midrash raises many questions. Why did Jacob want to reveal to his sons when the final exile would end? Why was he prevented from doing so? Also, there are discrepancies between the parable and the referent. It was God who concealed the end of days from Jacob; thus in the parable, it should have been the king who hid the deed from the servant, not the servant who hid the deed from his sons. Furthermore, the servant wanted his sons to be free – would Jacob have wanted his sons to abandon the yoke of Heaven? And why did God reprimand Jacob for not calling Him?

The Reason for the Lengthy Exile

We first need to examine why the exile has lasted so long. It is written that the people of Israel "were punished twice for all their sins" (Isaiah 40:2). How could God, the compassionate Father, punish the Jewish people more severely than they deserved to be punished?

The key to understanding this matter lies in the verse:

> I have only known you from all of the families of the earth. Therefore, I visit upon you all of your iniquities. (Amos 3:2)

If the Jewish people were like all other peoples, then the destruction of the Temple would have sufficed to atone for their sins. However, the Jewish people are destined to acquire a true, intimate love of God, permanently fixed in their hearts, as indicated by the phrase "I have only known you," which implies a unique relationship between God and the Jewish people. In order to achieve this level of unfailing, constant love, they need to undergo an intensive purification to purge all moral and spiritual failings. If not corrected, these dormant faults could be reawakened and induce moral relapses in future generations.

For this reason, the Sages wrote that the people of Israel sinned doubly, were punished doubly, and will be consoled doubly (*Pesikta deRav Kahana, Nachamu*). Their sin was twofold: besides the gravity of the sin itself, it led to their estrangement from God. They were also punished doubly: in order to cleanse them from the sin and to purify their hearts to love God. And they will also be consoled doubly: not only will their transgressions be forgiven, they will also merit a special closeness to God.

Calculating the End of Days

The second issue that must be clarified is: is it possible to know when the End of Days will come? The Sages interpreted the verse,

"A day of retribution is in My heart" (Isaiah 63:4) as follows: "to My heart I have revealed it, but not to My limbs" (*Sanhedrin* 97a). The term "My limbs" is a metaphor for the angels. How could Jacob have access to information which was hidden even from the angels?

Theoretically, if we were to know the spiritual level the Jewish people need to attain, the errors that future generations will commit, and the time needed to rectify those errors, then we would be able to calculate when the End of Days will occur. However, even this complex calculation is not so straightforward. Perhaps God will not wait until the Jewish people are worthy of redemption based on their own merits? Perhaps God will not delay the redemption until their sins have been fully expiated through exile, but will hasten the end, elevating Israel even before the people have properly prepared themselves to be redeemed?

In fact, this is precisely how Daniel interpreted King Nebuchadnezzar's dream, a dream foretelling "what will be at the End of Days." In the dream, Nebuchadnezzar saw that "a stone, broken off not by [human] hands, struck the statue" (Daniel 2:34). This great statue, wrought from four different metals, symbolized the four great empires[39] and the corresponding exiles of the Jewish people. The stone, the Divine instrument for destroying the statue and terminating the exile, was "broken off not by human hands," indicating that the final redemption will not be achieved solely through the efforts of the Jewish people. God desires that Israel will work toward rectifying its sins and moral deficiencies; but ultimately, it will be granted eternal spiritual greatness by God Himself (See Zohar, *Pekudei* 240).

---

[39] Commonly understood to be Babylon, Persia, Greece, and Rome.

Spiritual Growth versus Submission

The righteous who walk before God always try to attain spiritual perfection on their own, without "burdening" Heaven and expecting Divine assistance. Jacob wanted his family to acquire the final objective of constant love for God through their own efforts. By revealing the End of Days to them, Jacob intended to indicate the objective that they should strive for, so that they could attain this level through their own actions.

God, however, had different plans. Humanity was given free will so that they should not need to rely on *nehama dekisufa*, the "bread of shame." The necessity to labor and make correct choices in life gives us the satisfaction of earning our reward. Yet there is a drawback to attaining perfection through our own efforts. While the ultimate goal is to attain love of God, we also need to feel a sense of awe and submission before God. In truth, for all of our remarkable potential, we do not deserve to be called "God's servants." The Midrash teaches that God held Mount Sinai over the Israelites like a bucket, forcing them to accept the Torah (*Shabbat* 88a). This demonstrated that the Jewish people must also acknowledge their subservience to God.

Similarly, in the end of days, God will not wait until the people of Israel have perfected themselves, for then they would only have the merit of loving God, and would lack the necessary awe and servitude to Him. God will redeem the Jewish people before they are ready; the redemption will arrive like "a stone that was not broken off by [our own] hands." It is impossible to calculate the hour of redemption, for it will not occur when the Jewish people are ready, but when God deems it time. Thus Isaiah's prophecy indicates that the date is only revealed to "My heart" – i.e., only God knows.

Explaining the Parable

Now we may understand the parable. The king's servant wanted to free his sons from subservience to the king so that they would be able to serve the king purely out of love. When the king stood above him, however, the servant recognized that the majesty of the king is so great, that the highest level is in fact to be the king's servant. That is why God rebuked Jacob when he summoned his sons without Him. God was questioning Jacob: Do you want the redemption to be achieved only through your own efforts? Do you want it to be exclusively based on the quality of love for God?

Complete adherence to God's will, however, could only take place after the Torah was given at Sinai. Thus the Midrash concludes with God's rejoinder to Jacob: "This matter is not for you." True subservience to God will only be possible after the revelation of the Torah and its mitzvot.

When the faithful servant saw the king in all his majesty standing over him, he backtracked from his original plan of freeing his sons. Similarly, after God revealed Himself, Jacob recognized God's infinitely exalted nature. He realized that, even in the End of Days, the true goal is to combine love with submission and awe. Therefore, Jacob abandoned his plan to reveal the level of pure love of God that the Jewish people need to attain in the End of Days. Instead, Jacob admonished his sons to honor and fear God, just as he and his fathers had done.

VAYECHI: WHEN GREAT SOULS ERR[40]

Shortly before his death, Jacob blessed his sons. Some of these blessings, however, were more like reprimands:

> Reuben, you are my firstborn... first in rank and first in power. [But since you were] unstable as water, you will no longer be first, for you moved your father's beds. (Gen. 49:3-4)

According to some opinions, Reuben did not actually interfere with his father's sleeping arrangements.[41] He intended to do so, indignant at what he saw as a slight to his mother's honor and her position in the household. But at the last minute, Reuben restrained himself.

How did Reuben succeed in overcoming his intense feelings of injustice and dishonor?

Reuben's Fear of Punishment

One scholar inferred the method Reuben used to master his anger

---

[40] Adapted from *Ein Eyah* vol. IV, pp. 48-49.
[41] After Rachel's death, Jacob moved his bed to the tent of Rachel's handmaid. Reuben, deeply disturbed by what he saw as an affront to his mother's honor, moved his father's bed to Leah's tent (*Shabbat* 55a).

by reversing the letters of the word "פַּחַז" ("unstable") to "זחף" and reading it as an acronym: "זָכַרְתָּ – You reminded yourself of the punishment for this act; חָלִיתָ – you made yourself ill over it; and פֵּירַשְׁתָּ – you avoided sin" (*Shabbat* 55b).

This explanation is surprising. Was Reuben motivated by the lowest form of *yirat Shamayim* (awe of Heaven) – the fear of punishment? Was this the only way the *tzaddik* could prevent himself from wrongdoing? Could such a great individual not take advantage of more lofty incentives, evoking his natural love and awe of God in order to avoid sin?

The Achilles' Heel of Great Souls

Some people are blessed with such nobility of soul that their traits are naturally virtuous and good. Yet even these *tzaddikim* need to recognize their limitations as fallible human beings. They too may be misguided. Precisely because they rely so heavily on their innate integrity, they may more easily fall into the trap of deluding themselves and making terrible mistakes, inflicting great harm on themselves and those around them.

Truly great souls will avoid this mistake. They carefully examine the source of their moral outrage. Further examination may indeed reveal that their zealous response comes from a sense of true injustice. But if they have any doubts as to the source for their powerful emotions, they can adopt a different approach. Instead of examining the matter in terms of ideals and lofty visions of the future, they will take into account more commonplace moral considerations. Such unpretentious calculations are sometimes more effective than nobler considerations.

Reuben reminded himself that he would be held accountable for disrupting the delicate balance in the family and temporarily usurping his father's position. The simple reminder of the personal price to be paid helped Reuben clear his mind. He was then able to analyze more accurately his true motivations and arrive at the correct moral decision.

The resulting inner turmoil was tremendous. Reuben was accustomed to following the dictates of his innate integrity. The conflict between his sense of injustice and his awareness of the correct response was so great that he felt ill – emotionally, and even physically: "You made yourself ill over it."

This too indicates greatness of soul: the ability to acquiesce to moral imperatives. Truly great individuals are able, like Reuben, to rein in all of the soul's powers when necessary. They recognize the absolute justice of the Eternal Judge, before Whom there are no excuses and no exceptions. They follow the dictum that even if the entire world – your entire *inner* world – tells you that you are righteous, still consider yourself fallible (see *Niddah* 30b).

Much good can result from recalling the punishment for wrongdoing, even if this motivation may appear beneath one's spiritual stature. This simple reminder can overcome all the sophisticated calculations – calculations which may mislead even the noblest souls. In this fashion, Reuben succeeded in avoiding sin and retained his moral integrity

ספר שמות

THE BOOK OF

EXODUS

SHEMOT: "I WILL BE WHO I WILL BE"[42]

Moses was not happy that he had been given the task of leading the Jewish people out of Egypt. He foresaw many of the challenges involved, including the difficulty in gaining the trust of the Hebrew slaves.

> "So I will go to the Israelites and say to them, 'The God of your fathers sent me to you.' They will ask what His name is – what should I tell them?"

God replied to Moses:

> "'I Will Be Who I Will Be.' This is what you should tell the Israelites: 'I Will Be' sent me to you." (Ex. 3:13-14)

What do these peculiar names – "I Will Be Who I Will Be" and "I Will Be" – mean? Also, it appears that God gave Moses two different answers. Which name was Moses to use in identifying God to the people?

---

[42] Adapted from *Ein Eyah* vol. I, pp. 45-46.

I Will Be With You

The Talmud in *Berachot* 9b explains God's response as follows:

> "Go tell the Israelites, 'I Will Be Who I Will Be.' 'I Will Be' with you in this exile, and 'I Will Be' with you in future exiles."

> Moses exclaimed, "Master of the Universe, we have enough problems already! Why mention future suffering?"

> God agreed. "Go tell them 'I Will Be' sent me to you."

This explanation, however, creates new difficulties. Did God need Moses to explain human psychology to Him? Did Moses understand the people better than their Creator?

A Guide for All Times

God's message to the Jewish people was that the Torah and its mitzvot would enable them to attain their highest state of being. The Torah would guide them throughout history, in all situations, whether they were a subjugated people in exile or a free people in their own land.

God wanted the people to know that the redemption from slavery in Egypt was not a one-time rescue mission. They were leaving Egypt in order to receive the Torah at Sinai. The Divine name "I Will Be Who I Will Be" was meant to convey a fundamental message: the Torah is a guide for all times, a path that would sustain the people even during future exiles and troubled times.

God never intended, however, that Moses would use this name. Moses was not supposed to explicitly mention future exiles and further dishearten a downtrodden people. Rather, Moses was to tell them the shorter name, "I Will Be." The subjugated nation would be informed that God is with them now – "I Will Be" with you in this exile, and I will redeem you. And they would understand that the Torah will also guide their lives when they will live as an independent nation in their own land.

Implicitly, however, the name "I Will Be" contains a deeper message. As a free people in the Land of Israel, the Torah would prepare them to be an eternal nation, overcoming the challenges of future exiles. "'I Will Be' with them in this exile; and 'I Will Be' with them in future exiles."

SHEMOT: THE INNER TRAIT OF GOODNESS[43]

When Moses expressed his doubts as to whether the people would believe he was indeed God's messenger, God gave him a sign to prove his authenticity – but a sign which implied displeasure in Moses' lack of faith in his people.

What was the sign? Moses' hand temporarily became white with *tzara'at* (leprosy). A miraculous sign, to be sure, but *tzara'at* is an affliction that defiles – a clear indication that Moses was being chastised.

The Sages noted a subtle discrepancy between the Torah's description of Moses' hand turning leprous and its subsequent return to normalcy. The first time, Moses took out his hand "and behold! his hand was leprous like snow" (Ex. 4:6). Then Moses placed his hand inside his robes a second time, and when he had "removed it from his chest, his skin had [already] returned to normal" (Ex. 4:7).

A careful reading of the text indicates that the two transformations occurred differently. The leprosy took hold *after* Moses removed his hand from his robe; but his hand reverted to its normal color even *before* he had taken out his hand, while it was still inside his robe. Why should there be a difference between the two?

---

[43] Adapted from *Ein Eyah* vol. IV, p. 243.

From here, the Sages concluded, "The Divine trait of *tovah* [goodness] comes more quickly than the trait of *puranut* [suffering or punishment]" (*Shabbat* 97a).

What does this mean? Why should one trait be faster or better than another?

Transcending the Limits of Time

There is in fact an essential difference between these two facets of Divine providence. The attribute of *tovah* is the very foundation of the world. Divine goodness is the goal of all existence; it is united with the very source of life. For this reason, this trait transcends the restrictions of time and place. Even when it descends into our finite world, a reality bound by time and place, we may still sense its elevated, limitless source.

This is the meaning of the Talmudic statement, "The trait of goodness comes more quickly." The attribute of *tovah* reveals an inner light, free from the restrictions of time and place. Ezekiel described this phenomenon in his sublime vision of angelic creatures "running and returning, like rapid flashes of lightning" (Ez. 1:14).

The trait of *puranut* is a different story. *Puranut* is not an intrinsic aspect of reality. It is ancillary and transitory. Its value is only to serve the good, to 'refine the vessels' so that they will be able to receive the flow of Divine goodness in all of its abundance.

As a result, *puranut* is subject to the limitations of time and place, and its manifestation is delayed.

The True Nature of Israel

While Divine goodness is integrally connected to the inner essence of life, *puranut* relates to its superficial aspects. The more we distance ourselves from the true reality, the more our worldview becomes filtered through the lens of *puranut*. Seeing the world as a place of judgment and suffering is a perception emanating from distortions of the imagination. It does not focus on the true nature of reality, but on its external appearance.

Precisely here – as God taught Moses the true inner nature of Israel, beneath the cloak of outer appearances – the superficiality of *puranut* was unveiled. Moses' arm only looked leprous after it was exposed to the outside light. In the realm of true essence, there is no place for suffering and harsh punishments; this trait belongs to the realm of superficial appearances.

Moses' hand was restored to its original healthy state as soon as he placed it "inside his chest," indicating that the attribute of goodness reflects the inner essence of reality. It is connected to the root of creation, transcending all limitations of the finite universe. Therefore Divine beneficence is not restricted by the framework of time and "arrives quickly."

VA'EIRA: GOD'S NAME[44]

Why do we find different names for God in the Torah?

Different names correspond to the different ways in which God reveals Himself in the world. The Tetragrammaton, the special name composed of the four letters *Yud-Hey-Vav-Hey*, corresponds to a level of Divine revelation that was concealed before Moses' time.

> "I revealed Myself to Abraham, Isaac and Jacob as *'El Shaddai'* [God Almighty]. But I was not known to them through My name *Y-H-V-H*." (Ex. 6:3)

What is the significance of these two names of God? Why did only Moses' generation merit knowledge of the Tetragrammaton?

In the same prophetic communication to Moses, God contrasted the Patriarchs' ties to the Land of Israel with that of their descendants. Abraham, Isaac, and Jacob were only travelers and foreigners in the Land:

> "I made My covenant with them, giving them the Land of Canaan, the land of their wanderings, where they lived as foreigners." (Ex. 6:4)

---

[44] Adapted from *Midbar Shur*, pp. 293-297.

Their descendants, on the other hand, were destined to settle permanently in the Land: "I will give it to you as an eternal inheritance" (Ex. 6:8).

Is there some connection between the different names for God and residence in *Eretz Yisrael?*

A Higher Level of Providence

Dwelling in the Land of Israel means living with a greater degree of Divine providence. It is "a land constantly under the scrutiny of the Eternal, your God; the eyes of the Eternal your God are on it at all times" (Deut. 11:12). God gave *Eretz Yisrael* to the Jewish people as an eternal inheritance, so that they will always benefit from this unparalleled level of Divine providence. God's providence will never leave the people of Israel; their history transcends the laws of nature.

This level of Divine guidance was only possible after they became a nation. Individuals, even the most righteous, may waver and stumble.[45] Therefore, the Patriarchs could only be sojourners in *Eretz Yisrael.* They could only merit the Land's preternatural providence in a temporary, sporadic fashion.

The name "*Shaddai*" comes from the word "*shiddud,*" meaning "to intervene." This name for God implies occasional Divine

---

[45] Rav Kook held that "free will only applies to individuals. Regarding the Jewish people as a whole, however, God made a covenant, namely that it is absolutely impossible for the entire Jewish people to be separated and detached from the holiness of His great Name" (*Midbar Shur*, p. 314).

intervention in the natural realm. This was the degree of providence that the *Avot* experienced. They lived in a world of natural forces – with occasional miracles. They were but travelers in the Land of Israel. God was thus revealed to them as *El Shaddai*.

With the formation of Israel as a nation, however, the special providence of the Land of Israel became the Jewish people's permanent inheritance. The generation of Moses was granted a higher revelation of God's providence, as reflected in the name "Y-H-V-H." This Divine name comes from the word "*lehavot*," "to cause to exist." Their world was no longer a universe ruled by the forces of nature. They merited a constant, direct connection to the One Who continually creates and sustains all existence.

BO: THE BIRTH OF A NATION[46]

> This is how you must eat [the Passover offering]: with
> your waist belted, your shoes on your feet, and your
> staff in your hand. You must eat it with *chipazon* – in
> haste. (Ex. 12:11)

The word "*chipazon*" is an uncommon word. In the entire
Bible, it appears only three times. Twice it is used to describe the
Israelites' haste when they fled Egypt. Why did they need to be
ready to depart at a moment's notice?

According to the Midrash, there were in fact *three* parties who
were in a rush for the Israelites to leave Egypt. The Egyptians,
afraid of further plagues and catastrophes, wanted the Hebrew
slaves to clear out as quickly as possible. The Israelites were in a
hurry lest Pharaoh change his mind yet again and refuse to let
them leave.

And there was a third party in a state of urgency. The Midrash
speaks of the *chipazon* of the *Shechinah*. Why was God in a hurry?

A Hasty Redemption

The redemption from Egypt needed to be fast, like the swift

---

[46] Adapted from *Ma'amarei HaRe'iyah* vol. I, p. 164.

release of an arrow from a bow. Here was a group of slaves who had almost completely forgotten the greatness of their souls, a treasured inheritance from their ancestors who were widely respected as holy princes.[47] With a decisive wave of God's hand, a nation brimming with courage and nobility of spirit, unlike any people the world had ever seen, was formed. This was the dramatic birth "of a nation from the midst of another nation" on the stage of human history.

A meteoric exodus from Egypt with wonders and miracles was critical to protect this fledgling nation from the dark confusion of universal paganism. The Jewish people needed to be quickly extracted from the idolatrous Egyptian milieu in which they had lived for centuries so that they would be free to raise the banner of pure faith and enlightened ideals.

The Future Redemption

The word *chipazon* appears a third time in the Bible, in Isaiah's breathtaking description of the future redemption. Unlike the Exodus from Egypt,

> You will not leave with haste – *chipazon* – or go in flight. For the Eternal will go before you, and your rear guard will be the God of Israel. (52:12)

Unlike the miraculous upheaval that brought about the dramatic launch of the Jewish people, the future redemption will

---

[47] As the Hittites informed Abraham: "You are a prince of God in our midst" (Gen. 23:6).

be a gradual process, advancing step by step. Why will the future redemption be so different from the redemption from Egypt?

In Egypt, the Hebrew slaves had adopted the idolatrous culture of their neighbors. Their redemption required supernatural intervention, a Divine rescue from above. But the future redemption will take place within the laws of nature. It will emanate from the stirring of the human heart, אתערותא דלתתא – an awakening from below. The Jewish people will rise from their exilic slumber, return to their homeland, regain their independence, reclaim their forests and cities, defend themselves from enemies who seek to destroy them, recreate their academies of Torah, and reestablish their spiritual center in Jerusalem. Step by step, without overriding the laws of nature, so that even the *ba'al ha-neiss*, the beneficiary of the miracle, is unaware of the great miracle that is unfolding.

Unlike the dramatic exodus from Egypt, the future redemption is not an escape from the world and its influences. Over the centuries, the Jewish people have succeeded in illuminating many aspects of the world that were full of darkness. Our influence has refined the world on many levels. The impact of our Torah and lifestyle, which we observed with dedication and self-sacrifice throughout the exile, served as a beacon of light for many nations.

The goals of the future redemption are twofold. First: to complete our national mission of spreading the light of Torah throughout the world. This light needs to be projected in its purest, most pristine form, cleansed from the dregs that have accumulated during centuries of exposure to negative influences. The second goal is to purify ourselves from those foreign tendencies which we have adopted through contact with other nations during our lengthy exile.

When we will once again stand strong and free on the majestic heights of our land, ready to realize our spiritual potential – only then will the nations be able to see our light.

We must draw upon the heritage of our redemption from Egypt and our miraculous birth as the people of Israel. The current process of redemption, manifest in the revitalization of the Jewish people in the Land of Israel, must not be detached from our national mission as a light unto the nations. Then our future redemption will be not in haste, but will advance steadily, like the ever-spreading light of daybreak.[48]

---

[48] The Jerusalem Talmud (*Berachot* 1:1) relates that two scholars were walking in the Arbel Valley when they saw the first rays of dawn break forth over the valley. Rabbi Chiyya turned his colleague and said, "So will be the redemption of Israel. In the beginning it starts out slowly; then, as it progresses, it shines greater and greater."

BO: DONKEY-HOLINESS[49]

Immediately before leaving Egypt, the Israelites were commanded to commemorate the final plague of *makkat bechorot*, the death of the firstborn, by consecrating their firstborn, saying:

> When Pharaoh stubbornly refused to let us leave, God killed all the firstborns in Egypt, both man and beast. I therefore offer to God all male firstling animals, and redeem all the firstborns of my sons. (Ex. 13:15)

This mitzvah applies not only to firstborn babies, but also to kosher animals, and – surprisingly – to firstborn donkeys: "Every firstling donkey must be redeemed with a sheep" (Ex. 13:13).

Why are firstborn donkeys also included in this mitzvah?

This is even more surprising when we consider that some non-kosher animals, such as camels and pigs, have only one sign of impurity. Donkeys, however, exhibit both signs of impurity.[50] The Zohar teaches that the donkey is *avi avot ha-tumah*, the ultimate source of impurity.

---

[49] Adapted from *Igrot HaRe'iyah* vol. II, p. 188, letter 555 (1913); *Orot*, p. 85 (*Orot HaTechiyah*, sec. 45).

[50] Donkeys are not ruminants, nor do they have cloven hooves.

In addition, the Maharal of Prague[51] noted that the Hebrew word for "donkey" (*chamor*) shares the same root as the word for "material" (*chomer*). The donkey, he explained, is a symbol of materialism and crassness.

So why did God bestow the special holiness of *bechor* on this ignoble creature?

Hidden Holiness

One explanation proposed by the Sages in *Bechorot* 5b is that donkeys helped facilitate the Exodus, as they hauled the treasures of Egyptian gold and silver for the Hebrew slaves. Yet the Israelites could have used some other pack animal. It would appear that there is something special about the donkey, that it symbolizes an inner truth about the redemption of the Jewish people, both in Egypt and in the future national rebirth of the Messianic Era.

The Israelites in Egypt had sunk to the lowest levels of idolatry and impurity. Outwardly, they were indistinguishable from their Egyptian neighbors. According to the Midrash, even the angels were unable to distinguish between the two nations. They questioned God's decision to rescue the Israelites at the Red Sea, protesting, "Both the Egyptians and the Israelites worship idols!"

But as with the donkey, the impurity of the Jewish people was only on the surface, hiding a great inner holiness. It was a superficial defect, as it says, "Do not look upon me [disdainfully] because I am black; for [it is only] the sun that has darkened me"

---

[51] Rabbi Judah Loew ben Bezalel (1520-1609) in *Gevurot Hashem*, chapter 29.

(Song of Songs 1:6).

The Messianic Donkey

We find a similar idea with regard to the future redemption. The Sages noted that the prophets used conflicting metaphors to describe the Messianic Era. In Daniel's nighttime vision, the Messianic king arrives "on the clouds of the heaven" (7:13). The prophet Zechariah, on the hand, spoke of a righteous king who makes his appearance as "a pauper, riding on a donkey" (9:9). So how will the Messiah arrive – floating on clouds, or sitting on a donkey?

Rabbi Yehoshua ben Levi explained that the Messiah's form of transportation depends on us:

> If [the people of Israel] merit, he will come "on heavenly clouds." If they do not merit, then he will be "a pauper riding on a donkey." (*Sanhedrin* 98a)

In other words, if the Jewish people attain a spiritual level high enough, they will merit a supernatural redemption replete with wonders and miracles – the Messianic king on clouds. If, however, the redemption arrives because the final hour has come, but the Jewish people are not worthy – then the redemption will unfold through natural means (see *Ohr HaChaim* on Num. 24:17).

Thus, "a pauper riding on a donkey" is a metaphor for an undeserved redemption, a redemption which comes despite a poverty of merits. It is a redemption based on natural processes, as exemplified by the donkey, a symbol of the material world. Yet this donkey, while externally crass and impure, has a special holiness hidden within – the holiness of the firstborn.

According to Rav Kook, the image of the Messiah arriving on a donkey characterizes the period of *Ikveta deMashicha*, the generation when the "footsteps" (*ikvot*) of redemption are first heard. The Talmud (*Sotah* 49b) describes this era as a time of terrible spiritual decline, replete with brazenness, immorality, and corruption. But the Zohar asserts that, despite its external faults, the generation will be "good on the inside." This inner goodness is reflected in the unusual nature of the Jewish people in the pre-Messianic Era. Despite the darkness clouding their behavior and beliefs, they are characterized by an innate holiness, which finds expression in their great love for the Jewish people and the Land of Israel.

The Function of *Chevlei Mashiach*

The Sages indicated the deeply disturbing nature of *Ikveta deMashicha* with the term "*chevlei mashiach*," the 'birth pangs' that precede the Messianic Era. In his seminal work, *Orot*, Rav Kook discussed various reasons for the intensified degree of materialism that characterizes the era of national revival. His central argument is that the Messianic 'birth pangs' come to correct an imbalance stemming from centuries of stateless dispersion.

Rav Kook explained the process using the following analogy. The dregs at the bottom of a wine bottle help preserve the wine. If a bottle lacks dregs, and we wish to correct the situation by adding dregs, the initial result will be to muddy the entire bottle, temporarily ruining it. But as the dregs settle at the bottom, the wine regains its clarity and benefits from the preservative nature of the dregs.

So too, involvement in material pursuits is necessary to ensure the flow of normal life. The exile, with its concentration on spiritual matters, enervated the life-force of the Jewish people to such an extent that their national survival was in danger. The Jewish people needed to return to their land in order to survive as a nation. The return to the land and to a more balanced national life meant greater involvement in life's material aspects.[52] Initially, the crassness and brazenness of the pre-Messianic Era are cause for great consternation. But as the negative forces are subdued, like the settling of the wine dregs to the bottom of the bottle, their detrimental aspects dissipate.

Transforming Darkness to Light

The period of *Ikveta deMashicha* is a difficult time, and not all the Sages were eager to experience it. Rav Yosef, however, demonstrated great spiritual courage, saying, "Let the Messiah come; and may I merit to sit in the shadow of his donkey's dung" (*Sanhedrin* 98b). Once again, we find the metaphor of the donkey used in connection with the Messianic Era.

Rav Yosef was accustomed to looking at the inner essence of things. He recognized the tremendous inner holiness hidden in this problematic generation, as symbolized by the Messiah's

---

[52] Thus the early pioneers were occupied primarily with the *physical* revival of the Jewish people in *Eretz Yisrael* – draining swamps, planting crops, building cities, establishing defense organizations, political institutions, and so on.

donkey. Rav Yosef understood that the Messianic light will demonstrate how to utilize all forces, even the most coarse – "the donkey's dung" – for the sake of good. He knew that the darkness of national rebirth will lead to an even higher light of Torah and knowledge of God.

BESHALACH: THE SOUL'S INNER SONG[53]

The Talmud portrays *Shirat HaYam*, the Israelites' song of thanksgiving at their miraculous deliverance at the Red Sea, as a song of young children and babies:

> When the Israelites exited the sea, they wanted to sing. How did they sing? A young child was sitting on his mother's lap, and a baby was nursing at his mother's breast. When they witnessed the *Shechinah*, the young child lifted his neck and the baby stopped nursing, and they sang out, "This is my God and I will honor Him" (Ex. 15:2). (*Sotah* 30b)

Why did the Sages describe *Shirat HaYam* as a song breaking forth spontaneously from the mouths of babes?

Knowledge and Honor

Kri'at Yam Suf, when the Red Sea split so that the Hebrew slaves could pass through to freedom, was the culmination of the Exodus from Egypt. A careful examination of the text, however,

---

[53] Adapted from *Shemuot HaRe'iyah* (*Beshalach* 5630), quoted in *Peninei HaRe'iyah*, pp. 143-145.

indicates that the Exodus and the Splitting of the Sea had different objectives. The Ten Plagues and the Exodus were meant to ensure that "Egypt will know that I am God" (Ex. 7:5). The goal was *knowledge* of God. Through these wonders and miracles, the world would learn to acknowledge God's existence and recognize His control over the universe.

As the Israelites crossed the Red Sea, however, God announced, "I will be honored through Pharaoh and all his armies" (Ex. 14:17). The miracle at the sea aimed for a higher goal: not just *yedi'at Hashem*, knowing God, but *kevod Hashem* – *honoring* God.

From the Throat

The obligation to honor God is learned from Proverbs: "Honor God from your wealth" (3:9). The *Midrash Tanchuma* explains that in addition to honoring God with one's monetary wealth, one can also honor him with other gifts and talents, including song. For example, an individual blessed with a melodic voice should lead the communal prayers. Rashi explains that the word *"mei-honecha"* ("from your wealth"), may be read as *"mei-gronecha"* – "from your throat."

This leads us to a deeper understanding of what it means to honor God. Knowledge of God is a function of our intellectual faculties; but *kavod* comes from a deeper, more visceral part of our existence. Like the throat, it is connected to our essential life force – "If one's neck is removed, one cannot live" (*Midrash Shir HaShirim* 4:6).

For this reason, the Midrash describes *Shirat HaYam* as a song that burst forth from the mouths of infants. The song at the Red Sea was a natural expression of the Israelites' innate feeling of *kevod Hashem*. It emanated from their yearnings for God, even before they had proper knowledge of God, when they were like young children.

Beyond Set Measures

The Talmud teaches that one reciting the *Shema* prayer should mention both the Exodus and the Splitting of the Sea (Jer. Talmud *Berachot* 1:6). The commentaries explain that we mention both events, since the redemption from Egypt began with the plagues and was completed with the miracle at the sea. And yet the Sages taught a surprising rule: one who forgot to mention the Exodus must go back and recite the *Shema* again, but one who forgot to mention the Splitting of the Sea does not need to recite the *Shema* again (*Shemot Rabbah* 23). If the Splitting of the Sea was the consummation of the Exodus, why is it not a mandatory part of the prayers?

We may better understand the difference between knowing God and honoring Him by contrasting basic mitzvah performance with *hiddur mitzvah*, the elaboration and beautification of a mitzvah. Every mitzvah has parameters and minimum requirements in order to properly fulfill it. *Hiddur mitzvah* means going beyond those basic requirements. *Hiddur mitzvah* is a reflection of our inner aesthetic side and an expression of unrestricted *kevod Hashem*. The Sages derived the concept of *hiddur mitzvah* from the poetic Song at the Sea, "This is my God and I will honor [or: beautify] Him" (Ex. 15:2).

This enables us to understand why one who failed to mention the Splitting of the Sea does not repeat his prayers. Honoring God, unlike knowledge and wisdom, is not defined within a fixed framework. Precisely because of its loftiness, *kevod Hashem* cannot be bound by set limits. It reflects a deeper and more innate aspect of our essence – a stirring of the inner song of the soul.

BESHALACH: LISTENING TO THE OLD[54]

Truly Listening

At a place in the desert called Marah, Moses sweetened the bitter waters so the people would have water to drink. Then he admonished them that they should listen carefully – שָׁמוֹעַ תִּשְׁמַע – to God's voice (Ex. 15:26).

Why is the verb "to listen" (שָׁמוֹעַ תִּשְׁמַע) repeated? In Biblical Hebrew, the grammatical structure of combining the infinitive with the conjugated verb is used to place emphasis. Thus שָׁמוֹעַ תִּשְׁמַע means "you will listen carefully." The Talmud, however, often infers additional meanings from this repetition. In this case, the Sages derived an important lesson about Torah study:

> If "שָׁמוֹעַ" – if you listen to the old – then "תִּשְׁמַע" – you will merit listening to the new. But if you turn away [from the old], you will no longer hear. (*Berachot* 40a)

This statement needs clarification. What is meant by "old" and "new"? What special promise is hinted in the double verb, שָׁמוֹעַ תִּשְׁמַע?

---

[54] Adapted from *Ein Eyah* vol. II, p. 185.

Love of Torah

There are two reasons why people are drawn to study Torah. The first motivation is the natural desire to satisfy one's intellectual curiosity, just as with any other area of study.

However, the proper motivation for Torah study should be a love for Torah that is based on an awareness of the Torah's intrinsic value. This is called *Torah lishmah* – the study of Torah for its own sake.

Studying Torah *lishmah* means that one is aware of the holiness inherent in the very act of studying Torah. This level of Torah study requires one to see the universal light that permeates each and every detail of the Torah, and recognize the Torah's ability to elevate the individual and the entire world with the light of Divine morality.

> We must sense the Godly soul to be found within the ensemble of the Torah's details, perfecting the universe – in life, in the material and spiritual realms, for the collective and the individual. (*Orot HaTorah* 2:2)

Reviewing the Old

When is the disparity between different motivations for Torah study most pronounced? The true test comes with regard to "the old" – when reviewing material previously learned.

If our principal motive is merely intellectual curiosity, then such study will be unappealing and even burdensome. Why should one find reviewing old material to be interesting? If, however, we are studying the Torah because of its true inner value, because it is a revelation of God's blueprint for perfecting the world, then the newness of the material is not important. The value of Torah study comes from the very act of assimilating this Divine revelation, in uniting our thoughts with the holy concepts revealed in the Torah.

One who studies Torah *lishmah* internalizes its teachings. Thus, the Sages taught, one "possesses" the Torah he has studied, for it has become an integral part of him (see *Kiddushin* 32b). With this level of identification with the Torah and its teachings, "he will merit listening to the new" – he will be able to hear original Torah thoughts from within himself.

Rabbi Meir expressed this idea in *Avot* 6:1:

> All who engage in Torah study for its own sake merit many things.... The secrets of Torah are revealed to them. They become like a spring that flows with ever-increasing strength and a stream that never ceases.

The scholar who studies Torah *lishmah* becomes a fountain of creativity, contributing his own innovative explanations and insights. When the Sages taught that this person "will merit hearing the new," this "new" isn't just new to him, but new to the entire world.

One who is disinterested in reviewing previously learned material, on the other hand, is demonstrating that Torah study is only an intellectual pursuit. This person, the Sages warned, "will no longer hear." Even new ideas will fail to pique his interest, for he will come to lack even the normal measure of curiosity with regard to the Torah's wisdom.

YITRO: BLESSINGS ON MIRACLES[55]

Moses' father-in-law Jethro rejoiced when he heard of all that God had done for the Israelites:

> Blessed be God Who rescued you from hand of Egypt and from the hand of Pharaoh, Who liberated the people from Egypt's power. Now I know that God is the greatest of all deities: the very thing they plotted came on them! (Ex. 18:10-11)

The Sages learned from Jethro's blessing that when one sees a place where a miracle occurred for the Jewish people, one should recite the blessing "שֶׁעָשָׂה נִסִּים" – "Who made miracles for our fathers in this place" (*Berachot* 54a).

This statement, however, is difficult to understand in light of the fact that Jethro did not say this blessing when visiting the Red Sea, but when he met Moses and the Israelites in the Sinai desert. How could Jethro serve as an example for this *brachah*, which is only recited when seeing the location where a miracle took place?

---

[55] Adapted from *Ein Eyah* vol. II, pp. 243-244.

Appreciating all Aspects

We need to examine the concept of reciting a blessing over a miracle. Consider two different situations. In case A, a person was headed for the hospital and allowed a neighbor who was not feeling well to come along. The sick neighbor will be thankful for the assistance, but his gratefulness will be tempered by the fact that his benefactor was planning to go there anyway.

In case B, the benefactor, realizing that his neighbor was ill and needed to see a doctor, made a special trip to take him to the hospital. Clearly, the sick neighbor will feel much more thankful in this situation, where the assistance was rendered expressly for him.

If we consider the nature of a miracle, we will realize that it is similar to case B. When we bless God over a miraculous deliverance, we feel completely indebted and thankful to God, as this Divine intervention took place explicitly to help us.

But there is an additional aspect of Divine deliverance which should heighten our sense of gratitude. When an act comes directly from God, not only is the overall goal for the ultimate good, but also all the ramifications and side effects that result from the miracle. We should be appreciative not only for the actual deliverance, but also for any accompanying details. This even includes the location of the miracle, which at some point in time benefited (or will benefit) from the miracle.[56]

---

[56] Cf. the explanation given by Rabbi Nissim of Gerona (1320-1376) for the ancient custom of praying at the graves of great scholars and prophets. "Prayer at these locations is more desirable, since bodies that once experienced the Divine *shefa* [prophetic influence] are buried there." Sparks of holiness can still be found at their gravesites, "since

The Sages learned this from Jethro – that a blessing over a miracle should include recognition of the positive benefits gained from the miracle's accompanying details. Besides thanking God for the overall rescue ("Who liberated the people from Egypt's power"), Jethro also mentioned the details of that rescue: that they were saved from the hands of the Egyptian people and from the hands of Pharaoh.[57]

Furthermore, Jethro called attention to the poetic justice – *middah kneged middah* – in the way that the Egyptians were punished. "The very thing they plotted came upon them." The Egyptians drowned Jewish babies, so they were punished by drowning in the Red Sea. Here was an additional detail that reflected the ultimate justice of the miracle in all of its aspects.

---

their bones served as vessels for the Divine *shefa*" (*Drashot HaRan, Drush* 8).

[57] For one can suffer at the hands of a cruel people, even if the king is kind; and one can suffer at the hands of an evil king, even if the people are sympathetic. In Egypt, the Israelites were the victims of cruelty on the part of the people *and* the king.

YITRO: BREAKING BREAD WITH SCHOLARS[58]

A Meal Before God

When Moses' father-in-law Jethro met the Israelites in the desert, he rejoiced when he heard about the rescue of the Jewish people from Pharaoh's hand, and he brought offerings to God.

> And Aaron and all the elders of Israel came to share the meal with Moses' father-in-law before God. (Ex. 18:12)

The expression "before God" appears out of place here. In what way was this particular feast in God's presence?

The Talmudic sage Rabbi Avin explained:

> To partake of a meal where a Torah scholar is present is like enjoying the splendor of God's Divine Presence. After all, did Jethro, Aaron, and the elders of Israel eat before God? They ate before Moses! Rather, this verse teaches us that sharing a meal with a scholar [such as Moses] is like enjoying the splendor of God's Presence. (*Berachot* 64a)

---

[58] Adapted from *Ein Eyah* vol. II, pp. 395-396.

Rabbi Avin's statement needs to be clarified. What is so wonderful about eating with a Torah scholar? Wouldn't *studying* Torah with him be a much greater spiritual experience? And in what way is such a meal similar to "enjoying the splendor of God's Presence"?

Common Denominator

The human soul, for all its greatness, is limited in its ability to grasp and enjoy God's infinite wisdom. Whatever degree of pleasure we are able to derive from God's Presence is a function of our spiritual attainments. The greater our spiritual awareness, the greater the pleasure we feel in God's Presence. But while we will never gain complete mastery of Divine wisdom, even the small measure of comprehension that *is* possible is sufficient to fill the soul with tremendous light and joy.

A Torah scholar whose holiness is great, whose wisdom is profound, and whose conduct is lofty cannot be properly appreciated by the masses. Common folk will not understand his wisdom and may not be able to relate to his holiness. In what way can they connect with such a lofty scholar?

A scholar's greatest influence takes place in those spheres where others can best relate to him. Most people will be unable to follow his erudite lectures, but a meal forms a common bond between the most illustrious and the most ordinary. This connection allows everyone to experience some aspect of a great scholar's path in Torah and service of God.

When a Torah scholar reveals his great wisdom and holiness,

the average person will be overcome by a sense of unbridgeable distance from such sublime attainments. He may despair of ever reaching a level so far beyond his own limited capabilities. But when sharing a meal with a scholar, the common physical connection enables people to be more receptive to the scholar's noble traits and holy conduct.

Of course, those who are able to understand the scholar's wisdom can more fully appreciate his greatness. Those individuals will derive greater benefit and pleasure from him. This is precisely Rabbi Avin's point: just as the degree of pleasure gained from God's Presence depends on the soul's spiritual state, so too, the benefit we derive from a great scholar depends on our spiritual level and erudition.

MISHPATIM: PERMISSION FOR DOCTORS TO HEAL[59]

Medical Fees

Amongst the various laws in the *parashah* of *Mishpatim* – nearly all of which are of a societal or interpersonal nature – the Torah sets down the laws of compensation for physical damages. When one person injures another, he must compensate the other party with five payments. He must pay for (1) any permanent loss of income due to the injury, (2) embarrassment, (3) pain incurred, (4) loss of income while the victim was recovering, and (5) medical expenses.

This last payment, that he "provide for his complete healing" (Ex. 21:19), i.e., that he cover any medical fees incurred, is of particular interest. The word "to heal" appears 67 times in the Torah, almost always referring to God as the Healer. Only here, as an aside to the topic of damages, does the Torah indicate that we are expected to take active measures to heal ourselves, and not just leave the healing process to nature.

This detail did not escape the keen eyes of the Sages. "From here we see that the Torah gave permission to the doctor to heal" (*Berachot* 60a).

Yet we need to understand: why should the Torah need to

_____

[59] Adapted from *Olat Re'iyah* vol. I, p. 390.

explicitly grant such permission to doctors? If anything, we should expect all medical activity to be highly commended, as doctors ease pain and save lives.

Our Limited Medical Knowledge

The human being is an organic entity. The myriad functions of body and soul are intertwined and interdependent. Which person can claim that he thoroughly understands all of these functions, how they interrelate, and how they interact with the outside world? There is a danger that when we treat a medical problem in one part of the body, we may cause harm to another part. Sometimes the side effects of a particular medical treatment are relatively mild and acceptable. And sometimes the results of treatment may be catastrophic, causing problems far worse than the initial issue.[60]

One could thus conclude that there may be all sorts of hidden side effects, unknown to the doctor, which are far worse than the ailment we are seeking to cure. Therefore, it would be best to let the body heal on its own, relying on its natural powers of recuperation.

Relying on Available Knowledge

The Torah, however, rejects this view. Such an approach could easily be expanded to include all aspects of life. Any effort on our part to improve our lives, to use science and technology to

---

[60] The tragic example of birth defects as a result of treating morning sickness in pregnancy with thalidomide comes to mind.

advance the world, could be rebuffed on the grounds that we lack knowledge of all consequences of the change.

The Sages taught: "The judge can only base his decision on what he is able to see" (*Baba Batra* 131a). If the judge or doctor or engineer is a competent professional, we rely on his expertise and grasp of all available knowledge to reach the best decision possible. We do not allow concern for unknown factors hinder our efforts to better our lives.

> The progress of human knowledge, and all of the results of human inventions – is all the work of God. These advances make their appearance in the world according to mankind's needs, in their time and generation.

MISHPATIM: AN EYE FOR AN EYE[61]

Azar's Question

During the years that Rav Kook served as chief rabbi of Jaffa, he met and befriended many of the Hebrew writers and intellectuals of the time. His initial contact in that circle was the "elder" of the Hebrew writers, Alexander Ziskind Rabinowitz, better known by the abbreviation "Azar." Azar was one of the leaders of Po'alei Tzion, an anti-religious, Marxist party; but over the years, Azar developed strong ties with traditional Judaism. He met with Rav Kook many times, and they became close friends.

Azar once asked Rav Kook: How can the Sages interpret the verse "an eye for an eye" (Ex. 21:24) as referring to monetary compensation? Does this explanation not contradict the *peshat*, the simple meaning of the verse?

The Talmud (*Baba Kamma* 84a) brings a number of proofs that the phrase "eye for an eye" cannot be taken literally. How, for example, could justice be served if the person who poked out his neighbor's eyes was himself blind? Or what if one of the parties had only one functioning eye before the incident? Clearly, there are many cases in which such a punishment would be neither equitable nor just.

---

[61] Adapted from *Malachim Kivnei Adam* by R. Simcha Raz, pp. 351, 360.

What bothered Azar was the blatant discrepancy between the simple reading of the verse and the Talmudic interpretation. If "eye for an eye" in fact means monetary compensation, why does the Torah not state that explicitly?

The Parable

Rav Kook responded by way of a parable. The Kabbalists, he explained, compared the Written Torah to a father and the Oral Torah to a mother. When parents discover their son has committed a grave offense, how do they react?

The father immediately raises his hand to punish his son. But the mother, full of compassion, rushes to stop him. "Please, not in anger!" she pleads, and she convinces the father to mete out a lighter punishment.

An onlooker might conclude that all this drama was superfluous. In the end, the boy did not receive corporal punishment. Why make a big show of it?

In fact, the scene provided an important educational lesson for the errant son. Even though he was only lightly disciplined, the son was made to understand that his actions deserved a much more severe punishment.

A Fitting Punishment

This is exactly the case when one individual injures another. The offender needs to understand the gravity of his actions. In practice, he only pays monetary restitution, as the Oral Law rules. But he should not think that with money alone he can repair the damage he inflicted. As Maimonides explained, the Torah's intention is not that the court should actually injure him in the same way that he injured his neighbor, but rather "that *it is fitting* to amputate his limb or injure him, just as he did to the injured party" (*Mishneh Torah*, Laws of Personal Injuries 1:3).

Maimonides more fully developed the idea that monetary restitution alone cannot atone for physical damages in chapter 5:

> Causing bodily injury is not like causing monetary loss. One who causes monetary loss is exonerated as soon as he repays the damages. But if one injured his neighbor, even though he paid all five categories of monetary restitution – even if he offered to God all the rams of Nevayot [see Isaiah 60:7] – he is not exonerated until he has asked the injured party for forgiveness, and he agrees to forgive him. (Personal Injuries, 5:9)

Afterwards, Azar commented:

> Only Rav Kook could have given such an explanation, clarifying legal concepts in Jewish Law by way of Kabbalistic metaphors, for I once heard him say that the boundaries between *Nigleh* and *Nistar*, the exoteric and the esoteric areas of Torah, are not so rigid. For some people, Torah with Rashi's commentary is an esoteric study; while for others, even a chapter in the Kabbalistic work *Eitz Chayim* belongs to the revealed part of Torah.

MISHPATIM: LEGISLATING KINDNESS[62]

The Borrower's Liabilities

Rabbi S. R. Hirsch wrote that the laws governing a borrower are "perhaps the most difficult of all the rules of Jewish civil law to comprehend."[63] I borrowed a pencil from my friend, but it rolled off the table and broke in half. Do I need to pay for a new one?

> If a person borrows something and it breaks or dies... the [borrower] must make full restitution. However, if the owner was with him, he need not make restitution. (Ex. 22:13-14)

A borrower is accountable for all types of damage or loss — even for completely unpreventable accidents. Even if the pencil I borrowed was swept away in a tornado, I am still obligated to buy a new one for my friend.

This comprehensive liability appears to be unreasonable. If I had not borrowed the pencil, it would still have been lost when the tornado struck. Why should I have to pay? As the Talmud in *Baba Metzia* 36b puts it: "What difference does it make to the

---

[62] Adapted from *Otzarot HaRe'iyah* vol. II, p. 519.
[63] From Rabbi Hirsch's commentary to Exodus 22:13.

Angel of Death where it is located?"

Encouraging *Chessed*

Rav Kook explained that the Torah placed extra liabilities upon the borrower, even in cases when the article would have been lost even if it had not been borrowed, in order to encourage people to be helpful and lend to one another. This is similar to the rationale for special rabbinical legislation protecting those who lend money, so that "the door will not be closed for [would-be] borrowers" (*Sanhedrin* 32a). Since the lender receives nothing in return for his kindness, the Torah sought to counterbalance any selfish thoughts that might prevent him from assisting his neighbor.

Strange Exemption

This overall understanding helps explain the most peculiar aspect of the law of the borrower – his exemption from liability when *"be'alav imo"* – when "the owner was with him." The Torah rules that if the owner was working for the borrower at the time of the loan (whether for pay or just as a favor), the borrower is no longer responsible for damages.

One might think that the Torah is referring to a situation where the owner and borrower were working together with the borrowed object, such as driving a tractor to plow a field together. But the Sages explained in *Baba Metzia* 95b that it makes no difference what service the owner was performing for the borrower. Thus, if my neighbor was helping me with my computer when I asked to borrow his pencil, I am no longer liable for the pencil's damage or loss.

Even more surprising, the Sages taught that this exemption takes effect if the owner assisted the borrower *at the time of the loan*. What the owner was doing when the article broke, however, is irrelevant (*Baba Metzia* 94a-b).

Why should it matter if the owner was working for the borrower? We could understand that if the owner was present when the object was damaged; the borrower could exempt himself from liability by claiming that the owner was able to check that the borrowed object was used properly. But why should it make a difference if the owner was present at the time of the loan? This exemption is so illogical that one highly-respected authority[64] wrote in despair: "This is an unsolved problem which I have taxed my brain to make sense of and find a reason for – but in vain."

No Need for Extra Measures

The explanation presented above, however, provides a solution to this riddle. The reason why the Torah placed comprehensive liability upon the borrower was in order to encourage kindness and generosity. In the case of *"be'alav imo,"* however, we see that the owner assists the borrower to a greater degree than is common between neighbors. The lender's service for the borrower indicates that they are on friendly terms. In such a case, it is unlikely that the owner will refuse to lend out his possessions. Therefore, the Torah did not see a need to place extra liabilities upon the borrower in order to encourage the loan.

---

[64] Rabbi Yair Bachrach (1639-1702), prominent German rabbi and legal scholar, author of the collection of responsa entitled *Chavat Yair*.

For this reason, the verse concludes with the law of a rented article: "If the article was hired, [the loss] is covered by the rental payment" (Ex. 22:14). The juxtaposition of these two cases indicates that the borrower – when the owner is working with him – is similar to a person renting an object. What is common to these two cases? In both situations, the lender was the recipient of some benefit from the borrower. Therefore, the borrower is not liable for accidental loss or breakage.

Borrowing a Horse to Rob a Bank

Finally, this reasoning helps clarify the Talmud's question in *Baba Metzia* 96a. The Sages debated whether one who borrowed an animal for illicit purposes – say, to rob a bank – is also liable if the animal dies. Why should the purpose of borrowing be a factor in the extent of the liability?

According to the reasoning above, this question becomes clear. If the borrower's motives are improper, the Torah would not wish to encourage such a loan. It is preferable that the borrower *not* be made liable in all situations, thus discouraging the owner from lending out his property for improper or illegal purposes.

TERUMAH: "TAKE FOR ME AN OFFERING"[65]

In preparation for building the Tabernacle, God commanded Moses to collect the necessary materials:

> Speak to the Israelites and have them take for Me an offering. From every person whose heart inspires him to donate, you shall take My offering. (Ex. 25:2)

Why did God command Moses to *take* the donations? The verse should read that they must *give* an offering!

The language of "taking" might lead one to conclude that the materials could have been taken from the people by force. But this was not the case, for the Torah stresses that the offerings were donated freely – "from every person whose heart inspires him to donate."

Why, in fact, did this collection need to be voluntary? The Talmud in *Baba Batra* 8b teaches that a community may force members of the community to support the poor and the needy. Using our money to help others is a trait that needs to be trained and developed. So why did God command that these gifts for the Tabernacle, the first act of *tzedakah* (charity) on a national level, be donated solely out of sincere generosity?

---

[65] Adapted from *Otzarot HaRe'iyah* vol. II, pp. 189-190.

Two Goals of *Tzedakah*

The mitzvah of *tzedakah* is meant to accomplish two objectives. The first concerns the person receiving the charity. Through this mitzvah, the poor are provided with what they lack. The second objective concerns the one giving. By donating our time and money, we express our inner qualities of *chessed* and kindness in a concrete and tangible manner. The act of *tzedakah* actualizes our traits of generosity and contributes toward our own spiritual growth.

We can distinguish between these two objectives within the act itself. The first goal stresses the aspect of *giving* to the needy. The important factor here is that the poor person receives the assistance he needs. The second goal, on the other hand, stresses the aspect of *taking* from the benefactor. This is a special benefit of the mitzvah of *tzedakah*: by relinquishing our material possessions for the sake of others, we refine our character traits and elevate the soul.

Which of these two goals is the principal objective of *tzedakah*?

The Gimmel's Chase

The Sages in *Shabbat* 104a noted that the Hebrew letter *gimmel* (ג) appears to be facing the next letter in the alphabet, the *dalet* (ד), with its left 'leg' stretched out toward the *dalet*. Why is the *gimmel* running toward the *dalet*? The Sages explained that the *gimmel* is the benefactor (from the word "*gommeil*," meaning one who gives or supports). The *gimmel* is chasing after the impoverished *dalet* (from the word "*dal*," meaning "poor" or "needy") in order to help him.

Why is the benefactor running after the poor? Should it not be the other way around? The Sages wanted to teach us that the principal aim of *tzedakah* is connected to the very foundations of the universe. The true goal of *tzedakah* is to elevate the soul of the giver. After all, if the purpose was to help the poor, God could have provided other means for their support without having to rely on the generosity of society. The shapes of the Hebrew letters – letters which God used to create the universe – hint at this fundamental truth. The *gimmels*, the benefactors, need to pursue the *dalets*, the poor, in order to grow and develop spiritually.

Thus the Jewish people's very first philanthropic project emphasized that the central aspect of *tzedakah* is not giving to the needy, but taking from the donor. "Have them *take* for Me an offering." God commanded that the contributions to the Tabernacle be given freely – "every person whose heart inspires him to donate" – since the soul and its traits are only refined when one donates willingly.

TERUMAH: THE TACHASH AND THE EREV RAV[66]

The Talmud gives an account of the enigmatic *Tachash*, a mysterious creature whose beautiful multicolored hide was used as a covering for the Tabernacle:

> The *Tachash* that lived in the time of Moses was a unique species. The Sages could not determine whether it was domesticated or wild. It only appeared at that time for Moses, who used it for the Tabernacle. Then it vanished. (*Shabbat* 28b)

What is the significance of this unique animal? What was its special connection to Moses, that it made its appearance only during his lifetime? And why did Moses incorporate the colorful *Tachash* in the Tabernacle, albeit only for its outermost covering?

Mixed Blessings from Mixed Multitudes

In Aramaic, the *Tachash* is called "*Sasgona*," for it was proud ("*sas*") of its many vivid colors ("*gona*"). According to Rav Kook, the multihued *Tachash* is a metaphor, representing Moses' desire to include as many talents and gifts as possible when building the

---

[66] Adapted from *Ein Eyah* vol. III, pp. 105-107.

Jewish people – even talents that, on their own, might have a negative influence upon the people. The metaphor of the *Tachash* specifically relates to Moses' decision to allow the *Erev Rav* – "mixed multitudes" from other nations – join the Israelites as they left Egypt.

The *Erev Rav* were the source of much grief. They instigated the Sin of the Golden Calf and other rebellions against God in the wilderness. And their descendants throughout the generations continued to bring troubles upon Israel. Nevertheless, at the End of Days, all the troubles these difficult and diverse forces caused will be revealed as having been for the best, as the absorption of the *Erev Rav* served to enrich the Jewish people.

One disturbing aspect of the *Erev Rav* is the phenomenon of many dynamic forces abandoning the Jewish nation during its long exile among the nations. Yet this is not a true loss, since only that which was foreign to the inner spirit of Israel is cast off. These lost elements of the *Erev Rav* were ultimately incompatible with *Knesset Yisrael*, the national soul of Israel; thus they were unable to withstand the pressures and hardships of exile. It saddens us to lose that which we thought was part of Israel, but in fact, they were never truly assimilated within the nation's soul.

This outcome benefits the world at large. As these "fallen leaves" join the other nations, they bring with them much of what they absorbed from the holiness of Israel. As a result, other peoples have become more receptive to Israel's spiritual message.

Could the *Tachash* be Domesticated?

The Sages were in doubt as to the ultimate fate of the multi-talented *Erev Rav*. Would they be truly absorbed within Israel, enriching the people and remaining forever a part of it? Or would they only serve as a positive influence on the world, outside the camp of Israel?

The Sages expressed this uncertainty by questioning whether the *Tachash* was a domestic creature. A wild animal cannot be trained and will not permanently join man's home. It can only be guided indirectly. A domesticated animal, on the other hand, is completely subservient to man and is an integral part of his household. Would the *Erev Rav* ultimately be rejected, like wild animals which can never be truly at home with humanity? Or would they be domesticated and incorporated into the house of Israel?

Moses and the *Tachash*

Just as the *Tachash* only made its appearance in Moses' time, so too, this absorption of foreign talents was only possible in Moses' generation. No other generation could have taken it upon itself to accept alien forces into the nation. Once the contribution of the *Erev Rav* to Israel is complete, the nation's spiritual restoration requires that they will be purged from the Jewish people. "I will purge your dross... and then you will be called the city of righteousness, faithful city" (Isaiah 1: 25-26).

We usually avoid destructive forces which may delay and hinder the ultimate good. However, a far-reaching vision can detect the underlying purpose of all human activity, as all actions ultimately fulfill the Divine Will. The great hour of Exodus resonated with the highest vision; the first redemption of Israel initiated the historical process that will culminate with the final redemption. Moses, the master prophet, "the most faithful of all My house," saw fit to include those varied forces that ordinarily would be rejected. And yet, like the skins of the *Tachash*, they were only suitable for the most external covering.

> The new heavens and the new earth which I will make
> are standing before Me. (Isaiah 66:22)

All of the wonderful forces of the future – "the new heavens and the new earth" – are not really new. They already exist. Even now, they are "standing before Me." By accepting the *Erev Rav*, Moses planted these diverse gifts within the Jewish people. Like seeds, they decay in the ground; but ultimately they will sprout and bring forth new life. The brilliant future light, with all of its spectacular colors and breadth, is not new; it was secreted away long ago. This resplendent light is hidden, like the multi-hued *Tachash*, until the time will come for it to be revealed once more.

TETZAVEH: MOSES AND THE PRIESTLY GARMENTS[67]

Where was Moses?

The commentaries noted an unusual fact about the Torah portion of *Tetzaveh*: it is the only *parashah*, from when we first read of Moses' birth in the book of Exodus, in which Moses is not mentioned.

The Ba'al HaTurim (Rabbi Jacob ben Asher, 1269-1343), explained that this was a consequence of Moses' defense of the Jewish people after the Sin of the Golden Calf. At that precarious juncture, Moses pleaded with God to forgive the Israelites; and if not, then "please remove me from Your book that You have written" (Ex. 32:32).

The Sages taught that "The curse of a sage comes true, even if it was contingent on a condition [and that condition was not met]" (*Makkot* 11a). Thus, even though God did forgive the Jewish people, Moses' vow was partially fulfilled, and his name was removed from the portion of *Tetzaveh*.

The question arises: why was this *parashah*, which describes the special garments of the *kohanim*, chosen as the one in which

---

[67] Adapted from *Shemuot HaRe'iyah* (*Tetzaveh* 1929), quoted in *Peninei HaRe'iyah*, pp. 175-176.

Moses is not mentioned? Also, why was Moses punished for valiantly defending the Jewish people?

Concession for Weakness

According to the Midrash, God originally intended to appoint Moses and his descendants to be *kohanim*. God, however, became disappointed with Moses due to his repeated refusal to lead the Israelites out of Egypt, and He transferred the priesthood to his brother Aaron (*Zevachim* 102a on Ex. 4:14). But while Moses lost the priesthood, he still retained the *potential* to be a *kohen*.

In fact, when the Tabernacle was dedicated, Moses did serve as the *kohen*, bringing the dedication offerings (Ex. 29). It is surprising that Moses did not wear the special garments of a *kohen* during his one-time service. If a *kohen* does not wear these special clothes while serving in the Temple, his service is rendered invalid (*Zevachim* 17b); and yet Moses performed the dedication service just wearing a white robe (*Avodah Zarah* 34a). Why didn't Moses need to wear the priestly garments?

In general, clothing is a concession for human weakness. The Hebrew word בֶּגֶד ("clothing") comes from the root בגד, meaning "to betray." In the Garden of Eden, there was nothing wrong with being naked. It was only after Adam and Eve ate from the Tree of Knowledge of Good and Evil that they needed to hide behind clothes – a necessary but tragic betrayal of their natural purity.

The same is true for the priestly garments. Each of the eight garments, the Sages taught, comes to atone for a particular transgression: arrogance, slander, improper thoughts, and so on (*Zevachim* 88b). Were it not for these sins, the *kohanim* would have no need for these special clothes.

Beyond Clothing

The Talmud relates that the white robe that Moses wore when he served in the Tabernacle had no seams. In other words, his robe had no clear and distinct boundaries, nothing to emphasize its separation from his body. It was almost as if Moses needed no clothing at all.

Moses was not tainted by the Sin of the Golden Calf, a sin that the Midrash (*Shemot Rabbah* 32:1) links to the sin of Adam. Therefore Moses did not need the extra clothes of the *kohanim*. He understood that, due to the Sin of the Golden Calf, the *kohanim* would need to wear special garments. Therefore he asked God: "Please remove me from Your book" – please remove me from the portion of Your book that commands the *kohanim* to wear special clothes. I was not involved in the Sin of the Golden Calf, and I have no connection with the need for these clothes.

What is so terrible about the priestly garments? These clothes indicate that the *kohanim* suffer from a fundamental dissonance. While they wear their special clothes, the *kohanim* are *shluchei dedan* and *shluchei deRachmana*, our emissaries to God and God's emissaries to us. But when they remove the priestly garments, they become private individuals once again.

Moses, on the other hand, was a "servant of God" (Deut. 34:5). This was not an honorific title, but a description of his very essence, regardless of what clothes he wore. Divine service was not a duty that Moses took upon himself during certain hours of the day. It was his defining quality.

God heeded Moses' request and removed his name from the portion of *Tetzaveh*. And indeed Moses had no need for these clothes, but performed the Divine service wearing only a seamless white robe.

TETZAVEH: RAISING A CONSTANT FLAME[68]

Not just any oil was suitable for use in the Temple Menorah. The Torah stipulates that the oil be particularly refined, made from hand-crushed olives, so that it will "raise up a constant flame" (Ex. 27:20).

Why does the Torah use this unusual phrase, "to raise up the flame"? Why not say simply "to kindle the flame"?

Proper Oil and Wicks

The Sages explained that this phrase indicates that the lights of the Menorah must burn easily and naturally, necessitating that only the finest oil and wicks be used. The oil must be pure, produced from types of oil that are easily absorbed, and the wicks must be made from a material that burns smoothly. With such high quality oil and wicks, the flame will "raise itself up" and will not need to be fiddled with.

For Sabbath lights, the Sages similarly required that the oil come from a substance that is absorbed easily, and the wicks be made from a material that burns smoothly. "Those wicks and oils that the Sages disqualified from use on the Sabbath may also not be used in the Temple" (*Shabbat* 21a).

---

[68] Adapted from *Ein Eyah* vol. III, p. 57 on *Shabbat* 21a.

Elevating Body and Soul

Rav Kook explained that there is a deeper significance to this rule. The goal of the Sabbath is to perfect the individual, and the requirement for easily lit wicks and oil contains an important lesson about the path to spiritual growth.

If the body is overwhelmingly drawn toward physical pleasures, the intellect will not succeed in guiding it. One may become skilled in some craft, or gain proficiency in certain areas of wisdom, but wisdom will not reside in the heart. The overriding attraction to material pursuits will interfere with the illumination of the intellect.

Our body is like a wick. It must be refined so that it does not resist the light, but rather works together with the soul. Only then it will be illuminated easily and evenly. This is the essence of the Sabbath: a day set aside for harmonious living, so that we may naturally grow in holiness and true service of God.

The oil is a metaphor for the human intellect. The mind also needs guidance; not every intellectual pursuit leads to ethical and spiritual growth. Cases abound of brilliant individuals who led amoral, even corrupt lives. Just as the oil of the Menorah must be of a type that is readily absorbed by the wick, so too, we should immerse ourselves in a wisdom which provides practical guidance toward proper living. Such is the wisdom of Israel – the Torah.

Lights of the Individual and the Nation

The Sabbath day promotes the spiritual growth of the individual.

But what about the spiritual growth of the nation? What if the nation seeks to amass wealth and power, regardless of any injustices perpetrated along the way? Unfortunately, this is a common phenomenon: the individual aspires to justice and goodness, while his country ruthlessly pursues its objectives.

The heritage of the Jewish people, however, is different. Our national aspirations are at one with our individual aspirations. Both are rooted in God's law from Sinai. Both the individual and the nation pursue the same goals of justice and kindness. This is the significance of the association made between the Sabbath lights and the Temple Menorah, connecting the aspirations of the individual and the nation. Both Sabbath and Temple lights require oil and wicks that burn smoothly and easily. The Torah of the nation, like that of the individual, must guide its actions effectively, and not be limited to abstract philosophical inquiry.

Raising Itself Up

The Sages further explained that flame needs to be constant, a light that "raises itself up." What does this mean? Our impetus for seeking justice and good should be based on intrinsic, natural motives. This is accomplished by purifying the body through the sanctity of practical mitzvot, and the mind through the light of Torah study. Then we do not require artificial assistance to avoid evil. Our enlightened conscience will naturally lead us to the proper path.

TETZAVEH: CLOTHES OF DIGNITY AND BEAUTY[69]

Make sacred clothes for your brother Aaron, for dignity and beauty.... They will be used to consecrate him and make him a priest to Me. (Ex. 28:2-3)

Why Do We Wear Clothes?

Clothing has a dual purpose. Its first function is utilitarian, protecting us from the elements – the cold and the rain, the wind and the sun. In this respect, our apparel corresponds to the fur of beasts and the feathers of birds, except that the animals have it better. They never need to change clothes or worry about acquiring new ones when their garments wear out or no longer fit. Their wardrobe comes naturally.

The second function of clothing, on the other hand, is unique to humans. Our attire affects our state of mind; it influences how we feel about ourselves and the image that we wish to project. We feel unhappy when wearing unattractive or ill-fitting clothes, and feel good when wearing apparel that is flattering. We feel comfortable in casual clothing, and dignified in formal wear.

This second aspect of clothing has great ethical value. It

---

[69] Adapted from *Ein Eyah* vol. II, p. 354.

stresses those qualities that separate us from the animals and their simple physical needs. It enables us to attain a heightened sense of holiness and dignity. When we cover our heads, wear modest dress, and observe the mitzvot of *tefillin* and *tzitzit*, we deepen our awareness of God's constant presence.

David's Punishment

When King David was elderly, residing in his cold Jerusalem palace, he was unable to keep himself warm in the winter, no matter how many layers of clothing he wore (I Kings 1). Why was it that clothing no longer kept the king warm?

The Sages taught that David was punished in his old age for an act he had performed many years earlier. When King Saul was hunting for David in the caves of the Judean desert, David stole into the king's encampment and surreptitiously cut off a corner of the king's cloak while he slept. David paid a heavy price for this act of disrespect toward clothing. "One who treats clothing contemptuously will later find himself unable to derive benefit from them" (*Berachot* 62b).

In light of our analysis of clothes, the rationale behind King David's punishment becomes clearer. The two aspects of clothing – its utilitarian and ethical functions – are interrelated. If we fail to appreciate clothing's contribution to human dignity and morality, its role in raising us above the animals, then we have overlooked its principal benefit. It is only due to clothing's ethical value in helping us to acquire refined traits that we also enjoy its physical benefit – its provision of warmth and comfort. If clothes were meant only to protect us from the elements, we would have been better off with a good coat of fur.

When David tore the royal garments, he belittled the key purpose of clothing. His punishment demonstrates that, stripped of its ethical function, clothing loses its true value. And then, even its utilitarian value is lost.

KI TISSA: THE COPPER WASHSTAND[70]

Make a copper washstand, along with a copper base for it. Place it between the Altar and the Communion Tent, and fill it with water for washing. Aaron and his sons must wash their hands and feet from it. (Ex. 30:18-19)

Most of the Temple vessels were fashioned from gold and silver. Why was the *Kiyor*, the Washstand, made out of copper? Why was it placed between the Altar and the Sanctuary?

Preparation before Serving

Three metals were used in building the Tabernacle, and later, the Temple in Jerusalem: gold, silver, and copper. Each metal was employed according to its relative value. Gold, with its great ornamental value, was used to construct the innermost vessels: the Ark, the Table, the Menorah, and the Incense Altar. Silver is more utilitarian in nature. The sockets which formed the base for the Tabernacle's beams, the hooks and bands of the courtyard pillars, the wine libation decanters, and other sacred implements, were all fashioned from silver.

---

[70] Adapted from *Olat Re'iyah* vol. I, pp. 119-120.

Copper, the least valuable of the three metals, was used to make those vessels that were not used in the Temple service itself, but rather to *prepare* for it. Thus the Washstand, where the *kohanim* washed their hands and feet before starting their holy service, was fashioned out of copper.

Purifying Thought and Deed

What is the significance of the location of the Washstand? Why was it placed between the Altar and the Sanctuary? And why did the *kohanim* need to wash not only their hands, but their feet as well?

We serve God in two basic ways: with our minds, through Torah study; and with our actions, through practical mitzvot. Washing at the *Kiyor* purifies and prepares one for both forms of service.

The sanctuary was called the *Ohel Moed*, the Communion Tent where God told Moses, "I will meet with you" (Ex. 30:6). It was a place of Divine revelation and prophecy. God's word emanated from the Holy Ark, which held the two tablets of the Ten Commandments. This area of the Temple signifies our intellectual service of God through the revelation of prophecy and Torah.

The Altar, on the other hand, was the focal point for elevating the *ratzon* (the will or primal desire) and deed. The practical aspects of the Temple service were performed around the Altar. Offerings brought on the Altar served to refine the faculty of *ratzon* – they were to be *"lir'tzono lifnei Hashem,"* "for a desire [that is pleasing] before God" (Lev. 1:3).

The Washstand prepared the *kohanim* for their holy service on both levels, in thought and deed. It was situated between the Sanctuary and the Altar, as both forms of Divine service require appropriate preparation so that they will be performed in purity.

The hands and feet symbolize these two faculties. Our hands follow the dictates of the mind, while our feet move almost involuntarily, without conscious effort. When the *kohanim* washed their hands, they purified themselves for their intellectual service of God. And when they washed their feet, they purified themselves for their practical service in action and deed.

KI TISSA: MOSES' EXTRAORDINARY PRAYER[71]

Perhaps the lowest point in the history of the Jewish people occurred shortly after the Torah's revelation at Mount Sinai. Without Moses' leadership and guidance, the people turned to idolatry, worshipping a golden calf. Divine justice demanded that this terrible betrayal be punished severely, but Moses "pleaded before God" on their behalf (Ex. 32:11).

The word for "pleaded" – "*va-yechal*" – is not the usual expression for prayer. The Sages offered several explanations why the Torah used this particular word to describe Moses' prayer. Rabbi Elazar noted that "*va-yechal*" shares the same root as "*choleh*" ("sick"). Moses prayed for the sake of Israel so intensely that he became ill from the effort.

According to Rabbi Eliezer the Great, the word "*va-yechal*" even indicates the specific illness that afflicted Moses. Moses suffered from *achilu*, a fever in the bones.

Why should Moses' efforts for the sake of the Jewish people make him ill? What is the significance of a fever in his bones?

Intensity of Prayer

The gravity of the Sin of the Golden Calf should not be

---

[71] Adapted from *Ein Eyah* vol. I, pp. 144, 146 on *Berachot* 32a.

underestimated. It was not a foregone conclusion that God would forgive the Israelites. Divine justice dictated that the Jewish nation deserved to be destroyed for this calamitous breach of faith.

Moses could not offer just any prayer in their defense. Their sin was beyond the normal efforts of the great leader to rectify. In order to recover, to some extent, the spiritual state they had attained at Sinai, Moses needed to pray with an intensity that exceeded his natural powers. The exertion was so great that Moses became ill. This is one implication of the word *"va-yechal"* – a pleading so intense that it disrupted his body's normal functioning.

Awakening the Fire in the Bones

Rabbi Eliezer the Great provided an additional insight into Moses' extraordinary prayer. Although bones are not particularly sensitive, they nevertheless contain a condensed essence of life. (The word *"etzem"* in Hebrew means both "bone" and "essence.") When the life-force has left all other parts of the body, it still remains in the bones. A starved individual, just barely alive, will appear to be a walking skeleton.

Thus bones are a metaphor for the marrow of life, stored deep inside the body. This life-force is not normally felt, unless it is awakened by a very powerful force. Ezekiel thus described the national revival of the Jewish people with a vision of dry bones coming back to life.

Moses was unable to plead the case of the Jewish people using only his natural powers. He needed to awaken all of his powers, even those hidden deeply within. His extraordinary effort was in equal measure to the people's cataclysmic spiritual breakdown. The nation's descent into idolatry could not be corrected by the regular influence of ethical life alone. It was necessary that powers from the soul's essence – from the people's inner goodness and holiness, hidden deeply in their bones – be awakened.

Since these aspects of life are ordinarily hidden, their awakening is an unnatural, even extreme measure. Moses' plea for the sake of Israel at that critical time was thus based on a special fire – a fire of holiness, smoldering inside their very bones.

KI TISSA: THE KNOT OF GOD'S TEFILLIN[72]

Moses' Vision

One of the more enigmatic passages in the Torah describes a mysterious encounter that took place following the Sin of the Golden Calf. After successfully pleading on behalf of the Jewish people, Moses took advantage of this special time of Divine favor. "Please let me have a vision of Your Glory!"

God replied that it is impossible for mortal man "to have a vision of Me and live." However, God agreed to protect Moses in a mountain crevice as He "passed by."

"You will then have a vision of My back. My face, however, will not be seen." (Ex. 33:17-23)

This account raises many questions. The most obvious problem concerns the story's anthropomorphic elements. God has no body; what do the allegorical terms "back" and "face" mean?

The Talmudic commentary for this puzzling incident only adds to our confusion. The Sages explained that God revealed His "back" to Moses by showing him the knot of God's *tefillah shel rosh*.[73]

---

[72] Adapted from *Ein Eyah* vol. I, p. 33, on *Berachot* 7a.

[73] The *tefillah shel rosh*, the phylactery worn on the head, is held in place by means of a leather strap tied to the back of the head with a special

What is the significance of God's *tefillin* knot? Why did God choose to reveal that particular part of His *tefillin* to Moses?

Knowing God

There are two levels of knowledge. The first is an accurate knowledge of an object's true nature. The second is a limited knowledge, restricted by our intellectual or physical limitations. Regarding tangible objects, there may not be a significant difference between the two levels of knowledge. But when dealing with abstract concepts, especially with regard to the nature of God, the difference will be great – perhaps infinitely so.

The Torah is based on the second type of knowledge. It presents us with a perception of God according to our limited grasp, since only this type of knowledge can provide ethical guidance. Knowledge of God's true nature, on the other hand, is not a form of comprehension at all. As God informed Moses: "Man cannot have a vision of Me and live."

Bound to the Human Intellect

Now we may begin to understand the metaphor of God's *tefillin*. Contained inside *tefillin* are scrolls with verses declaring God's unity and Divine nature. These verses signify a comprehension of God's true reality. This truth, however, is beyond human understanding. How can we relate to this infinite truth? What brings it down to the level of our intellectual capabilities, enabling this knowledge to enlighten us and provide moral direction?

---

knot.

The function of the knot is to bind the *tefillah shel rosh* to the head – and intellect. The knot symbolizes a level of comprehension that takes into account the abilities of those contemplating, so that they may grasp and utilize this knowledge.

The imagery of God's "face" and "back" corresponds to these two levels of knowledge. "Face" in Hebrew is פָּנִים, similar to the word פְּנִים, meaning inner essence. True knowledge of God's infinite reality is God's "face."

Knowledge of God's reality according to our limited understanding, on the other hand, is referred to as God's "back." Moses was granted this partial, indirect knowledge – a grasp of the Divine that we are able to appreciate and apply in our finite world.

VAYAKHEIL: TWO LAYERS OF WISDOM[74]

Two woven coverings stretched out across the roof of the *Mishkan*, the Tabernacle designated for worshipping God in the wilderness. The inner covering was a resplendent work of fine linen and colorful wool, dyed indigo, purple, and crimson. The outer covering was a simpler affair, made solely of goat wool. One might think that the magnificent inner covering was the greater of the two. The Talmud, however, notes that weaving the outer wool covering required greater wisdom.

The Torah describes the women involved in spinning the colorful inner covering as being "wise-hearted." Regarding the simpler, outer covering, on the other hand, the Torah indicates that the women employed an especially lofty wisdom. They were "women whose hearts *uplifted them in wisdom*" (Ex. 35:25).

What was this special wisdom? According to the Talmud in *Shabbat* 99a, the wool was washed and spun – while still attached to the goats!

Abstract and Practical Wisdom

The Sages compared the building of the *Mishkan* to the creation of heaven and earth. The details of how the Tabernacle was

---

[74] Adapted from *Ein Eyah* vol. IV, pp. 245-246.

constructed correspond to the configuration of the universe, both physically and spiritually.

Rav Kook explained that these two Tabernacle coverings relate to two spheres of wisdom in the world, the basis of Divine influence and holiness. The first level of wisdom is abstract and general, while the second is practical and detailed. The abstract wisdom shines with brilliant flashes of the intellect and variegated hues of the imagination. This wisdom deals with inner, sublime matters, and therefore corresponds to the colorful inner covering.

Practical wisdom, on the other hand, would appear to be a simpler matter, serving primarily to protect and watch over the abstract concepts of the inner wisdom. But in truth, the practical wisdom of how to apply abstract principles in everyday life is profound and rare. Spiritual abstractions may be revealed through prophecy and Divine inspiration. But the practical Torah of mitzvot could only be revealed through the unique clarity of Moses' prophetic vision.

"The women whose hearts uplifted them in wisdom" – these women were blessed with the gift of the highest wisdom. By virtue of its profound insight, their "hearts were uplifted," thus elevating all feelings and emotions, all actions and deeds, all aspects of life. Their wisdom was so great that "they spun [on] the goats." They were able to elevate the material world – even life's vexing aspects, as symbolized by a mischievous goat – binding and tying it to the lofty eternal light.

VAYAKHEIL: ART AND CREATION[75]

Moses informed the Israelites: "God has selected Betzalel... and has filled him with a Divine spirit of wisdom, insight, and knowledge in all craftsmanship." (Ex. 36:30-31)

What exactly were these three gifts of wisdom, insight, and knowledge that God bestowed upon Betzalel? The Sages wrote that the master craftsman was privy to the very secrets of creation. Betzalel knew how to "combine the letters with which the heavens and the earth were created," and utilized this esoteric knowledge to construct the Tabernacle (*Berachot* 55a).

We find that King Solomon mentioned the same three qualities when describing the creation of the universe:

> God founded the earth with *wisdom*; He established the heavens with *insight*. With His *knowledge*, the depths opened, and the heavens drip dew. (Proverbs 3:19-20)

What is the difference between wisdom, insight, and knowledge? How do they apply both to the Creator of the universe and to the human artist?

---

[75] Adapted from *Ein Eyah* vol. II, pp. 263-264.

Chochmah, Binah, and Da'at

Chochmah (wisdom) is needed to design the fundamental structure. In terms of the creation of the world, this refers to the laws of nature which govern the universe. The intricate balance of natural forces, the finely-tuned ecosystems of life – this is the underlying chochmah of creation.

In art, chochmah fulfills a similar function, determining the work's underlying structure. Using wisdom, the artist decides on the overall composition, the balance of light and shade, colors, perspective, and so on.

Binah (insight) refers to the future vision, the ultimate goal. The Hebrew word "binah" is related to the word "boneh" ("to build"). The emphasis is not on the current reality, but on the process of gradually building and progressing toward the final, complete form. Therefore, Solomon ascribed chochmah to forming the earth, and binah to establishing the Heavens. The foundation of the earth – its current physical structure – is based on chochmah. Binah, on the other hand, corresponds to the Heavens, the spiritual content that reflects its final form.

What is binah in art? The spiritual aspect of art is the sense of wonder that a great artist can awaken through his work. Betzalel was able to imbue the Tabernacle with magnificent splendor, thus inspiring the observer to feel profound reverence and holiness. The great beauty of his work succeeded in elevating the emotions, as it projected a majestic image of God's grandeur.

The third attribute, da'at (knowledge), refers to a thorough attention to detail. "With His knowledge... the heavens drip dew."

The rain and dew were created with *da'at*. They sustain every plant, every blade of grass, every creature. God created the universe not only with its fundamental laws of nature (*chochmah*) and spiritual direction (*binah*), but also with meticulous care for its myriad details – *da'at*.

Attention to detail is also important in art. The artist should make sure that the finest details correspond to the overall composition and heighten the work's impact.

Betzalel knew the letters of creation, the secret wisdom used to create the universe. With his gifts of *chochmah*, *binah*, and *da'at*, Betzalel was able to ensure perfection in the Tabernacle's structure, its vision, and its details. His holy sanctuary became a suitable vessel for God's Presence, completing the sanctity of the Jewish people by facilitating their special closeness to God.

PIKUDEI: THE HIGH PRIEST'S CROWN[76]

Perhaps most striking of the special garments worn by the *Kohen Gadol* (High Priest) was the *tzitz.* This was a gold plate tied around the forehead, engraved with the words "Holy to God." What was the significance of this priestly crown?

Rav Kook explained that the *tzitz,* fashioned out of pure gold, reflected the loftiest spiritual riches. The crown's placement on the forehead – the location of our inner drive (*ratzon*) for good and holiness – symbolized the *kohen's* aspirations for the highest good contained within his inner soul.[77]

The Talmud teaches that the *tzitz* encircled the *kohen's* forehead "from one ear to the other" (*Shabbat* 63b). What is the significance of the ears in relation to the *tzitz?*

Two Types of Listening

The ear is an organ which we use to hear and listen. One aspect of listening, represented by one ear, is directed above – receptive to the inner voice of elevated thought. The *tzitz* extended from this ear to the forehead, indicating that its function was to conduct

---

[76] Adapted from *Ein Eyah* vol. IV, *Shabbat* 6:72, p. 113.

[77] Located directly behind the forehead is the *prefrontal cortex*, the center of cognitive analysis and abstract thought. It is responsible for the ability to postpone immediate gratification for higher, long-term goals.

these lofty thoughts to the *kohen's* inner will. In short, it symbolized the *kohen's* aspirations to actualize his loftiest goals, implementing them in life, character traits, and deeds.

The second aspect of listening, our awareness of the physical world below, is represented by the second ear. This connection allows the physical world to acquire a new inner content, while providing practical knowledge which could not be attained in the spiritual realm. Here the spiritual is enriched through insight into the material world, its actions and emotions.

The *tzitz* encompassed both types of listening – receptiveness to lofty ideals from above, and practical understanding from the physical world below. It provided a channel connecting these two realms, uniting the world with all of its disparate parts.

In this way, the *Kohen Gadol* became whole and integrated, aware of how the physical can extend and enrich the spiritual realm. He could serve as a unifying force for the people, who share this yearning for complete unity.

This ability to bridge the physical and spiritual worlds corresponds to the essence of the mission of the *kohanim*. They are a conduit, connecting the Jewish people to God and God to the Jewish people. The Talmud describes them as *sheluchei dedan –* our representatives, as they bring Israel's offerings to God. And they are also *sheluchei deRachamana* – God's emissaries, bringing God's blessings and Torah to Israel.

The placement of the *tzitz,* encompassing both ears, indicated that the *Kohen Gadol* should not suffer from a disconnect between his spiritual and physical sides. As a conduit between humanity and God, he needed to be attuned to the spiritual, while still in touch with the material world.

ספר ויקרא

THE BOOK OF

LEVITICUS

VAYIKRA: THE GOAL OF SACRIFICES[78]

Sacrifices are not an innovation of the Jewish people. Noah also offered sacrifices to God. However, not all offerings are equal. The Midrash employs the following parable to illustrate this idea:

> There was once a king who hired two chefs. The first chef cooked a meal that the king ate and enjoyed. Then the second chef cooked a meal that the king ate and enjoyed. How can we know which meal the king enjoyed more? When the king subsequently commanded the second chef, "Make for me again the dish that you prepared," we realize that the second meal was the king's preferred dish.

In other words, by the fact that God commanded the Jewish people to offer sacrifices, we know that God prefers their offerings to those which Noah initiated on his own accord.

But how do we evaluate the relative worth of different sacrifices? What distinguishes the service of Israel from that of Noah?

---

[78] Adapted from *Midbar Shur*, pp. 155-158.

Two Goals of Offerings

The key to assessing an offering is to examine its purpose. The more elevated the goal, the more acceptable the offering. Noah's objective in offering sacrifices after the Flood was very different than that of the Jewish people. Noah sought to preserve the physical world, to protect it from Divine retribution. Noah's offerings achieved their goal – "God smelled the appeasing fragrance and said to Himself, 'Never again will I curse the soil because of man'" (Gen. 8:21).

The offerings of the Jewish people aspire to a far greater objective. Their goal is to enable Israel to merit heightened levels of Divine providence and prophecy. The Torah explicitly sets out the purpose of the Temple service: "Make for Me a sanctuary, and I will dwell in their midst" (Ex. 8:25).

Fragrance and Bread

The difference between Noah's offerings and those of Israel is reflected in the metaphors that the Torah uses to describe them. Noah's offerings had an "appeasing fragrance," while those of Israel are referred as "My bread." What is the difference between a fragrance and food?

When an animal consumes vegetation, the plant life is absorbed into the animal and becomes part of it. In this way, the plant has attained a higher state of being. When a human consumes an animal, the animal is similarly elevated as it becomes part of that human being. This transformation to a higher state through consumption parallels bringing an offering with the objective of attaining a higher state of existence. The offerings of the Jewish people are called "My bread," since the magnitude of change to which they aspire — perfection as prophetic beings — is similar to the transformations of plant to animal and animal to human.

The offerings of Noah, on the other hand, had only an "appeasing fragrance." They produced a wonderful scent and appealed to the natural senses, but they did not attempt to effect a fundamental change in nature. Their purpose was to maintain the world, to refine humanity within the framework of its natural moral and intellectual capabilities.

In fact, the offerings of the Jewish people encompass both of these objectives. They are described both as "appeasing fragrance" and as "My bread," since we aspire to perfection in two areas — natural wisdom and Divine prophecy.

VAYIKRA: MAIMONIDES AND KORBANOT[79]

Why did God command that we offer *korbanot* (sacrifices)? What is the purpose of this form of serving God?

Maimonides' Explanation

Much has been written about Maimonides' controversial analysis of the Temple service in his *Guide to the Perplexed*. At the core of Maimonides' explanation is his recognition of the difficulty in changing human nature. Deeply entrenched habits and beliefs cannot be uprooted overnight. It would have been futile for the Torah to command the Israelite slaves to abruptly discontinue all forms of worship which they had known in Egypt. Such a revolutionary demand would be like a present-day religious leader demanding that we suspend all external displays of worshipping God – no fasts and festivals, no prayers and petitions in times of trouble – just a mental service of God through reflection and meditation, without action or speech.

For this reason, the Torah permitted forms of worship that were practiced in those times. However, the Torah required that all worship be directed toward God alone. In this way, the nation would be weaned from idolatry, without being stripped of those

---

[79] Adapted from *Midbar Shur*, pp. 158-159.

practices they used to express themselves spiritually.

> It is unreasonable to expect that one who grew up as a slave, laboring in mud and bricks, should one day wash his hands from the dirt and straight off [without any preparation] do battle with the giants. Therefore, God did not immediately bring the people into the Land of Israel, and did not lead them [along the direct route], "the way of the Land of the Philistines" (Ex. 13:17). Similarly, it is unnatural for one who is accustomed to many forms of service and practices, so ingrained that they are like unquestionable laws, to abruptly desist from them. (*Guide to the Perplexed* 3:32)

Nachmanides Objects

Other medieval scholars rejected Maimonides' approach out of hand. Nachmanides (on Lev. 1:9) in particular vociferously attacked this position. He refuted Maimonides' explanation with two major arguments:

1) The Torah describes *korbanot* as a "pleasant fragrance to God." This phrase indicates that this form of Divine service has an intrinsic positive value, and is not just a means to wean the people from mistaken beliefs and habits.

2) We find that long before the idolatrous Egyptians, Noah offered sacrifices to God, and they were accepted: "God smelled the appeasing fragrance" (Gen. 8:21). Similarly, we find that God accepted Abel's offerings of sheep long before idolatrous practices had spread throughout the world.

To Reform a Prince

And yet it appears that we find support for Maimonides' explanation in the Midrash. The Midrash explains the purpose of *korbanot* by way of a parable:

> This is like an uncouth prince who was given to devouring unslaughtered meat. The king said: "Let him always be at my table, and he will be reformed on his own." So too, since the Israelites were keenly devoted to idolatry in Egypt... the Holy One said: Let them offer their sacrifices before Me at all times. (*Vayikra Rabbah* 22:8)

A careful reading of the Midrash, however, indicates an approach quite different than that of Maimonides. The parable speaks of the prince eating all of his meals at the king's table. Clearly, dining with the king is in itself a great privilege and honor, besides its secondary benefit as a means to reform the prince's coarse habits.

The parable is describing a situation where the son, due to his inappropriate behavior, does not deserve to dine with the king. Dining with the king is certainly a great honor, but eating *exclusively* at the royal table is a special measure designed to refine the prince's behavior. So too, offering *korbanot* is a lofty form of worshipping God. Through this service, we merit a spiritual elevation, like one who dines with the King Himself, gaining the special favor of the King of the universe.

This parable does not come to explain the concept of *korbanot* in general, but rather refers to a temporary edict that was in force only while the Israelites sojourned in the desert. For those 40 years, they were forbidden to slaughter meat for their own personal consumption. They were only allowed to eat from the *Shelamim* (Peace offerings) brought to the Tabernacle (see Deut. 12:20). The Midrash explains that this provisional decree was meant to wean the recently liberated slaves away from idolatrous practices, ensuring that none would continue the idolatrous practices of Egypt in the privacy of his home.

Jeremiah's Clarification

This may be the true meaning of the verse which Maimonides quoted as a source text: "For I did not speak with your fathers, nor did I command them when I took them out of Egypt, regarding offerings and sacrifices" (Jeremiah 7:22).

This verse is problematic. How could Jeremiah claim that the Torah does not command us to offer *korbanot?* We find many chapters in Leviticus devoted to the Temple service. And why does the verse stress, "When I took them out of Egypt"?

The verse cannot be referring to those offerings which are explicitly commanded in the Torah. Rather, it refers to the special situation that existed "when I took them out of the Land of Egypt," when meat was permitted only when brought as a *Shelamim* offering in the Tabernacle. One might think that this is the ideal, and we should emulate the actions of that exceptional generation. Jeremiah therefore explained that this abundance of offerings was not an end unto itself, but only a temporary decree of that generation, in order to wean them from the idolatrous practices they had adopted in Egypt.

VAYIKRA: THE INNER LIGHT OF DESTRUCTION[80]

Flooding, wars, earthquakes – every day we are bombarded with news of catastrophe and disaster. Is this how God envisioned His world? How can we relate to the many destructive forces in the world?

The offering of a *korban* in the Temple culminated in the ritual of *zerikat ha-dam*, as the *kohen* sprinkled the animal's blood – its life-force – around the Altar.

> He will slaughter [the offering] near the Altar's base, on the north side before God. The *kohanim*, descendants of Aaron, will then dash its blood all around the Altar. (Lev. 1:11)

What is the significance of the offering being slaughtered on the *northern* side of the Temple compound? Why does the verse note that the *kohanim* are "descendants of Aaron" – is that not well-known? And why does it say the blood was dashed all around the Altar, when in fact it was just sprinkled twice, on the two diagonally opposite corners of the Altar?

---

[80] Adapted from *Olat Re'iyah* vol. I, p. 134.

Concealed Before God

Slaughter is an act of severe judgment. When performed on an offering, it serves to connect all the terrible decrees, disasters, and destruction that take place in the world to the hidden Divine rule of the universe. Everything emanates from the secret ways of the merciful God. All is ultimately good, leading to blessing and kindness.

From our limited perspective, slaughtering is held in low regard. It is thus performed near the *base* of the Altar. But it conceals a hidden light of kindness. The offering was slaughtered *"tzafonah lifnei Hashem."* Literally, this means "on the northern side, before God." But the word *tzafon* also means "hidden," so the verse may be translated as "concealed – before God alone."

The task of revealing the inner light in the forces of destruction was given to the *kohanim*, the descendants of Aaron. Why the emphasis on Aaron's lineage? Aaron was renowned for his compassion and kindness. "Be a disciple of Aaron: Love peace and pursue peace; love people, and draw them to Torah" (*Avot* 1:12). Aaron's descendants inherited the special qualities necessary to uncover this hidden light.

The Temple service teaches us that destruction of life has a place even in the holiest of services. It is precisely due to their connection to the highest level – the most all-encompassing perspective of reality – that phenomena which appear inexplicable and destructive from our limited outlook may be seen as contributing to the world. Our physical perception can discern only a sliver of reality; it is severely limited in terms of time, space, and true understanding of events. We lack knowledge of the overall context, and are unable to see the full picture.

The method the *kohanim* used to dash the blood is a fitting metaphor for our superficial perception. The physical eye only sees a partial reality, broken and disconnected. It sees the *kohen* dashing blood on two opposite corners. But on a higher plane, the vision is continuous and complete. The sprinkling encompasses the entire Altar.

Thus the compassionate children of Aaron, as they performed the service of *zerikat ha-dam* around the Altar, provided a glimpse of the hidden source of good and kindness in the universe.

TZAV: APPRECIATING BOUNDARIES[81]

One type of offering brought in the Temple was the *korban Todah*, the Thanksgiving offering:

> This is the law of the Peace offering (*Shelamim*)... If offered as a thanksgiving offering, then it is presented along with unleavened loaves. (Lev. 7:11-12)

Who brought this offering? The Talmud mentions several examples:

> Four need to give thanks: those who sail the seas, those who travel through deserts, the sick who are cured, and prisoners who are freed. (*Berachot* 54b)

Why did the Sages choose these four situations as examples of individuals who need to publicly thank God?

Testing Limits

Appreciation does not come naturally to us. The human soul is programmed to constantly strive for more, as it says, "The soul is

---

[81] Adapted from *Ein Eyah* vol. II, p. 252.

never satisfied" (Ecc. 6:7). We look ahead, not behind. We are always trying to improve our lot, to experiment and discover new horizons. Thus it is more natural for us to take for granted than to take stock. Often we feel gratitude for what we have by way of contrast: only when we no longer have it, or hear of others who lack, do we begin to truly appreciate it.

Another consequence of the human characteristic to constantly strive for more is our tendency to challenge accepted rules. The testing of limits is particularly pronounced in transitional periods (two-year-olds in their passage from infancy to childhood, and teenagers in their passage from adolescence to adulthood). While this is necessary for personal growth, certain restrictions may only be ignored at great risk. Generally speaking, there are four types of boundaries that people, in their quest for independence, attempt to ignore. They suffer the results of rebelling against natural or moral limits, and their experiences provide a lesson to others.

The first group consists of those who attempt to defy the basic laws of nature that govern humanity. One example of this are those who abandon the land, risking their lives by sailing the seas. Outside of their natural habitat, they will come to appreciate the safety and normalcy of life on land.

The second group includes those who rebel against the laws of the state. Governmental rules help regulate communal life. Those who abandon the rule of law by escaping to the desert (or the frontier) will quickly learn to appreciate the necessity for law and order.

The third group is comprised those who ignore guidelines for personal health care. Their interests and desires override the need to attend to their physical needs. Only when they suffer from illness do they come to appreciate the importance of heeding the rules of health and hygiene.

The final group is made up those who, in their greed for unfettered freedom, reject the ethical laws of society. Their actions pose a threat to others in the community. They must be imprisoned to prevent them from harming others. Hopefully, they will come to the realization that it is better to settle for a limited freedom outside the walls of prison than no freedom at all.

These four types publicly give thanks – if they survive their folly! – and serve as an example to others to appreciate the natural, societal, physical, and moral boundaries that make life livable.

TZAV: THE COMMUNITY'S PRAYER OF THANKS[82]

After Rav Yehudah recovered from a serious illness, a delegation of rabbis and students paid the illustrious scholar a visit.

> "Blessed is the merciful God Who has given you back to us," they exclaimed, "and not to the dust!"
>
> Rav Yehudah responded: "[By your statement], you have exempted me from the obligation of offering a prayer of thanks." (*Berachot* 54a)

The Sages taught that one who survived a perilous situation — imprisonment in jail, crossing an ocean, traversing a desert, or recovering from a serious illness — should recite *Birkat haGomeil*. This "Blessing of Deliverance" expresses our appreciation to the "One Who bestows kindnesses to those who are not deserving."

The episode with Rav Yehudah is quite baffling. How could his visitors' somewhat peculiar greeting qualify as a substitute for Rav Yehudah's own offering of thanks for his recovery to health?

---

[82] Adapted from *Ein Eyah* vol. III, on *Berachot* 54a, sec. 9:20.

For the Community's Benefit

Dangerous circumstances are frequently the result of some moral fault or social failing. Those who find themselves in jail, sick, or crossing the desert are often individuals who defied the laws of society, who have neglected their health, or who seek to evade the restrictions of organized communal life.

This, however, was not the case with a righteous man like Rav Yehudah. Rav Yehudah was the leading scholar of third-century Babylonia; he was the founder and dean of the famed Talmudic academy at Pumbedita. His illness was not due to his own personal shortcomings, but rather to those of the society in which he lived. His local community failed to properly appreciate the tremendous privilege of hosting such an eminent scholar. Rav Yehudah's illness was a wake-up call that jolted the people. As the possibility of losing their rabbi became very real, they became more aware of the benefits to be gained from him.

The community's visit after his recovery reflected their recognition that thanksgiving really should come – not from Rav Yehudah – but from them. They expressed their appreciation for him in simple, artless words. In this way, they emphasized that without his guidance – in Torah, wisdom, and ethical living – they would be unable to aspire to higher values.

The visitors did not speak in Hebrew, the language designated to express lofty feelings of holiness, the holy language that angels speak. They used the language of the masses – Aramaic – an indication of their lowly state without Rav Yehudah's elevating influence.

Due to his illness, the community had gained a heightened

awareness of the great benefit that God provided in sending them such a holy and pious man. "Blessed is the merciful God Who has given you to us" to provide us with spiritual leadership.

"And did not give you to the dust." They employed a plain, even coarse description of death, stripped of any deeper insight. In this way they expressed their awareness, after the shock of nearly losing their beloved leader, of their lowly spiritual and intellectual state. Until now, they realized, they had failed to fully avail themselves of everything his pure spirit could provide. Thus they portrayed the possibility of his death as being "given to the dust," since his lofty influence would be irretrievably lost.

By their visit and unusual announcement, the community demonstrated that they now better recognized Rav Yehudah's contribution, and that they would make a greater effort to follow his teachings and moral example.

The Scholar's Response

Rav Yehudah was obligated to give thanks for his recovery. But after seeing this positive result of his illness – an awakening of the community's thirst for Torah and wisdom – he realized that his illness was in fact a kindness from God, "Who bestows kindnesses to those who are not deserving."

By answering "Amen" to their declaration, Rav Yehudah acknowledged that he willingly accepted his suffering, knowing that it had been a source of blessing for the community as a whole. As the Sages noted, "More than the calf wants to suckle, the mother cow wants to nurse" (*Pesachim* 112a).

SHEMINI: MOURNING FOR NADAV AND AVIHU[83]

After the tragic deaths of Aaron's sons Nadav and Avihu, Moses instructed Aaron and his remaining sons not to display any public signs of mourning:

> Do not let your hair grow untended, and do not rend your garments.... And as far as your brothers are concerned, the entire house of Israel will mourn the ones whom God has burned. (Lev. 10:6)

Why was Aaron not allowed to publicly mourn the death of his sons?

The Death of Rabbi Yehudah HaNasi

To better understand Moses' unusual instructions, we must examine the Talmudic account of the passing of another prominent individual: Rabbi Yehudah HaNasi ("the Prince"). Rabbi Yehudah HaNasi was the second-century redactor of the Mishnah, and a pivotal religious and political figure. His influence

---

[83] Adapted from *Midbar Shur*, pp. 332-336, 341-342.

was so great that he was universally referred to as "Rebbi" – "my teacher." No other name was needed to identify him.

Rabbi Yehudah's death was a traumatic event for the entire nation. The Talmud in *Ketubot* 104a relates the story of his final hours:

> When Rebbi became deathly ill, the scholars declared a public fast. His students and colleagues prayed for his recovery.
>
> Rebbi's maidservant went up to the roof and pleaded: "On high, the [angels] want Rebbi [to join them]; and down below, they want Rebbi [to stay]. May it be Your will that those down below should prevail." But when she saw that Rebbi was suffering, she changed her prayer: "May it be Your will that those above will prevail."
>
> The scholars however continued their constant prayers for Rebbi's recovery. The maidservant grabbed a jar and hurled it from the roof. The sudden crash startled the scholars and momentarily disrupted their prayers. Rebbi's soul promptly departed.
>
> The sages asked Bar Kappara to investigate. He went and found Rebbi had passed away. Bar Kappara tore his garment and reported back: "The angels and the mortals struggled over the Holy Ark. But the angels vanquished the mortals, and the Holy Ark has been captured."

Why did the scholars and the maidservant disagree over

whether to pray for Rabbi Yehudah HaNasi to live? Who was right? And why did Bar Kappara refer to his illustrious teacher as "the Holy Ark"?

The Benefits of *Tzaddikim*

The key to understanding this account is recognizing that there are two ways in which Torah scholars benefit the world. The first contribution is obvious to all: they disseminate Torah and provide guidance in the proper path.

In addition to these activities, however, there is an intrinsic quality based on the inner holiness of the Torah itself. *Tzaddikim* provide a hidden benefit, as they refine and elevate society by their very presence.

The Talmud in *Sanhedrin* 99b teaches that one who complains, "What do Torah scholars do for society? They only study for themselves" should be considered a heretic. Even if we do not see how scholars contribute to society, the intrinsic holiness of their Torah provides blessing and merit for all. Even the evil city of Sodom would have been spared had ten righteous people lived there, as God informed Abraham: "I will spare the entire region for their sake" (Gen. 18:26).

Bar Kappara's Message

Now we may understand the story of Rabbi Yehudah HaNasi's death, and the disagreement between his disciples and his maidservant.

There are instances when it is proper to pray for the release of those gravely ill – when they are suffering greatly and there is no hope for their recovery (see *Nedarim* 40a). This, however, does not apply to a *tzaddik*. With regard to Torah scholars, the very existence of their Torah in the world is a hidden treasure that outweighs considerations of their own personal pain and discomfort. For these righteous individuals, it is proper to pray even for *chayei sha'ah*, for a limited extension of life. For this reason, the scholars continued praying for Rebbi, even though his illness was terminal.

At first, Rebbi's maidservant also prayed for his recovery, but her motivation was that her master should be able to continue to disseminate Torah. When she realized that his illness was so grave that he would no longer be able to teach, and that the only possible gain prayer could achieve was a temporary reprieve from death, she decided – mistakenly – that Rebbi no longer served a purpose in this world. Since he could no longer benefit this world and was wanted in the next, she prayed that the angels and the righteous souls in the next world would prevail.

Bar Kappara, however, recognized Rebbi's lofty inner qualities and his hidden benefit to the world. For this reason he referred to his teacher as "the Holy Ark." Bar Kappara wanted the people to recognize that this inner holiness was in fact Rebbi's primary benefit to the world. In this aspect, a *tzaddik* is like the Holy Ark. The Ark contained the original *luchot* (tablets) from Mount Sinai, and was a symbol for the Torah. Yet the Ark was covered with a heavy plate of gold; it was impossible to actually study from the *luchot* within. Thus the Holy Ark represents, not the Torah's practical benefit to the world, but its intrinsic holiness. From its location in the Temple's inner sanctum, it emanated holiness to the nation and the entire world.

We must appreciate Rebbi, Bar Kappara was saying, not just as the redactor of the Mishnah and a teacher of Torah, but primarily as a Holy Ark, as a receptacle of Torah and holiness.

Mourning for Nadav and Avihu

Now we can understand why Aaron and his family were not permitted to publicly mourn for Nadav and Avihu. The benefit that the inner holiness of *tzaddikim* provides to the world is so great that it cannot be expressed in words. External displays of mourning cannot do justice to the magnitude of this loss. Public signs of mourning only express our sorrow at the cessation of their public activities.

Since the people were unable to truly appreciate the inner qualities of Nadav and Avihu, it was appropriate for the nation to publicly mourn the loss of their outward contributions to society. But Aaron, who recognized the lofty nature of his sons, realized that this terrible loss could never be conveyed in human language. Thus "Aaron was silent" (Lev. 10:3).

Moses instructed Aaron not to eulogize his sons even for their public activities, because this was a minor benefit compared to the value of their inner holiness. Since this hidden quality cannot be expressed in words, it was preferable for Aaron to remain silent.

Often we eulogize a great individual so that people will come to recognize the magnitude of the loss to society. In this instance, however, Moses explained that public mourning was unnecessary. Even without public eulogies, "The entire house of Israel will mourn the ones whom God has burned." The entire nation was aware of Nadav and Avihu's greatness, and would surely lament their absence.

SHEMINI: THE ERROR OF NADAV AND AVIHU[84]

In the midst of the great public joy during the Tabernacle dedication, tragedy struck the family of the *Kohen Gadol*:

> Aaron's sons, Nadav and Avihu, each took his fire pan, placed fire on it and then incense. They offered before God a strange fire that God had not instructed them. Fire came forth from before God and consumed them; and they died before God. (Lev. 10:1-2)

Why did Nadav and Avihu die? What was their sin?

Chochmah and *Binah*

The Kabbalists explained that Nadav and Avihu erred by separating the spiritual realm of *binah* (insight) from the higher realm of *chochmah* (wisdom). To understand this statement, we must first clarify the concepts of *chochmah* and *binah*.

Chochmah is the very essence of holiness. It is pure awareness, a flash of intuitive understanding. This lofty perception contains the

---

[84] Adapted from *Orot HaKodesh*, vol. II, pp. 283-286; vol. III, pp. 360-361.

splendor of sublime ideals at their highest level, before they are applied to the detailed characteristics of reality. Compared to the infinite expanse of *chochmah*, all else is small and inconsequential.

Below *chochmah* lies the spiritual realm of *binah*. *Binah* is an elaboration and extension of *chochmah*. This realm is created when the light of *chochmah* is ready to realize the ideals that govern finite content, enabling the formation of worlds and souls. *Binah* reflects reality in its most idealized form. It corresponds to the sublime purpose of creation and the culmination of life.

Exquisite beauty and delight are revealed in the realm of *binah*. Enlightenment through prophecy emanates from this realm. The absolute holiness of *chochmah*, on the other hand, transcends all forms of spiritual pleasure.

Israel draws its inner spirit from the transcendent realm of *chochmah*. As the Zohar states, "*Oraita me-chochmah nafkat* – the Torah emanates from *chochmah*." The source of Israel's faith is beyond all spiritual delight, beyond all ideals. Ideals belong to the realm of *binah*. Ultimately, they restrict our aspirations and are unable provide an absolute and constant level of morality.

Separating *Binah* from *Chochmah*

Nadav and Avihu drew their inspiration from the wellsprings of *binah*. They sought the sublime experiences that characterize this realm, a spiritual grandeur that is accessible in our world. Due to their heightened awareness of their own greatness, however, they mistakenly saw in the holy realm of *binah* the ultimate source of reality. They placed all of their aspirations in this spiritual realm.

By doing so, they abandoned the higher source of light that

transcends all spiritual freedom and joy. The true basis of life is rooted in the supernal realm of *chochmah* and Torah. Unpunished, their mistake would have brought about the collapse of the world's moral foundations. History is testimony to movements dedicated to great ideals that, because they were not anchored to the elevated source of *chochmah*, descended into the darkest depths of ignorance and cruelty.[85]

Nadav and Avihu erred by pursuing the spiritual joys of prophecy and inspiration in a form detached from Torah and its practical teachings. This is what the Kabbalists meant by saying that Nadav and Avihu divided *binah* from *chochmah*. They tried to attain closeness to the Holy on their own initiative, offering a fire "that God had not instructed them." The various explanations for their behavior suggested by the Sages – that they were inebriated, that their heads were uncovered (a sign that they lacked proper awe of Heaven), that they taught Torah in front of their teacher – all reflect the same basic flaw. Nadav and Avihu concentrated their efforts on their own spiritual attainments, without integrating the discipline of Torah. They were highly aware of their own spiritual greatness, but personal holiness must be negated before the higher light of Torah.

Repairing the Mistake of Nadav and Avihu

The Torah stresses that Nadav and Avihu had no children. Their service of God was not one that could be transmitted to future generations. And yet their independent spirit and idealism has an

---

[85] How many million have perished in wars over religious beliefs, as well as political ideologies such as communism and fascism?

important   place   in   the   future   Messianic   Era:

> Remember the Torah of Moses My servant, which I enjoined him on Horev, laws and statutes for all of Israel. Behold, I am sending you the prophet Elijah before God's great and terrible day. He will restore the hearts of the fathers to the children, and the hearts of the children to their fathers. (Malachi 3:22-24)

Malachi envisioned a future reconciliation between fathers and children. His prophecy also mentions Elijah the prophet and the Torah of Moses. What is the connection between these different themes?

The pre-Messianic Era is a time characterized by a tragic rift between the younger generation, idealistic and independent in spirit, and the older generation, faithful to the old traditions and the Torah of Moses. This divide parallels the sin of Nadav and Avihu, who separated *binah* from *chochmah*, dividing the ideals from their eternal source.

But the unique personality of Elijah, combining the prophetic ideals of justice with zeal for God's covenant and Torah, will repair this rift. It is Elijah's synthesis of Torah and idealism that will reconcile the generations. And together, the passionate spirit of youth (*binah*), together with the orderly and practical wisdom of the elders (*chochmah*), will bring about the final redemption.

TAZRIA: MAN VERSUS MOSQUITO[86]

Why does the Torah discuss the laws of *taharah* (ritual purity) for humans only after teaching the analogous laws concerning animals, differentiating between those animals which may be eaten and those which are unclean? Should not humanity, the crown of creation, come first?

Third-century scholar Rabbi Simlai explained: "Just as mankind was created after all the animals... so too, the laws pertaining to mankind were given after the laws regarding animals" (*Vayikra Rabbah* 14:1).

In short, the order here in Leviticus parallels the account of Creation in Genesis. But is there a deeper significance to this order? The Midrash elaborates the lesson to be learned from this:

> If one is deserving, he is told: "You came before all of creation." But if not, he is reminded: "[Even] the mosquito preceded you."

What sort of a contest is this, between man and mosquito?

---

[86] Adapted from *Shemu'ot HaRe'iyah, Tazria* (1929).

Quantity versus Quality

We find in Psalms two nearly identical verses, but with small – and significant – differences:

> How many are Your works, God! The earth is full of Your creations. (Ps. 104:24)

> How great are Your works, God! Your thoughts are very profound. (Ps. 92:6)

What is the difference between these two similar verses? The first verse expresses our wonder at the variety and diversity of God's works. "How *many* are Your works!" The second verse expresses our amazement at their greatness and profundity. "How *great* are your works!" The first verse refers to quantity; the second, quality.

In other words, we may look at the world in two ways. We can be amazed by its detailed, multifaceted nature – its abundance of species and life forms, the remarkable diversity in the world of nature. This viewpoint focuses on the diverse physical aspect of the universe. "The earth is full of Your creations."

Or we may reflect on the universe's inner side. We may perceive its wonderful sophistication and delicate balance, a reflection of the profundity of its design and purpose. This view perceives the underlying spiritual nature of the universe, focusing on the preliminary design – God's 'thoughts' – which preceded the physical creation. "Your thoughts are very profound."

Back and Front

The Midrash which contrasts man and mosquito opens with the verse, "You formed me back and front" (Ps. 139:5). What does it mean that humanity was formed with two aspects, "back and front"?

"Back" refers to the culmination of the world's physical manifestation. This is the process of creation by contraction (*tzimtzum*), step by step, until a detailed physical universe, filled with multitudes of diverse creatures, was formed. From this viewpoint, the ubiquitous mosquito is the superior species. If we are not deserving – if we lack our qualitative, spiritual advantage – then we are reminded: "The mosquito preceded you." In a contest of numerical strength and survival skills, the mosquito wins hands down. From the viewpoint of "How *many* are Your works," even the lowly mosquito comes before us.

"Front," on the other hand, refers to the conceptual design that preceded the actual physical creation. If we are deserving – if we put our efforts into developing our spiritual side – then we belong to the realm of God's thoughts that transcend the physical world. On the qualitative basis of "How *great* are Your works," we may take our place before the rest of creation.

METZORA: THE POWER OF SPEECH[87]

Only in Israel

What is the root cause of the disease of *tzara'at,* as described in the Torah? The Midrash explains that this skin disorder is a punishment for malicious gossip and slander. A person suffering from *tzara'at* is called a *"metzora"* because he is *"motzee shem ra"* — he spreads derogatory reports.[88]

Given that *tzara'at* is brought about by slander, one would expect that all peoples would be afflicted, since even non-Jews are culpable for personal damages. Maimonides, however, wrote that *tzara'at* is not a natural phenomenon, but a unique sign found only among the people of Israel. Why should only the Jewish people suffer from this ailment?

Divine Speech

There are two types of speech. There is everyday speech, based on

---

[87] Adapted from *Mo'adei HaRe'iyah,* pp. 295-296; *Olat Re'iyah* vol. I, p. 192.

[88] *Vayikra Rabbah* 16:1. See Maimonides, Laws of *Tzara'at* (16:15), that one observes the commandment "Be careful regarding *tzara'at"* (Deut. 24:8-9) by avoiding gossip.

and limited to that which occurs in the material universe. And there is a higher form of speech, a holy speech that God bestowed upon Israel. This elevated speech does not originate in the physical world. On the contrary, the world originates from it. This is the speech through which God created the world. "Through the word of God, the heavens were made; and through the breath of His mouth, all of their hosts" (Ps. 33:6).

God granted us the power of His speech, the speech that preceded the world, when He gave us the Torah, the blueprint of creation. "He looked in the Torah and created the universe" (*Zohar Terumah* 161b). The transmission of Divine speech to the Jewish people is alluded to in the verse: "I put My speech in your mouth... to plant the heavens and lay the foundations of the earth" (Isaiah 51:16).

Redemption of Speech

The Kabbalists explained that the Hebrew name for Passover, *Pesach*, is a combination of the words *"peh sach"* – "the mouth speaks." The redemption from Egypt, which paved the way for the Torah's revelation at Sinai, also redeemed the faculty of speech. For this reason, Passover is commemorated through a mitzvah involving speech, the mitzvah to retell the story of the Exodus. And we find that Moses, aware of this aspect of the redemption from Egypt, tried to disqualify himself by protesting, "I am not a man of speech" (Ex. 4:10).

In an essay entitled "The Redemption of Speech," Rav Kook wrote:

Sometimes we can sense the connection between our speech and the universe. This is the initial step to redeem speech from its exile.

As the soul is elevated, we become acutely aware of the tremendous power that lies in our faculty of speech. We recognize clearly the tremendous significance of each utterance; the value of our prayers and blessings, the value of our Torah study and of all of our discourse. We learn to recognize the overall impact of speech. We sense the transformation and great stirring of the world that comes about through speech. (*Orot HaKodesh* vol. III, p. 285)

Two Mouths

The most striking expression of the difference between these two levels of speech is the remarkable statement of Rabbi Shimon Bar-Yochai:

> "Had I been present at Mount Sinai, I would have requested that God create us with two mouths: one mouth to say words of Torah, and one mouth for all of our mundane needs." (Jerusalem Talmud, *Berachot* 1:2)

We may lack a mouth dedicated exclusively to Torah and prayer, but we can still deepen our awareness of the extraordinary nature of holy speech. At the start of the morning prayers, we recite a wonderful formula as we focus our *kavanah* (mental state):

"I hereby ready my mouth to thank and praise my Creator." With this short declaration, we ready ourselves to make use of our mouth for a totally different form of speech. We prepare ourselves to employ the lofty speech that is rooted in the source of Divine wisdom. Since our prayers come from the elevated speech which was used to create the universe, they have the ability to influence the world and change its course.

With this appreciation for the power of holy speech, we may understand why *tzara'at* only afflicts the Jewish people. Our faculty of elevated speech, based on the Divine speech which transcends the universe, can influence the world – for good and for bad. When we misuse this great power, we harm the world and are held responsible. The affliction of *tzara'at*, and the process of purifying oneself from it, comes to repair the damage.

The verbal communication of other nations, however, is rooted in the realm of the physical universe. Since it lacks the power of elevated speech, the nations are not held responsible for its misuse.

ACHAREI MOT: TRIPLE MEASURE OF INCENSE[89]

A Cloud in the Holy of Holies

The High Priest was only permitted to enter the inner sanctuary of the Temple on one day of the year – on Yom Kippur.

> Speak to your brother Aaron, that he may not enter the sanctuary within the partition at any time... so that he may not die, for I appear over the Ark cover in a cloud. (Lev. 16:2)

What exactly was this cloud inside the Holy of Holies? In *Yoma* 53a, the Talmud explains that this was a cloud of incense smoke. The *ketoret* (incense) played a central role in the special service of Yom Kippur. Only after burning the *ketoret* inside the Holy of Holies was the High Priest allowed to enter, as it says:

> Then he shall take a fire pan full of burning coals... together with both hands' full of finely pulverized incense... so that the cloud from the incense will envelope the Ark cover. (Lev. 16:12-13)

---

[89] Adapted from *Olat Re'iyah* vol. I, pp. 139-141.

What is this special connection between the *ketoret* and the Yom Kippur service? And why did it need to be finely pulverized to a greater degree than the incense that was offered on other days?

Beyond Time

Once a year, the *kohanim* would produce enough *ketoret* for the entire year. They would prepare 368 portions of *ketoret* – one portion for each day of the year, plus an extra three portions for Yom Kippur. Why did the service on Yom Kippur require an extra three measures of incense?

The central theme of Yom Kippur is *teshuvah* (repentance) and *kapparah* (atonement). What is remarkable about these concepts is that they allow us, in a sense, to rewrite the past. *Teshuvah* is not just about attaining forgiveness for past misdeeds. The Sages taught (*Yoma* 86b) that there is a level of elevated *teshuvah* through which "sins are transformed into merits." They further explained that "*itzumo shel yom mechapeir*" – the very day of Yom Kippur, even without the Temple service, provides atonement (*Yoma* 85b). What gives Yom Kippur this unique ability to transcend time and change history?

The inner essence of the entire year is contained within Yom Kippur. The Torah employs an unusual phrase to describe Yom Kippur: "*achat ba-shanah*" – "once in the year" (Lev. 16:34). Yom Kippur has a singular quality that illuminates during the entire year. Thus the paradox: the special nature of Yom Kippur appears "*achat*" – once a year, within the framework of time – but at the same time, it is "*ba-shanah*" – it influences and elevates the entire year, transcending the normal boundaries of time.

We may distinguish between three aspects of Yom Kippur and its special relationship to time:

1) The special nature of the day itself – *itzumo shel yom* – with its own unique holiness.

2) Its ability to repair and redeem the previous year.

3) Its potential to influence and uplift the coming year.

Since Yom Kippur affects time in three directions – present, past, and future – the Yom Kippur service requires three extra measures of *ketoret*, in addition to the regular daily quota.

Extra Fine

Why did the *ketoret* of Yom Kippur need to be finely pulverized when it was prepared on the day before Yom Kippur?

Despite the fact that the scent of incense engages our most refined sense,[90] the daily *ketoret* is offered within the framework of time and thus relates to our physical reality. But on Yom Kippur, the incense needs to be *dakah min hadakah*. It is returned to the mortar and pounded until it becomes a fine powder. The *ketoret* of Yom Kippur must match the singular holiness of the day. It must be extraordinarily refined, unfettered by the limitations of physicality and material needs. Only then will the *ketoret* correspond to Yom Kippur's lofty goals of pure thought and holy aspirations.

---

[90] "What is it that the soul enjoys and not the body? It is fragrant smells" (*Berachot* 43b).

KEDOSHIM: LESSONS IN TZEDAKAH[91]

The Last Edge Harvested

One form of assistance which the Torah mandates to be given to the needy is the mitzvah of *pei'ah*. The farmer must leave over a corner (*pei'ah*) of his field for the poor.

> When you reap your land's harvest, do not completely harvest the corners of your fields. ... Leave them for the poor and the stranger. (Lev. 19:9-10)

The Sages stressed that the area left over for the poor must be the very last edge harvested. One may not set aside a section at the start or in the middle of the harvesting process. Why not? By requiring *pei'ah* to be the final section of the field that was harvested, the Torah establishes a set time for the poor to claim their portion. The Talmud (*Shabbat* 23a) notes that this provision prevents four potential problems:

1) *Stealing from the poor.* The landowner could set aside the *pei'ah* at some pre-arranged hour, in order to make sure the corner produce will go to friends or relatives

---

[91] Adapted from *Ein Eyah* vol. III, pp.74-75.

instead of the needy.

2) *Lost time*. The needy will not need to hang around the field, waiting until the moment the owner arbitrarily decides to declare a section of his field to be *pei'ah*.

3) *Unwarranted suspicions*. People might not know that the farmer set aside his *pei'ah* earlier, and suspect him of not fulfilling the mitzvah.

4) *Swindlers*. Unscrupulous farmers could claim they set aside *pei'ah* earlier, when they never did so.

Rav Kook wrote that these four concerns clarify the Torah's views on charity.

Moral Duty

The very phrase, "stealing from the poor," is instructive. Helping the needy is not simply a matter of generosity. It is a social and moral obligation. The Hebrew word for charity (*tzedakah*) comes from the root "*tzedek*," meaning justice. One who refuses to assist the poor does not just lack the quality of generosity. He is a thief, stealing from what rightfully belongs to others!

In general, the existence of poverty in the world should not be looked upon as a purely negative phenomenon. There are many purposes to poverty, including its contribution to our spiritual growth.[92]

---

[92] See more about the goal of *tzedakah* in *Terumah*: "Take for Me an Offering."

Empathy for the Poor

If we only emphasize the obligatory aspect of *tzedakah*, we are concentrating solely on the donor's standpoint and overlooking the needs of the one receiving. This mitzvah also requires an attitude of generosity and kindness. We need to have empathy for the needy and their troubles. For this reason, the Torah expresses concern for the poor person's time and his sense of self-respect. He should not have to wait until the owner finally decides to provide him with produce from the *pei'ah*.

In short, the foundation of Jewish charity is duty. But an attitude of empathy and understanding is also necessary to fully attain the goal of *tzedakah*.

Social Obligation

Social mores can serve to protect the weak and the destitute. Some people give because they are embarrassed to be seen as stingy and uncaring. In addition, society honors generous donors and benefactors.

The first two aspects mentioned, our moral obligation and the need to develop empathy, comprise the internal incentive to help the poor. Only taking these aspects into account, however, minimizes the contribution of social pressure to encourage people to support the needy. One who is fully aware of the importance of charity does not require this external motivation. Not everyone, however, achieves this level of enlightenment. For the good of society as a whole, the Torah affirms the importance of social obligations to give and help others. With regard to the mitzvah of *pei'ah*, this is expressed by our concern that society may unjustly place suspicions on those who in fact did set aside *pei'ah*.

Stopping Swindlers

The fourth problem – closing off a potential loophole for swindlers – only applies to the lowest, most corrupt segments of society. Nonetheless, this is a sufficient reason to obligate all members of society. An organic unity exists within society. People are influenced by one another, and an enlightened individual cannot claim to be impervious to the overall moral decay that such a loophole might bring about in society's lower elements.

KEDOSHIM: LOVE YOUR NEIGHBOR[93]

Do not take revenge nor bear a grudge against the children of your people. You must love your neighbor as you love yourself. (Lev. 19:18)

Is the mitzvah of loving one's neighbor realistic? Is it possible to truly love another person as much as we love ourselves?

Practical Steps

In his magnum opus, *Orot HaKodesh*, Rav Kook gave practical advice on how to achieve this love for others:

❖ Love for the Jewish people does not start from the heart, but from the head. To truly love and understand the Jewish people – each individual Jew and the nation as a whole – requires a wisdom that is both insightful and multifaceted. This intellectual inquiry is an important discipline of Torah study.

❖ Loving others does not mean that we should be indifferent to their moral faults. Our goal is to awaken

---

[93] Adapted from *Orot HaKodesh* vol. III, pp. 324–334.

qualities of morality, integrity, refinement, and understanding. We need to clearly delineate the purpose of life, its purity and holiness. Even our acts of kindness should be rooted in a hidden *gevurah*, an inner outrage at the world's – and thus our own – flaws.

❖ If we take note of others' positive traits, we will come to appreciate and love them. This is not a form of insincere flattery, nor does it mean white-washing their faults and foibles. But by concentrating on their positive characteristics – and each person has a good side – the negative aspects become less significant.

This approach provides an additional benefit. The Sages cautioned against associating with the wicked and exposing oneself to negative influences. But if we connect to their positive traits, then this contact will not endanger our own moral and spiritual purity.

❖ We can attain a heightened level of love for Israel by deepening our awareness of the inner ties that bind all the souls of the Jewish people together, throughout all the generations. In the following entry from his notebooks, Rav Kook revealed his own profound sense of connection and love for every fellow Jew:

"Listen to me, my people! I speak to you from my soul, from within my innermost soul. I call out to you from the living connection by which I am bound to all of you, and by which all of you are bound to me. I feel this more deeply than any other feeling: that only you – all of you, all of your souls, throughout all of your generations – you alone are the meaning of my life. In you I live. In the aggregation of all of you, my life acquires that content that is called 'life.' Without you, I have nothing. All hopes, all aspirations, all purpose in life, all that I find inside myself – these are only when I am with you. I need to connect with all of your souls. I must love you with a boundless love... Each one of you, each individual soul from the aggregation of all of you, is a great spark from the torch of infinite light which enlightens my existence. You give meaning to life and work, to Torah and prayer, to song and hope. It is through the conduit of your being that I sense everything and love everything." (*Shemonah Kevatzim*, vol. I, sec. 163)

EMOR: AGENTS OF HOLINESS[94]

The Talmud in *Nedarim* 35b describes the *kohanim* as *sheluchei didan,* our agents. When they perform the Temple service, the *kohanim* act as our emissaries.

Yet this idea – that the *kohanim* act as agents for the Jewish people – appears to violate the legal definition of a *shaliach*. An agent acts on behalf of the one sending him (the principal), executing his wishes. The agent, however, can only do that which the principal himself is authorized to do. So how can the *kohanim* perform the Temple service on our behalf, when we as non-*kohanim* are not permitted to serve there?

Potential vs. Actual

The *parashah* opens with a set of special directives for *kohanim*: "God spoke to Moses: Tell the *kohanim*, the sons of Aaron..." (Lev. 21:1). The text appears repetitive – "the *kohanim*, the sons of Aaron." Why does the text need to emphasize that the *kohanim* are descendants of Aaron?

These two terms – "*kohanim*" and "sons of Aaron" – indicate two different aspects of the special sanctity of *kohanim*. The first is an intrinsic holiness, passed down from father to son. The phrase

---

94 Adapted from *Shemuot HaRe'iyah, Emor* (1930).

"sons of Aaron" refers to this inherent holiness.

The second aspect is an additional layer of holiness as expressed by a *kohen's* actual service in the Temple. This aspect is designated by the term *"kohanim."* The verb *le-khahein* means "to serve," so the word *"kohanim"* refers to their actual service in the Temple. Thus the term "sons of Aaron" refers to the *kohanim's* inherited potential, while *"kohanim"* refers to their actualized state of priestly service.

The *Chalal*

Usually a *kohen* will have both potential and actual *kohanic*-holiness. Yet there are certain situations that allow us to distinguish between the two.

A *kohen* is forbidden to marry a divorced woman. Should he nonetheless marry a divorcee, his son falls into a special category. He is called a *chalal*, from the word *"chilul,"* "to defile holiness." Despite his lineage as the son of a *kohen*, a *chalal* may not serve in the Temple.

Yet if a *chalal* went ahead and offered a *korban*, his offerings are accepted after the fact (Maimonides, *Hilchot Bi'at Mikdash* 6:10). This is quite surprising. In general, a *chalal* has the legal status of a non-*kohen*. If a non-*kohen* brought an offering, his service would be disqualified. Why are a *chalal's* offerings accepted?

The distinction between potential and actual kohanic status, between "sons of Aaron" and *"kohanim,"* allows us to understand the unusual status of a *chalal*. Due to the fact that he is the son of a divorcee, he has lost the actualized sanctity of a functioning *kohen*. But he still retains the inherited sanctity as a "son of Aaron."[95]

This intrinsic sanctity cannot be revoked. Therefore, while a *chalal* should not serve in the Temple, his offerings are accepted after the fact.

The Sages derived this ruling from Moses' blessing of the tribe of Levi: "May God bless his strength (*cheilo*), and favor the acts of his hands" (Deut. 33:11). Even the acts of those who are *chulin*, who have lost part of their kohanic sanctity, are still acceptable to God (*Kiddushin* 66b).

Our Agents

We may now understand the description of *kohanim* as *sheluchei didan*, "our agents." How can they be our emissaries in their Temple service when we ourselves are forbidden to perform this service?

In fact, the Torah speaks of the entire Jewish people as "a kingdom of *kohanim*" (Ex. 19:6). And Isaiah foresaw a future time in which "You will be called God's *kohanim*. They will speak of you as the ministers of our God" (Isaiah 61:6).

Non-*kohanim* may not serve in the Temple, for they lack the holiness of actual priesthood. Yet every Jew has the quality of *potential* kohanic holiness. Because this inner holiness will be revealed in the future, the entire people of Israel are called "God's *kohanim*." And it is due to this potential holiness that the *kohanim* are able to serve as our agents and perform the Temple service on

---

[95] That a *chalal* falls under the category of "the sons of Aaron" but not "*kohanim*" is seen in the Midrash Halachah quoted by Rashi: "One might think that *chalalim* are included. Therefore the verse says, 'the *kohanim*' – excluding *chalalim* [from the special laws of *kohanim*]."

our behalf.

Israel's Future Holiness

This understanding of the role of *kohanim* sheds a new light on the ceremony of *Birkat Kohanim*, the special priestly benediction (as described in Num. 6:23-27). The purpose of their blessing is to awaken the latent kohanic holiness that resides within each member of the Jewish people. As the *kohanim* extend their arms to bless the people, they reach out toward Israel's future state of holiness. Their outstretched arms – their *zero'a netuyah* – point to a future era, whose seeds (*"zera"*) are planted in the present.

> Via the established sanctity of *kohanim* in the nation, the entire nation will come to be a complete "kingdom of *kohanim* and a holy people" (*Olat Re'iyah* vol. I, p. 61)

EMOR: THE OMER CONTROVERSY[96]

When to Bring the *Omer?*

During the Second Temple Period, a fierce controversy raged concerning the date for bringing *Omer*, the springtime offering of barley.[97]

> When you come to the land that I am giving you, and you reap its harvest, you must bring an *omer* of your first reaping... The *kohen* shall perform this wave-offering on the day after the Sabbath. (Lev. 23:10-11)

The verse says the *Omer* is to be offered "on the day after the Sabbath" – but which Sabbath? According to the Oral Tradition, this "Sabbath" is the first day of the Passover holiday.

But the Boethusians, a heretical Jewish sect during the Second Temple period, rejected this tradition. In general, the Boethusians did not accept the Oral Law, and they favored a more literal understanding of the text. They argued that the Sabbath

---

[96] Adapted from *Mishpat Kohen*, pp. 273-274.

[97] An *omer* is a measure of volume between two and four liters; this was the amount of barley flour baked and then brought in the Temple as a meal offering.

mentioned in the verse is the seventh day of the week; so the *Omer* must be offered on the day after the Sabbath, i.e., the first Sunday after Passover.[98]

The objection of the Boethusians cannot be ignored out of hand. Why indeed does the Torah speak of offering the *Omer* on the day "after the Sabbath"? If the verse had just used the word "Passover" or "holiday," the whole controversy could have been avoided!

The National Holiness of Israel

What is at the heart of the dispute between the Boethusians and the Sages? The Talmud in *Menachot* 65a records that the Boethusians disagreed with another accepted Halachah. The Sages taught that the daily Temple offering (the *Tamid*) must be purchased with public funds. The Boethusians – many of whom were wealthy – argued that any individual was allowed to cover the cost for the daily offering. Why did they disagree with the Sages?

These three controversies – regarding the authority of the Oral Law, whether the word "Sabbath" mentioned with regard to the *Omer* is Passover, and whether the *Tamid* must be paid for using public funds – are all connected to one fundamental question: what is the nature of the Jewish people? Is the nation merely the combined contribution of each individual Jew? Or are the Jewish people as a whole a national collective with its own special holiness?

The Boethusians did not recognize the concept of *Knesset*

---

[98] This dispute also determines the date for Shavuot, since the Shavuot holiday is celebrated seven weeks after the *Omer* is offered.

Yisrael, the collective soul of Israel, as an entity with its own intrinsic holiness. Rather, they viewed the Jewish people as any other people. For them, a nation is in essence a partnership, formed by way of social contract, in order to benefit its members. The primary goal of this partnership is to help the individual – to provide the civil rights and benefits that each member gains by joining the partnership.

Halachah in fact distinguishes between two concepts: *tzibur* (the collective) and *shutafut* (partnership). We find the Talmud in *Temurah* 13a rules that a *korban tzibur*, a public Temple offering, belongs to the entire Jewish people. Such an offering may not be substituted by an offering of partners, no matter how many people join in. Why not? Clearly, the collective aspect of the Jewish people is holy in and of itself, an intrinsic holiness above and beyond the combined holiness of all of its individual members. For this reason, the Sages insisted that public offerings be purchased through public funds, for only then will these offerings represent the entire nation.

The Boethusians rejected this idea of national sanctity. They held that any individual may donate the daily *Tamid* offering, even though this is a *korban tzibur* of the entire people.

In general, the Boethusians rejected the authority of the Oral Torah. This stance was similarly based on their view of the Jewish people. Unlike the Written Torah, which came directly from God, the Oral Torah is transmitted through the Sages of Israel. The Oral Torah thus reflects the holiness of the Jewish people. As Rav Kook wrote in the opening paragraph of *Orot HaTorah*:

One can sense the spirit of the nation – bound to the

Torah's light like a flame is bound to a glowing coal –
that shaped the unique form of the Oral Torah.

But how does this relate to the disagreement over when to bring the *Omer* offering?

The relationship between the Sabbath and the holidays parallels the relationship between the Written and the Oral Torah. The Sabbath has a Divinely assigned, permanent holiness – *keviya vekiyma* – always set on the seventh day of the week. The holidays, on the other hand, are bound to the holiness of the Jewish people. Their dates are established according to the Jewish court's declaration of the start of each month and its decision to add a leap month. For this reason, the holiday prayers conclude with the words, "Who sanctifies Israel and the holidays." Why is Israel mentioned here? The Talmud in *Berachot* 49a explains: God sanctifies the Jewish people, who in turn sanctify the holidays.

Rooted in the Sabbath

The holiness of the nation is rooted in the holiness of the Torah. Similarly, the holiness of the holidays is rooted in the permanent holiness of the Sabbath, the first instance of holiness within the dimension of time, sanctified by God immediately following the Six Days of Creation. Thus the *kiddush* blessing refers to the Sabbath as "the first of the holy convocations."

Now we can understand why the verse refers to the Passover holiday as the "Sabbath." The first day of Passover is the very first holiday of the year,[99] and the Torah wanted to teach us that the

---

[99] The year begins with Rosh Hashanah, as it recalls the creation of the

holiness of the holidays is based on the eternal holiness of Shabbat.

The Boethusians wanted to be like all other nations, with a national identity based on the rights of the individual and the principle of social contract. Therefore they could not accept the binding nature of the Oral Law, and they refused to acknowledge that the holidays are based on the intrinsic sanctity of the Sabbath. But with Divine assistance, the Sages were victorious. They succeeded in establishing for all times the Halachah regarding the public funding of the *korban Tamid*, as well as the date for offering the *Omer* and the holiday of Shavuot.

---

world. But Passover, commemorating the formation of the Jewish people, is the first of the Jewish holidays. God informed Moses in Egypt, "This month will be for you the beginning of months, the first month of the year" (Ex. 12:2), designating Nissan as the first month in the Jewish calendar.

BEHAR: THE INTRINSIC SANCTITY OF THE LAND OF ISRAEL[100]

The Objection of the Ridbaz

Rabbi Yaakov David Willowski of Safed (the 'Ridbaz') was one of the most vociferous opponents to the *hetter mechirah* – the temporary sale of land in Israel to a non-Jew in order to avoid the restrictions of working the land during the Sabbatical year. More interesting than his Halachic objections to the sale, however, is the philosophical argument that the rabbi of Safed raised.

The stated purpose of the *hetter*, the Ridbaz wrote, is to uphold the mitzvah of *Yishuv Ha'aretz*, settling the Land, by allowing the fledgling agricultural settlements in the Land of Israel to grow and prosper. But if the legal sale is indeed effective, then the Land would lose its sanctity and the special agricultural mitzvot – tithes, the Sabbatical year, and so on – would no longer apply. And if the Land is not holy, there is no longer a mitzvah to settle the Land. Thus the *hetter* in effect undermines the very goal it was designed to support!

To paraphrase the Ridbaz: the whole purpose of our return to *Eretz Yisrael* is to fulfill its special mitzvot and experience its unique sanctity. If we use loopholes and legal fictions to avoid

---

[100] Adapted from the Preface to *Shabbat Ha'aretz*, pp. 61-63.

these mitzvot, we may as well be living in Warsaw or New York!

Rav Kook and the *Hetter*

Despite common belief, Rav Kook was not in fact the author of the *hetter mechirah*. This legal mechanism was first designed for the Sabbatical year of 1889. At that time, Jewish farmers in *Eretz Yisrael*, whose livelihood depended upon the export of wine and citrus fruits, turned to the leading Halachic authorities in Europe to find a way to avoid the ruin of the fragile industry they were struggling to develop. Were they to let the land lie fallow, the young orchards would suffer greatly, and the export business they had built up would be lost. They also feared that land left fallow could be lost to squatters and thieves.[101]

In response to this difficult situation, three prominent rabbis met in Vilna and devised the *hetter mechirah*, based on similar legal sales to avoid the prohibitions involved with *bechorot* (firstborn animals) and *chametz* on Passover. The *hetter* was approved by famed Halachic authority Rabbi Yitzchak Elchanan Spector. However, many prominent rabbis opposed it, including some of the greatest authorities of the time – and the controversy over the *hetter mechirah* was born.

As rabbi of the town of Jaffa and its surrounding communities, Rav Kook needed to take a position regarding the *hetter*. While still in Europe, he had discussed the issue with his father-in-law (later chief rabbi of Jerusalem), and they both decided against

---

[101] This was particularly problematic due to Ottoman Empire land laws, which allowed ownership of uncultivated land to be challenged by squatters.

supporting it.

But after coming to *Eretz Yisrael* and seeing first-hand the great need for the *hetter*, Rav Kook changed his mind and became a staunch supporter of the leniency. Prior to the Sabbatical year of 1910, he penned a Halachic treatise in defense of the *hetter mechirah*, entitled *Shabbat Ha'aretz*.

The Sanctity of the Land

In his remarks defending the *hetter*, Rav Kook responded to the Ridbaz's objection that the *hetter* undermines its own stated goal – supporting the settlement of the Land of Israel – because selling the Land to non-Jews annuls its sanctity and circumvents its special mitzvot.

This argument, Rav Kook explained, is based on the false premise that the special holiness of *Eretz Yisrael* is limited to *mitzvot ha-teluyot ba'aretz*, those mitzvot that only apply in the Land. According to this view, once these special mitzvot are no longer binding, there is no longer any holiness to the Land and no mitzvah to settle it.

But this is not the true outlook of the Torah. Instead, we should compare the mitzvah of settling the Land of Israel to the mitzvah of studying Torah. While it is true that Torah study enables one to learn how to properly discharge all mitzvot, one cannot say that the value of Torah study is only as a preparation to fulfilling mitzvot. In fact, there is an intrinsic holiness in the act of studying Torah. Even when studying subjects which have no current practical application, this study is nonetheless invaluable. As the Sages taught: "One who studies the laws of the *Chatat* offering is considered as if he offered a *Chatat*" (*Menachot* 110a).

The holiness of the Land of Israel is independent of those mitzvot that may be fulfilled while living there. Just the opposite: the primary holiness of the Land is reflected in the mitzvah to settle it, and the obligation of *mitzvot ha-teluyot ba'aretz* is an *expression* of this special holiness. As the Sages taught, merely living in *Eretz Yisrael* is equal to all the mitzvot in the Torah – and this 'equation' includes those mitzvot that only apply in the Land.

Equal to all the Mitzvot

This statement about the overriding value of living in the Land appears in the *Sifri* (sec. 80) in the context of the following story:

> Rabbi Elazar ben Shamua and Rabbi Yochanan HaSandlar set out to travel to Nitzivim [in Babylonia] in order to study Torah from Rabbi Yehudah ben Beteira. But when they arrived in Sidon, they remembered the Land of Israel. They lifted their eyes, and their tears flowed. They rent their garments and quoted the verse: "You will expel them and dwell in their land" (Deut. 12:29). Then they returned home and declared: Dwelling in the Land of Israel is equivalent to all of the mitzvot of the Torah.

These scholars had pure motives for leaving *Eretz Yisrael*. They sought to learn Torah from one of the leading sages of the generation. Yet in the end, they decided that the mitzvah of dwelling in the Land takes precedence. They placed greater value on living in *Eretz Yisrael*, even at a time when the country suffered from foreign rule and economic hardship. The mitzvah of living in the Land was still in force, even though the Sages of that time found legal loopholes – similar to the *heter mechirah* – to lighten the financial burden of certain mitzvot (such as Hillel's *pruzbul*, and avoiding tithes by bringing produce into the house by way of the courtyard or the roof (see *Berachot* 35b)).

Why did these scholars quote this particular verse, "You will expel them and dwell in their land"? Apparently, they noted that the word "their" is extraneous; it could have just read "and dwell in *the* land." They deduced from here that even when the Land of Israel has not been fully released from the control of foreign nations – even when it was still considered *"their* land," the land of the Canaanite nations, and many of the land-dependent mitzvot were not yet incumbent – we are nonetheless obligated to dwell in the Land.

This lesson was also valid during the time of Rabbi Elazar ben Shamua and Rabbi Yochanan HaSandlar. Even after the destruction of the Temple, even in a time of foreign rule, the mitzvah of dwelling in the Land is still equal to all the mitzvot.

The author of *Kaftor VaFerach*[102] similarly wrote (ch. 10) that the sanctity of the Land of Israel is independent of the *mitzvot ha-teluyot ba'aretz*. His proof: why did Jacob, Joseph, and Moses all seek to be buried in the Land when it had not yet been conquered and sanctified?

In summary, Rav Kook concluded, it is not only possible to be lenient in our days, it is proper to do so, in order to encourage settlement of the Land. Furthermore, the *heter* does not cancel all

---

[102] Rabbi Ishtori (Isaac) HaParchi (1280-1355).

aspects of the Sabbatical year. It only permits those types of agricultural labor that are rabbinically prohibited. Thus the Sabbatical year is not completely uprooted. This *hetter*, Rav Kook explained, is similar to the permission – and obligation – to desecrate the Sabbath in life-threatening situations. As the Sages wrote: "The Torah teaches that we should desecrate a single Sabbath for one whose life is in danger, so that he will be able to keep many future Sabbaths" (*Yoma* 85b). Similarly, by permitting certain agricultural work now, we will enable the full observance of the Sabbatical year in the future.

BECHUKOTAI: JUDICIAL CORRUPTION[103]

The *parashah* describes terrible calamities – disease, war, famine, and exile – that occur when the Jewish people abandon the Torah. According to Talmudic tradition, a primary cause for punishment is one particular offense: judicial corruption.

> As a punishment for [unnecessary] delay in executing judgment, perversion of judgment, and neglect of Torah – sword and plunder increase, pestilence and famine ensue. People eat, yet remain hungry; and they eat their bread by weight. (*Shabbat* 33a)

Uprooting Corruption

Why does judicial abuse bring about such harsh punishments?

When the court system is corrupt, acquitting the guilty and convicting the innocent, instead of advancing social justice, it promotes injustice and exploitation. A dishonest judicial system indicates that the fundamental social order has unraveled; society has degenerated to gangs of rapacious wolves, as the rich and powerful prey upon the weak and unprotected. In such a disastrous situation, the institutions of society must be completely

---

[103] Adapted from *Ein Eyah* vol. III, pp. 185-186.

revamped. If society refuses on its own to champion justice, Divine providence intervenes to uproot society, so that it may be rebuilt on foundations of justice and truth.

Neglect of Torah

What did the Sages mean by *"bitul Torah"* – "neglect of Torah"? How is this connected to judicial corruption?

The term *bitul Torah* refers to a moral decay in society's inner spirit, when the people reject the Torah as an inspiration to seek justice. Its teachings no longer serve as a guideline for spiritual and ethical goals. Bereft of spiritual aspirations, life degenerates into the self-centered pursuit of materialism. Goals are reduced to the mere fulfillment of physical wants and desires. This egocentric attitude undermines one's willingness to work for the communal good and the proper respect for the rights of others.

Hunger of the Soul

The Sages taught that people suffer by "eating, yet remaining hungry." Why this particular punishment?

Our sense of self-worth is based on feelings of honor and integrity. When the principles of law and order are ignored, our positive self-image is damaged. The human soul naturally aspires to the ideals of goodness, enlightenment, and fairness. When our goals are limited only to that which the hand may grab and the tooth may chew, the soul becomes unfulfilled and dissatisfied. We eat to fill our bellies, yet remain feeling empty and discontented.

Bread by Weight

The Sages also taught that "they eat their bread by weight." What is the nature of this hardship?

Bread is usually sold by unit, not by weight. But in times of famine, bread becomes a scarce commodity and is sold by weight. This change helps reinforce a heightened sensitivity toward the property rights of others. Our former unconcern regarding theft, our indifference toward the property of others, is corrected by a keen awareness of the value of every gram of a loaf of bread.

ספר במדבר

THE BOOK OF

NUMBERS

BAMIDBAR: THE HOLINESS OF SINAI[104]

Transient Holiness

Our sense of holiness and closeness to God is not constant; there are times when we experience a heightened spiritual awareness. These moments reflect a transient holiness – *kedushat sha'ah*.

Also in the life of the nation, there are special times of *kedushat sha'ah*. This is the central theme of *sefer Bamidbar* (the Book of Numbers), which recounts Israel's unique experiences during their forty-year sojourn in the Sinai desert – a time when bread fell from the heavens and water spouted from rocks, a time of Divine protection and unparalleled prophetic revelation.

The book of *Bamidbar* opens with the words:

> God spoke to Moses in the Sinai Desert in the Communion Tent. (Num. 1:1)

The terms "Sinai Desert" and "*Ohel Mo'ed*" ("Communion Tent") are motifs repeated throughout *Sefer Bamidbar*. They call our attention to the special *kedushat sha'ah* of that generation.

Unlike Jerusalem's permanent holiness, the holiness of Mount Sinai was temporary, lasting only for the duration of *Matan Torah*,

---

[104] Adapted from *Shemuot HaRe'iyah* 5689 (1929).

the Revelation of the Torah at Sinai. Unlike the permanence of the Temple – a durable structure – the Tabernacle was provisional – a portable tent. And unlike the 613 mitzvot that apply in all ages, the special mitzvot that God commanded the Israelites in the desert – how to encamp, the signal blasts, the order of transporting the Tabernacle – only obligated that generation.

One should not think that *kedushat sha'ah* is on a lower level than permanent holiness. On the contrary, it is precisely because of its loftiness that this holiness cannot last forever. The deficiency is not in it, but in we who experience it. We are unable to maintain this level of holiness on a continual basis.

One example of the temporary holiness of *Sefer Bamidbar* was the Israelites' use of special banners for each tribe in the encampment. The Midrash explains that these flags were given to Israel due to their desire to emulate the angels. Angels appeared at *Matan Torah* in chariots bedecked with flags, and the Israelites wanted to have similar flags. These flags correspond to the temporary holiness of Mount Sinai and *Matan Torah*. They reflect the special holiness of angels, a holiness beyond the reach of the human soul.

Moses and Aaron

The dichotomy between temporary and permanent holiness also existed in that generation's leaders: Moses and Aaron. Moses served as the *kohen* during the Tabernacle's dedication – a priesthood of *kedushat sha'ah* lasting only one week. Aaron, on the other hand, commenced a lineage of *kohanim* for all generations. Even today, *kohanim* emphasize their connection to Aaron's permanent holiness in the blessing they recite, "Who sanctified us with the sanctity of Aaron."

The founding of the Jewish people required both types of holiness. They needed both Moses and Aaron, both *kedushat sha'ah* and *kedushah la-dorot*. The events recorded in *Sefer Bamidbar* took place during an era of miracles and unique Divine providence, the historic revelation at Sinai, and Moses' unparalleled prophetic vision in the provisional *Ohel Mo'ed*. But it was also the time to establish the foundations for Israel's permanent holiness, to set down the Torah and mitzvot that would guide all future generations.

NASO: THE BENEFITS OF THE SOTAH WATERS[105]

The Suspected Adulteress

The integrity of the family unit is of primary importance in Judaism. For this unit to function properly, the husband-and-wife relationship must be one of trust and constancy. But what happens when this trust, so vital for a healthy marriage, is broken?

The Torah discusses the situation of the *Sotah*, the suspected adulteress. This tragic case occurs when a woman, previously cautioned by her husband not to seclude herself with a particular man, violates his warning and is seen alone with that man.

The Torah prescribes an unusual ceremony to deal with this potentially explosive situation. The woman is brought to the entrance of the Temple, and she brings an offering of barley meal. The *kohen* uncovers her hair and administers a special oath. If the suspected adulteress insists on her innocence, the *kohen* gives her to drink from the *Sotah* waters.[106] If the wife was unfaithful to her husband, these waters poisoned her. But if she was innocent, the

---

[105] Adapted from *Ein Eyah* vol. I, p.135.

[106] Water from the Temple washstand was mixed with earth from the Temple grounds. A bitter root was then soaked in the water. The text of the curse was written on parchment, and the ink was dissolved in the water.

waters did not harm her. In fact, they were beneficial – "she will remain unharmed and will become pregnant" (Num. 5:28).

The Benefit of the Waters

The Sages disagreed on the exact nature of the positive effect of the *Sotah* waters. Rabbi Yishmael understood the verse literally: if she was barren, she became pregnant. Rabbi Akiva, however, disagreed. If that were the case, childless women would purposely seclude themselves with another man and drink the *Sotah* waters in order to bear children! Rather, Rabbi Akiva explained, the waters would ease the pain of childbirth, or produce healthier babies, or induce multiple births (*Berachot* 31a).

Rabbi Akiva had a good point – the law of the *Sotah* could potentially turn the holy Temple into a fertility clinic. In fact, the Talmud tells us that one famous woman threatened to do just that. Hannah, the barren wife of Elkana, threatened to go through the *Sotah* process if her prayers for a child went unanswered. (Her prayers were in fact granted, and her son became the famous prophet Samuel.) Why was Rabbi Yishmael unconcerned with Rabbi Akiva's objection?

Rav Kook explained that the ritual for suspected adulteresses was so degrading and terrifying, no woman would willingly submit to it – not even a barren woman desperate for children.

Hannah's Exceptional Yearning

Hannah, however, was a special case. This amazing woman foresaw that her child was destined for spiritual greatness.

Hannah's profound yearning for a child went far beyond the natural desire of a barren woman to have children. She was motivated by spiritual aspirations greater than her own personal needs and wants. Hannah was willing to actively demonstrate that her longing for a child surpassed the normal desire of a barren woman. Thus Hannah was ready to undergo the ordeal of the *Sotah* ceremony. And by merit of her extraordinary yearning, her prayers were miraculously answered.

Only in this unique case was the natural deterrent of the ordeal of the *Sotah* insufficient.

NASO: THREE PRIESTLY BLESSINGS[107]

Birkat Kohanim

Aaron and his descendants, the *kohanim*, were commanded to bless the Jewish people with three special blessings:

> Speak to Aaron and his sons, saying: This is how you must bless the Israelites. Say to them:
> "May God bless you and watch over you.
> May God's Presence enlighten you and bestow grace to you.
> May God lift His face toward you and grant you peace." (Num. 6:23-26)

The third blessing in particular needs clarification. What does it mean that God will "lift His face toward you"?

The Need for Divine Favor

While the first blessing refers to God's assistance in the material realm, the second blessing speaks of enlightenment and spiritual attainments. Greater enlightenment, however, brings with it

---

[107] Adapted from *Olat Re'iyah* vol. I, p. 62.

greater responsibility. As we grow in knowledge and wisdom, we are expected to display a higher level of moral sensitivity. Our thoughts should be purer, our character traits more refined, and our lives more ethical.

If one takes into account the resulting moral demands, one may become apprehensive and even discouraged. In order to assuage this concern, the *kohanim* bestow a third blessing: "May God lift His face toward you."

To "lift one's face" is a Hebrew idiom meaning to give special consideration or leniency. The Torah cautions a judge, for example, not to "lift his face" toward one of the litigants (Lev. 19:15). The judge must be careful to avoid giving the impression of favoring one side. The other litigant may feel that the case is already lost and lose heart.

The *kohanim* bless us that, despite the expectations which come with a higher spiritual level, we should not lose heart. God will be lenient, taking into account the physical reality in which we live.

One may, however, feel embarrassed or uneasy with this Divine leniency. Therefore, the final blessing closes with the gift of peace – peace of mind. "And may He grant you peace."

BEHA'ALOTECHA: GREAT DREAMS[108]

Unlike the unique clarity of Moses' prophecy, ordinary prophecy is communicated through the medium of visions and dreams:

> If someone among you experiences Divine prophecy,
> I will make Myself known to him in a vision; I will
> speak to him in a dream. (Num. 12:6)

Why Dreams?

Dreams, Rav Kook wrote, perform a vital function in the world. Great dreams are the very foundation of the universe. Dreams exist on many levels. There are the prescient dreams of prophets, and the conscious dreaming of poets. There are the idealistic dreams of great visionaries for a better world; and there are our national dreams of redemption – "When God will return the captivity of Zion, we will be like dreamers" (Ps. 126:1).

Of course, not every dream falls under the category of a great dream. Most dreams are petty or pointless, as it says, "Dreams speak falsely" (Zechariah 10:2). What determines whether a dream is meaningless or prophetic?

---

[108] Adapted from *Orot HaKodesh* vol. I, p. 226; *Ein Eyah* vol. II, p. 279.

True Dreams and False Dreams

Those who are truly servants of God concentrate their aspirations and efforts on rectifying the world. When one's thoughts and actions are devoted exclusively to perfecting all of creation, then one's imagination will only be stimulated by matters that relate to the universal reality. The dreams of such individuals will naturally be of great significance. Their dreams relate to the inner truth of reality, to its past, present, and future.

But the imaginative faculties of people preoccupied with private concerns will be limited – like their waking thoughts and actions – to personal matters. What great truth could be revealed in imaginings that never succeeded in rising above the vain thoughts and desires of a self-centered individual?

The Sages expressed this idea allegorically by explaining that angels bring prophetic dreams and demons bring false dreams (*Berachot* 55b). What does this mean? Angels are constant forces in the universe, pre-arranged to perfect the world. True dreams relate to these underlying positive forces. Demons, on the other hand, are unholy forces rooted in private desires which are inconsistent with the overall universal order. False dreams are the resultant fantasies of such personal wishes.

The True Reality of Dreams

What would the world be like without dreams? Life immersed solely in materialism is coarse and bleak. It lacks the inspiring grandeur of expansive horizons; like a bird with clipped wings, it cannot raise itself above the bitter harshness of the present reality.

We are only able to free ourselves from these shackles through the power of dreams.

Some foolishly take pride in being 'realists.' They insist on taking into account only the present state of the world – a partial and fragmented view of reality. In fact, it is our dreams which liberate us from the limitations of the current reality. It is our dreams that accurately reveal the inner truth of the universe.

As that future reality is revealed, we merit an increasing clarity of vision. Our perception begins to approach the *aspaklaria hame'irah*, the clear vision of Moses, with whom God spoke "face to face, in a vision not containing allegory, so that he could see a true image of God" (Num. 12:8).

BEHA'ALOTECHA: MOSES' UNIQUE PROPHECY[109]

Separating from Tzipporah

> Miriam and Aaron spoke against Moses regarding the dark-skinned woman he had married. (Num. 12:1)

What was their complaint against Moses? The rabbinic commentaries explain that they were upset that Moses had separated from his wife Tzipporah, the dark-skinned daughter of Jethro. Miriam and Aaron were able to receive prophecy without resorting to celibacy. Why did Moses feel he needed to separate from his wife?

The separation was in fact Moses' idea; God had not commanded him to do this. The Talmud explains that Moses decided it was necessary after witnessing God's revelation to the Jewish people at Mount Sinai. Moses reasoned:

> The *Shechinah* spoke with all of Israel only on one occasion and at a predetermined hour. Nevertheless, the Torah cautioned [the Israelites at Sinai], "Do not go near a woman." Certainly I, with whom the

[109] Adapted from *Ein Eyah* vol. IV, p. 174; *Orot HaKodesh* vol. I, p. 275.

Shechinah speaks at all times and with no set hour, must do the same. (*Shabbat* 87a)

The Sages noted that Moses' reasoning was sound and God approved of his decision. Their proof: after the revelation at Sinai, God told the people, "Return to your tents" [i.e., return to your families]. But to Moses He said: "You, however, shall stay here with Me" (Deut. 5:27-28).

Why was this separation something that Moses needed to work out for himself? And why was Moses the only prophet obligated to separate from his wife?

Divine Perspective

Despite the innate greatness of the human soul, we are limited by our personal issues and concerns. Compared to the *Shechinah*'s all-encompassing light – a brilliant light that illuminates all worlds and everything they contain – our private lives are like the feeble light of a candle before the blazing sun. The cosmos are brimming with holiness – in all of their minutiae, in their transformations and advances, in their physical and spiritual paths. All of their heights and depths are holy; all is God's treasure.

In order to attain this higher perspective, a prophet must free himself from his own narrow viewpoint. The pristine dawn of lofty *da'at* (knowledge) must be guarded from those influences that induce the prophet to withdraw to the private circle of his own family.

Moses, the faithful shepherd, could not be confined to the limited framework of private life – not even momentarily. His entire world was God's universe, where everything is holy.

It was Moses who recognized the need to separate himself from matters pertaining to his private existence. From the Divine perspective, all is holy, and thus such measures are unnecessary. For Moses, however, it was essential. It allowed him to raise his sights and acquire a more elevated outlook. Separating from his family allowed Moses' soul to constantly commune with the Soul of all worlds. It enabled Moses to attain his uniquely pure prophetic vision.

Continual Light of Moses' Vision

What was so special about Moses' prophecy that, unlike all other prophets, he needed to detach himself from private life? We may use the analogy of lightning to illustrate the qualitative difference between the prophecy of Moses and that of other prophets.

Imagine living in a pitch-black world where the only source of light is that which is emitted by an occasional bolt of lightning. It would be impossible to truly identify one's surroundings in such a dark world. Even if the lightning occurs repeatedly, the lack of constant illumination makes this form of light inadequate. If, however, the lightning is extremely frequent – like a strobe light set to flash at a fast frequency – its illumination is transformed into a source of constant light.

This analogy may be applied to spiritual enlightenment. One cannot truly recognize the elevated realm, its holiness and eternal morality, the rule of justice and the influence of the sublime, without the illumination of continual prophecy.

Ordinary prophecy is like the intermittent light of an occasional lightning bolt. Only the Torah, the singular prophecy of Moses, is a light that radiates continually. We are able to perceive the truth of the world's inner essence through this constant light and live our lives accordingly.

SHELACH: REPAIRING THE SIN OF THE SPIES[110]

One of the greatest tragedies in the long history of the Jewish people occurred when the spies sent by Moses returned with a frightening report about the Land of Israel. Their dire warnings of fierce giants and a "land that consumes its inhabitants" convinced the people that they would be better off returning to Egypt.

Unlike other incidents in which the Israelites rebelled against God, on this occasion, Moses was unable to annul God's decree. The entire generation died in the desert, never reaching the Promised Land. The best Moses was able to do was delay the punishment for forty years.

Rav Kook wrote that even today we still suffer the consequences of this catastrophic error. The root cause for the exiles and humiliations of the Jewish people, throughout the generations, is due to our failure to correct the sin of the spies.

How can we rectify the sin of the spies?

To repair this national failure, a *teshuvat hamishkal* is needed, a penance commensurate with the sin which will "balance the scales." The spies defamed the Land of Israel, as it says, "They despised the desirable land" (Ps. 106:24). We must do the

---

[110] Adapted from *Malachim Kivnei Adam*, pp. 221, 222, 237.

opposite and show our unwavering love for the Land.

> [We must] declare to the entire world [the Land's] magnificence and beauty, its holiness and grandeur. If only we could express (with what may appear to us to be greatly exaggerated) even a ten-thousandth of the desirability of the beloved Land, the splendorous light of its Torah, and the superior light of its wisdom and prophecy!
>
> The quality of wonderful holiness that Torah scholars seeking holiness may find in the Land of Israel does not exist at all outside the Land. I myself can attest to this unique quality, to a degree commensurate with my meager worth. (*Igrot HaRe'iyah*, vol. I, pp. 112-113)

For Rav Kook, this recommendation on how to address the sin of the spies was not just a nice homily. Stories abound of his burning love for the Land of Israel and his indefatigable attempts to encourage fellow Jews to move to *Eretz Yisrael*.

Kissing the Rocks of Acre

The Talmud in *Ketubot* 112a records that Rabbi Abba would demonstrate his great love for the Land of Israel by kissing the rocks of Acre as he returned to Israel. What was so special about these rocks?

Rav Kook explained that if Rabbi Abba had bent down and kissed the *soil* of *Eretz Yisrael*, we would understand that his love for the Land was based on the special mitzvot that are fulfilled with its fruit – tithes, first fruits, the Sabbatical year, and so on. The soil, which produces fruit, signifies the importance and holiness of the Land through the *mitzvot hateluyot ba'aretz*.

But Rabbi Abba's love for the Land was not dependent on any external factors – not even the Land's special mitzvot (see *Avot* 5:16; *Orot*, p. 9). Rabbi Abba cherished the intrinsic holiness of *Eretz Yisrael*. He recognized that the special qualities of the Land of Israel, such as its receptivity to prophecy and enlightenment, go far beyond those mitzvot connected to agriculture. Therefore, he made a point of kissing its barren rocks and stones.

SHELACH: THE LESSON OF SHILOH[111]

A certain Torah scholar, recently arrived from America, was greatly agitated. He went to visit Rav Kook, unburdening his complaints and severe disappointment in the state of religious observance in *Eretz Yisrael*. He was shocked by the sight of irreligious Jews desecrating the Sabbath, eating non-kosher foods, and rebelling against Jewish traditions in the Holy Land. How could he raise his children in such an environment? He was so disturbed by what he saw that he contemplated returning to America.

Traveling to Shiloh

Rav Kook told him:

> Surely you remember the story from the beginning of the book of Samuel, a story which you studied as a child. It is related how Elkanah, the father of the prophet Samuel, "would ascend each year from his town to prostrate himself and bring offerings to God at Shiloh. There [in Shiloh], Eli's two sons Hophni

---
[111] Adapted from *Chayei HaRe'iyah* by Rabbi Moshe Zvi Neriah, pp. 211-212.

and Pinchas served as *kohanim* to God" (I Sam. 1:3).

It is curious that the verse mentions the High Priest's sons, Hophni and Pinchas. What did they have to do with Elkanah's yearly pilgrimage to Shiloh?

The Midrash teaches that Elkanah did not just travel to Shiloh. Elkanah wanted to encourage others to fulfill the mitzvah of *aliyah la-regel*, of visiting the Sanctuary on the holidays. In order to publicize the mitzvah and encourage others to join him, each year Elkanah would take to a different route to Shiloh.

One might ask: What caused the people of this generation to become so lax in their observance of the mitzvah of *aliyah la-regel* – a mitzvah mentioned several times in the Torah – that Elkanah felt it necessary to promote its observance?

The second question answers the first question. Hophni and Pinchas were unscrupulous men who were punished severely for their actions in the Shiloh sanctuary. The fact that they served as *kohanim* was the reason that many chose not to visit Shiloh. With *kohanim* like Hophni and Pinchas, people reasoned, it is preferable not to travel to Shiloh and be exposed to such scandalous behavior.

Elkanah, however, saw the matter differently. He told the people that, despite Hophni and Pinchas' improper behavior, we should not sever our connection to this holy place. We may not abandon this mitzvah. Rather, it is our duty to ascend to Shiloh and strengthen the holiness of the place.

It was due to his noble efforts that Elkanah was rewarded with a son who became one of the greatest leaders of the Jewish people – the prophet Samuel.

Strengthening Holiness in the Land

At this point, Rav Kook turned to his guest:

> We learn an important lesson regarding *Eretz Yisrael* from this story. The fact that there are irreligious Jews living here should not be a reason for us to abandon the mitzvah of dwelling in the Land of Israel. And certainly one should not consider leaving the country. Every person who lives in *Eretz Yisrael* and observes Torah and mitzvot adds greater holiness to the Land.
>
> Those who dwell in *Eretz Yisrael* in holiness – Rav Kook reassured the scholar – will merit children about whom they will be able to say with pride, like Hannah, Samuel's mother, "It was for this child that I prayed" (Sam. 1:27).

SHELACH: OFFERING WINE AND FLOUR[112]

Bringing an offering in the Temple requires more than just a bull, goat, or sheep. In Num. 15:1-16, the Torah commands that *korbanot* be accompanied by wine libations, called *Nesachim*, and flour offerings, called *Menachot*. What was the purpose of these additional offerings of wine and flour?

The answer to this question may be found in a Talmudic statement comparing the Temple service with our own daily service of prayer. Rabbi Yochanan taught:

> Reciting the Shema without tefillin is like offering an *Olah* [a burnt-offering] without its flour offering, or a sacrifice without wine. (*Berachot* 14b)

What is the connection between an incomplete Temple offering and reciting the Shema while not wearing tefillin?

Engaging All of Our Faculties

The Temple service, Rav Kook explained, was meant to encompass all aspects of creation. Every offering contained elements from each of the four basic realms of the universe:

---

[112] Adapted from *Ein Eyah* vol. I, p. 72.

human, animal, vegetable, and mineral. The service involved the individual who brought the offering (human), the sacrifice (animal), the wine and flour offerings (vegetable), and the altar (which was filled with earth from the mineral realm). Without wine and flour, the offering would lack a component from the plant kingdom.

Including wine and flour is an important lesson in how we should serve God. We are blessed with higher faculties – our intellect and power of speech – as well as lower, physical powers. Just as the Temple service incorporated all aspects of the universe, so too, our service of God should engage all of our powers and talents. If we were to serve God only with our more elevated faculties, we would not grow spiritually in all aspects of our being.

What does this have to do with reciting the Shema while wearing tefillin? The Shema proclaims God's unity and the obligation to love Him, "with all your heart, all your soul, and all your might" (Deut. 6:5). By saying these verses while wearing the tefillin on our arm and head, we demonstrate that we are serving God with our entire being – with our physical powers, as represented by the arm, as well as our higher faculties, as represented by the head.

Now Rabbi Yochanan's comparison is clearer. Reciting the Shema without tefillin is like offering a *korban* without the wine and flour. Such a person only utilizes his more refined faculties – his mind and speech – in his service of God. This is like an offering that lacks an element from the lower level of life, from the vegetable realm.

Turn From Evil, Do Good

This explanation also clarifies a puzzling Halachah. The Talmud in *Menachot* 90b rules that some *korbanot* are not accompanied by wine and flour. Offerings brought to atone for sins – the *Chatat* and *Asham* – do not have *Nesachim*. Why not?

Our spiritual service may be divided into two components. There are our efforts to avoid evil, as we abstain from committing the acts delineated by the 365 negative mitzvot; and there are our strivings to draw closer to God through performance of the 248 positive mitzvot. The psalmist summarized this idea in four short words: סוּר מֵרָע ("shun evil") וַעֲשֵׂה טוֹב ("and do good") (Ps. 34:15).

The idea that we should serve God with all aspects of our being, even our lower, physical powers, applies specifically to our positive efforts for spiritual growth. The Talmud in *Nedarim* 32b notes that, with the mitzvah of *brit milah*, "God gave Abraham control over all of his 248 organs." The number "248" alludes to the 248 positive mitzvot. With *brit milah*, even his lowest, most physical nature was directed toward that which is good and holy.

With regard to avoiding evil, however, the situation is different. When we stumble and sin, it is our intellectual faculties that are at fault. Our lower forces do not determine our moral choices; they are not rewarded or punished for their behavior. The body can digest forbidden food just as easily as kosher food. The service of סוּר מֵרָע, shunning evil, only reflects how well our higher faculties are functioning.

Now we understand why sin offerings are not accompanied by wine and flour. These *korbanot* come to atone for our failure to avoid bad choices, and only our moral/intellectual side is at fault.

But voluntary offerings such as the *Olah* and *Shelamim* are brought to attain a special closeness to God. They are a positive service of God – "and do good" – and should be accompanied by flour and wine, demonstrating that this service should engage all levels of our being.

KORACH: SEPARATION AND CONNECTION[113]

The entire congregation is holy, and God is with them. Why do you raise yourselves over God's community? (Num. 16:3)

This was the battle cry of Korach's rebellion – a complaint that, at first glance, seems perfectly justified. Did not the entire people hear God speak at Sinai? It would seem that Korach was only paraphrasing what God Himself told Moses: "Speak to the entire community of Israel and tell them: you shall be holy, for I, your God, am holy" (Lev. 19:2). Why indeed should only the Levites and the *kohanim* serve in the Temple? Why not open up the service of God to the entire nation?

Havdalah and *Chibur*

In our individual lives, and in society and the nation as a whole, we find two general principles at work. This first is *havdalah*, meaning "withdrawal" or "separation." The second is *chibur*, meaning "connection" or "belonging."

These are contradictory traits, yet we need both. This is most evident on the individual level. In order to reflect on our thoughts

---

[113] Adapted from *Orot HaKodesh* vol. II, p. 439.

and feelings, we need privacy. To develop and clarify ideas, we need solitude. To attain our spiritual aspirations, we need to withdraw within our inner selves.

Only by separating from society can we achieve these goals. The distracting company of others robs us of seclusion's lofty gifts. It restricts and diminishes the creative flow from our inner wellspring of purity and joy.

This same principle applies to the nation as a whole. In order for the Jewish people to actualize their spiritual potential, they require *havdalah* from the other nations — as "a nation that dwells alone" (Num. 23:9).

Similarly, within the Jewish people it is necessary to separate the tribe of Levi — and within Levi, the *kohanim* — from the rest of the nation. These groups have special obligations and responsibilities, a reflection of their inner character and purpose.

Separation in Order to Connect

Yet separation is not a goal in and of itself. Within the depths of *havdalah* lies the hidden objective of *chibur*: being part of the whole and influencing it. The isolated forces will provide a positive impact on the whole, enabling a qualitative advance in holiness. These forces specialize in developing talents and ideas that, as they spread, become a source of blessing for all. As they establish their unique traits and paths, life itself progresses and acquires purpose.

We find this theme of *havdalah/chibur* on many levels. The human race is separate from all other species of life. Through this *havdalah*, humanity is able to elevate itself and attain a comprehensive quality that encompasses the elevation of the entire world. The Jewish people are separate from the other nations; this separateness enables them to act as a catalyst to elevate all of humanity, to function as a "kingdom of priests and a holy nation" (Ex. 19:6).

The tribe of Levi is separated from the rest of the nation through their special responsibilities; this distinction ennobles the members of the tribe to fulfill their unique role. The Levites sanctify themselves and become a blessing for the entire nation. And the *kohanim*, with their special holiness, are elevated until they draw forth *ruach hakodesh* (prophetic inspiration) for the benefit of the entire nation, thus actualizing the nation's highest spiritual abilities.

The Correct Order

Now we may understand the source of Korach's error. The Zohar (*Mishpatim* 95a) teaches:

> The *Sitra Achra* [literally, the 'Other Side' – the forces of evil] begins with *chibur* [connection] and ends with *pirud* [division]. But the *Sitra deKedushah* ('Side of Holiness') begins with *pirud* and ends with *chibur*.

The correct path, the path of holiness, follows the order of first separating and then connecting. In other words, the separation is for the sake of connection. But Korach's philosophy (and similar ideologies, such as communism) took the opposite approach. He sought a simplistic inclusiveness of all, binding all people into one uniform group from the outset. He boastfully claimed to unite all together – "The entire congregation is holy." This approach, however, replaces the splendor of diversity with dull uniformity. In the end, this totalitarian approach leads to disunity, as all parts yearn to break apart in order to express their unique individuality. "The *Sitra Achra* begins with *chibur* and ends with *pirud*."

KORACH: WHO NEEDS THE PRIESTHOOD?[114]

> You have taken too much upon yourselves! All the people in the community are holy, and God is with them. Why do you set yourselves above God's congregation? (Num. 16:3)

Korach's call for religious equality resonates well with modern, egalitarian sensibilities. Why indeed do the Jewish people need a special caste of priests? Why cannot each member of the nation participate in the holy service, personally bringing his own offerings to God? Why do we need *kohanim* to serve as intermediaries?

Specialized Sectors

To answer this question, Rav Kook employed the paradigm of the human body. Each organ performs a unique function, providing for the health and general welfare of the body. Despite their different characteristics and tasks, the organs work together, functioning harmoniously as an organic whole.

Human society is also a living body, composed of different sectors and groups. Each profession – farmers, scientists, doctors,

---

[114] Adapted from *Orot*, pp. 53-55.

and so on – provides a specific service for the collective whole. These communal 'organs' provide for society's various needs according to their particular talents and training. As they work together and acknowledge the contribution of other sectors, they ensure the harmonious functioning and flourishing of society as a whole.

The analogy may be extended further. Just as each individual is blessed with certain strengths and ambitions, so too each nation has specific talents and ideals. These national aspirations may be expressed in the sciences, art, philosophy, economic prowess, etc.

Not every limb of a gifted individual is directly involved in his chosen profession. Artists use their hands and eyes, Olympic athletes use their legs, opera singers use their voices, and scientists use their intellect. It is similarly impossible for the entire nation to be directly involved in advancing the nation's ideals. Each nation needs a cadre of leaders who cultivate the soul of the nation. These spiritual elite allow the other sectors to attend to society's material needs, confident that the unique content which gives the nation its distinctive character will not be neglected.

Guarding Israel's Spiritual State

The need for a spiritual leadership is even more pronounced when it comes to the Jewish people, whose national ideology transcends the physical world in which we live. Efforts made to advance the nation's material welfare run the risk of diverting energy from the nation's spiritual aspirations. As a mediaeval Jewish moralist cautioned, "Whatever builds up the material will detract from the spiritual" (*Chovot HaLevavot* 9:2).

Due to this concern, practical affairs are often attended to in desultory fashion. In the end, both aspects, the physical and the spiritual, are harmed. The nation's spiritual efforts become disoriented due to its chaotic material state; and its physical state is weakened due to the coerced admixture of concern for spiritual matters.

Therefore, we need a cadre of lofty *tzaddikim*, gifted with intellectual greatness, who are charged with securing the spiritual state of the nation. These elite are not perturbed if the rest of society cannot not fully share in the richness of their spiritual life due to preoccupation with material matters. They know that spirituality will automatically permeate the nation due to the people's natural inclination to holiness. These public servants represent all of society, and they safeguard its spiritual treasure. The nation in return regards them as its most important assets, and honors them accordingly.

Radical Agents of Godliness

The *kohanim* are mistakenly thought of as intermediaries between man and God. In fact, they are not meant to be *intermediaries*, but rather to enable *immediacy* to God.

When we draw close to God, we do not approach Him with our basest drives and inclinations, but with our holiest aspirations and desires. It is our elevated qualities which draw our entire being toward a Godly, enlightened life.

The same is true for the national organism. It is not right or even possible to approach God using society's basest elements. The nation cannot draw near to God through those who are preoccupied by lives immersed in physical sensations and upheavals. This would lead to a weakened state of enlightenment, spiritually impoverishing the nation and the world at large.

We therefore designate a select group to empower the entire nation to approach God. The lofty, righteous *kohanim*, steeped in elevated knowledge, truly know God. The rest of the nation relies on their holiness and wisdom. The nation takes pride in the spiritual greatness of the *kohanim*; it is blessed through their blessing and sanctified through their sanctity. The people are strengthened and inspired as they labor to attain their material, social, and national objectives.

The need to appoint a cadre of spiritual leaders reflects an innate aspect of human nature. Only after an extended period of time will this institution be truly revealed in all of its nobility – but we are not deterred by lengthy processes. We continue along the path we embarked upon so long ago, and we look forward to its completion and perfection.

Korach's platform – to designate the entire people as priests, without distinctions, all equally wise and spiritually enlightened – is not feasible in the world's present state. Currently we need to aspire to a national spirit of holiness, by virtue of the nation's noblest parts. The *kohanim* will serve as radical agents for sanctity and spirituality, enabling the entire nation to flourish in all endeavors, in its renascence of life in its homeland.

KORACH: UNLIMITED BLESSINGS[115]

Korach, with his motto, "All the people in the community are holy" (Num. 16:3), contested the idea of a select group dedicated to serving God. After the rebellion was put down – quite literally, as it turned out – God affirmed the nation's need for Levites and *kohanim* to serve in the Temple and instruct the people.

Twenty-Four *Matnot Kehunah*

Since the tribe of Levi was dedicated to fostering the spiritual aspirations of the Jewish people, they were not meant to spend their days working the land. Instead, they were supported through a system of *terumot* and *ma'aserot* (tithes). For this reason, the story of Korach's rebellion is followed by a detailed description of the twenty-four *matnot kehunah*, gifts bestowed to the *kohanim*.

Not all people, however, are equally enthusiastic about giving these gifts.

Our eagerness to perform a mitzvah depends on how well we comprehend its goal and purpose. If the objective of a mitzvah is not clearly understood, then its fulfillment will suffer from a lethargic, lackadaisical attitude.

The institution of *kehunah*, the priesthood, and the various

---

[115] Adapted from *Ein Eyah* vol. III, pp. 183-184.

methods of supporting it, will be better appreciated when the entire nation is on a high spiritual level. Only then will we truly recognize the benefit of their influence. And we will realize that our lives are blessed to the extent that we are connected to the spiritual life of the nation.

We may discern three attitudes toward *matnot kehunah*.

1. Refusal to Tithe

The lowest level is one of outright refusal to support the *kohanim*. This attitude stems from a spiritual crisis in which one fails to appreciate the benefit of a spiritual life in general, and the positive influence of the *kohanim*, knowledgeable in God's Torah, in particular. Such a person lacks a connection to the special covenant of the *kehunah* and its overall goal, which encompasses all generations of the Jewish people, past, present, and future. This is a terrible tragedy, the result of a profound emptiness and estrangement from Torah.

2. Fulfilling the Letter of the Law

The second attitude is one of disinterest, even neglect. At this level, appreciation for the institution of *kehunah* is limited to its future place in the lofty state promised to the Jewish people. Since we have not yet merited this long-awaited state, the resulting attitude is to observe the bare minimum, fulfilling only the letter of the law so as not to violate any legal obligations. Such an individual will seek loopholes to avoid tithing, like bringing produce into the house via the roof or the courtyard (see *Berachot*

35b).

While this outlook is not so callous that it reflects a life tragically distant from Torah, it is still very far from a life of blessing. These individuals have not clarified for themselves the purpose of life. They do not appreciate the true value of eternal goals. They fail to grasp how these goals transcend any particular time, how they form a collective activity composed of the combined service of many generations – beautiful structures built through continuous efforts of Torah and mitzvot over time.

Sadly, with such an attitude, life appears as something that must be accepted against our will. Life's greatness and vitality, its essential holiness and beauty, are hidden. As long as one's outlook is so limited, life offers little satisfaction, and the soul will not be content with any of its accomplishments. What good is material success, when life's inner content is empty, incapable of nourishing our higher feelings and thoughts?

3. The Broad Outlook

The highest level is when one acquires the broader outlook that encompasses the overall expanse of life, embracing all generations and all times. From this viewpoint, the current state of the institution of *kehunah* is not the decisive factor. The *kehunah* is respected and cherished due to its future greatness, and from the overall good that comes from the accumulation of all of its contributions in the past, present, and future.

With such an outlook, the nation is ready to receive a profusion of blessings, both spiritual and material. It is with regard to this approach toward tithing that it is written:

Bring all the tithes to the storehouse, so that there is food in My house. Test Me in this, says the Lord of hosts: if I will not open for you the windows of Heaven, and pour out to you blessing *ad bli dai* – until there is more than enough. (Malachi 3:10)

The blessing is extraordinary, encompassing all of life's material aspects. But its source is the collective blessing that revitalizes life's inner depths: the blessing of inner peace, enabling us to feel the goodness of life itself. Life is not limited to the flawed present. As a result, nothing is lacking, and we receive unlimited blessings – *"ad bli dai."* As the Sages interpreted homiletically: "Until one's lips are exhausted from protesting: 'Enough!'" (*Shabbat* 32b)

CHUKAT: BEYOND HUMAN LOGIC[116]

Even King Solomon, renowned for his profound wisdom, failed to grasp its meaning. "I thought I would attain wisdom," he admitted, "but it is distant from me" (Ecc. 7:23).

What was it that eluded Solomon's powerful intellect? The Talmud in *Niddah* 9a explains that he was referring to the *Parah Adumah*, the red heifer whose ashes were used for ritual purification. The true meaning of this ritual is uniquely profound, beyond the grasp of the human intellect.

Why is this mitzvah so difficult to understand?

Repairing the Sin of the Golden Calf

According to the Sages, the *Parah Adumah* comes to atone for the Sin of the Golden Calf. The Midrash (*Bamidbar Rabbah* 19:8) explains this by way of a parable: when the maidservant's son sullied the king's palace, it was his mother who needed to come and clean up the mess.

What exactly is the connection between the ritual of the Red Heifer and the Sin of the Golden Calf? After all, the golden calf was formed out of gold jewelry donated by the people; it was not born to a cow.

---

[116] Adapted from *Midbar Shur*, pp. 317-320.

What was the essence of the Sin of the Golden Calf? Rabbi Yehuda HaLevi (*Kuzari* 1:97) and other medieval commentators explained that only when taking into account the unique spiritual level of the Jewish people at that time does their action count as a grievous offense. For other peoples, not only would it not have been deemed a sin, it might have even been considered a meritorious deed.

The people's motivations were sincere. They did not wish to abandon God. On the contrary, they sought to remain close to Him. They created an image – the prevalent form of worship at that time, like a house of prayer nowadays – in order to have a tangible focal point toward which they could direct their offerings and prayers. Even those who erred by praying directly to the golden image did not reject God. They announced, "O Israel! This is your God, Who brought you out of Egypt" (Ex. 32:8).

If so, what was their mistake? They erred in their attempt to gain closeness to God through actions dictated by their own logic and reasoning. God specifically forbade this form of worship. The image they created – despite their good intentions – contradicted God's command, and it became a stumbling block for those who worshipped the Golden Calf as an actual idol.

Understanding God's Rule

Why did God forbid us from using our powers of reason to establish new mitzvot and modify existing ones, using methods that, according to our understanding, would allow us to become closer to God?

If we want to know what God wants, we need to examine His

actions and the ways through which He governs the world. Theoretically, the percipient individual should be able to discern wonderful aspects of God's rule of the universe, and thereby understand His ways and Divine Will. This would work had God organized creation in such a way that all paths leading to the final goal reflect Divine perfection. Then all aspects of the universe would provide an accurate understanding of God and His Will, allowing us to recognize the proper way to serve Him.

God, however, in His lofty wisdom, organized the universe differently. He decreed that purity might be the end result of impure paths. Even those means which contravene God's Will will lead toward the final goal. Thus it is impossible to deduce what God truly wants simply by observing the ways of the world. Our service of God can only be guided by those directives which God explicitly transmitted through His Torah.

Acknowledging Our Limitations

How is this connected to the purifying ashes of the Red Heifer? Purity and impurity are a function of closeness or distance from God. True purity is the ability to draw near to God and fulfill His will. Death, on the other hand, is *avi avot ha-tum'ah*, the primary source of impurity. Death is an example of a phenomenon in the world that is diametrically opposed to the genuine intention of God, Who desires life. A person noting the phenomenon of death could deduce the exact opposite of God's true intention in the world, concluding that God does not wish that His creations live.

How do we purify ourselves from the impurity of death? To correct the misleading impression of death, we need to recognize the limits of the human intellect in understanding God's rule in the world. By performing the ritual of *Parah Adumah*, a mitzvah that by definition transcends logic, we acknowledge the limitations of our intellect, and avoid the pitfall of inferring God's will from the phenomenon of death.

We can also understand why those who prepare the purifying ashes of the Red Heifer become defiled in the process. God's Will cannot be deduced from the ways of the world, only from the final goal; so too, the process of the *Parah Adumah* generates impurity, and only the end result provides purification.

CHUKAT: SPEAK TO THE ROCK[117]

What is the meaning of God's instruction to Moses to speak to the rock? Can rocks hear us?

The short answer is – yes! Nature and all of its laws are listening. They listen for the call of redemption. They yearn for the redemptive light that preceded the creation of the universe. When this unifying light is revealed, the world's divided factions become linked and bound to their underlying foundation.[118]

As Moses approached to speak to the rock, all of creation was listening. Tragically, instead of speaking, Moses hit the rock. The waters, meant to revive and nourish the people, instead became *"Mei Merivah"* – "Waters of Dispute," bringing conflict and discord into the world. With his impatience and anger, Moses introduced a framework of coercion and force into the world, thus debasing the universe. The world was no longer ready to listen in attentive quietude to the inner voice of the Infinite.

The paradigm shifted from speaking to striking, from receptive

---

[117] Adapted from *Shemonah Kevatzim*, vol. VII, sec. 28.

[118] "Those who rule over themselves and cleave to their Creator, utilizing the world only to aid them in serving the Creator – they uplift themselves and the universe with them…. It is like the statement of the Sages, that the rocks united together [to form a bed for Jacob], each one saying: Let the *tzaddik* rest his head on me (*Chulin* 91)" (*Mesillat Yesharim*, chap. 1).

listening to coercive force.

A World That Listens

This tragic discord will be healed through the Divine spirit that flows within the wisdom of Israel. The flowing waters of Israel's wellspring – the Torah – will heal the discord of *Mei Merivah*. Every Jewish soul has a part in revealing this wisdom. It will arise powerfully, enabling the living word of God to penetrate all hearts. The return to patient communication will awaken the world's latent state of listening in all its splendor.

> You have opened my ears…. Then I said, "Behold, I
> have come, with a scroll of a book written for me."
> (Ps. 40:7-8)

We yearn for a world that listens with open ears, ears that are able to hear the inner call. We aspire for a world where our inner truth, the light of the Life of the worlds, is expressed, not through force and coercion, but through words and literature. "Behold, I have come, with a scroll of a book written for me."

The *Tikunei Zohar* identifies the staff which Moses used to redeem the Jewish people as a pen. "'The staff of God' – that is the pen." Moses' staff, used to strike the rock, will be transformed into a tool of communication and dialogue. And the art of literature will flourish, redeemed from its waywardness.

BALAK: AN ETERNAL PEOPLE[119]

Together with Shema

In the *parashah* of Balak, we find prophetic verses of exquisite beauty and an inspiring story of God's vigilant watch over the Jewish people. But to truly appreciate this Torah portion, consider this remarkable teaching of the Sages.

The Talmud (*Berachot* 12b) relates that at one time the rabbis contemplated incorporating the *parashah* of Balak into the daily prayers, alongside the recitation of the Shema. This is truly astounding. What lesson is contained in the words of Balaam – a villainous prophet, steeped in blind hatred for the Jewish people – that could possibly compare to the Torah's most fundamental beliefs, as delineated in the Shema, the centerpiece of Jewish prayer?

Fortunately, the Talmud clues us in to what makes this *parashah* so special. Its unique message may be found in the following verse, comparing the Jewish people to a fearsome lion:

> [Israel] crouches; he lies like a lion and a lioness. Who dares rouse him? (Num. 24:9)

---

[119] Adapted from *Ein Eyah* vol. I, pp. 67-68.

Yes, it is a beautiful metaphor describing the timeless strength and vitality of the Jewish people. But does this verse justify reading the entire portion of Balak twice a day, together with the Shema?

The Missing Link

Clearly, the Sages saw an inner link between Balak and the Shema. In order to understand this connection, we must first analyze the principal themes of the Shema. The Sages taught (*Berachot* 13a) that the first passage of the Shema expresses God's unity and our acceptance of His rule; and that the theme of the second passage is our acceptance of the mitzvot.

However, these two axioms of Judaism – accepting God's reign and accepting His mitzvot – are missing a common link. What is it that combines them, leading to universal acceptance of God through the performance of mitzvot? The missing link is the Jewish people.

The lofty aspirations expressed in the Shema necessitate the existence of a nation who, throughout the generations, observes the mitzvot and introduces the concept of God's unity to the world. This is the mission of the Jewish people. In fact, they were created specifically for this purpose: "This people I created for Me, [so that] they will proclaim My praise" (Isaiah 43:21).

Now we can understand why the Sages wanted to add this particular verse to the recital of the Shema. Balaam poetically compared the Jewish people to a sleeping lion that none dare disturb. Everyone fears the formidable powers of this majestic creature, even when it sleeps. The latent power of the Jewish people is such that, even when 'sleeping' – even when they are exiled from their land and many of their unique national institutions (the Temple, Sanhedrin, *kohanim*, prophets, etc.) are dormant – nonetheless, their eternal nature is legendary.[120]

The survival of the Jewish people throughout the generations, despite all odds, and in violation of all laws of history, enables them to persist in their mission of proclaiming God's unity. Their indestructible nature is in itself a sanctification of God's Name.

Jewish Nationalism

If the significance of the *parashah* of Balak can be reduced to this single verse, then why not just add that verse to the daily prayers? Why add the entire section?

The Talmud explains that we may not add the verse by itself, since the Torah should not be broken up arbitrarily. "Any section that Moses did not divide, we may not divide."

This explanation is difficult to understand. We find many

---

[120] "[The Jew] has made a marvelous fight in the world, in all the ages; and has done it with his hands tied behind him. He could be vain of himself, and be excused for it. The Egyptian, the Babylonian, and the Persian rose, filled the planet with sound and splendor, then faded to dream-stuff and passed away; the Greek and the Roman followed, and made a vast noise, and they are gone; other peoples have sprung up and held their torch high for a time, but it burned out, and they sit in twilight now, or have vanished. The Jew saw them all, beat them all, and is now what he always was, exhibiting no decadence, no infirmities of age, no weakening of his parts, no slowing of his energies, no dulling of his alert and aggressive mind. All things are mortal but the Jew; all other forces pass, but he remains. What is the secret of his immortality?" (Mark Twain, "Concerning The Jews," *Harper's Magazine*, March 1898).

individual verses incorporated in the liturgy. Why not this one?

It appears that detaching this particular verse from the rest of Balaam's prophecy poses a special danger. By itself, the verse could be construed as extolling nationalism for its own sake. The unique strength of the Jewish people is not meant to serve the goals of self-centered nationalism, military conquest, or national aggrandizement. The eternal nature of Israel must be understood within the context of their unique mission: to promulgate God's Name in the world. Therefore we must take care not to separate this verse from the rest of the portion.

Appreciating the Message of Balak

In the end, the Sages did not add the *parashah* of Balak to the daily prayers. They felt that such a lengthy addition would be too great a burden for the people.

Reading this portion would be a burden, since its message is not applicable to every generation. Not every generation is able to appreciate the role that Israel's timeless vitality plays in achieving its spiritual goals. Yet the very fact that the Sages wanted to incorporate it in the prayers indicates that a time will come when this message will be accepted and internalized by the nation as a whole.

BALAK: SWEET DREAMS[121]

Have you ever dreamt a disturbing dream, but cannot remember it? The Talmud recommends reciting the following prayer while the *kohanim* bless the people:

> Master of the World! My dreams and I belong to You.
> If the dreams are good – bolster them like the dreams
> of Joseph. And if they need to be remedied – fix them
> like the bitter waters that Moses sweetened. Just as
> You transformed wicked Balaam's curses into
> blessings, so too, make all of my dreams be for the
> best. (*Berachot* 55b)

Transforming Bad Dreams

There are two ways in which evil tidings may be transformed into good ones. In the first way, the means remain disturbing, but the final outcome is good. One example of this is the sale of Joseph into slavery and his subsequent imprisonment in Egypt. All of the various causes were adverse, incurring much hardship for Joseph. But the ultimate result – Joseph's rise to greatness, and his ability to provide sustenance during the years of famine – was certainly

---

[121] Adapted from *Ein Eyah* vol. II, p. 274.

for the best.

However, it is even more impressive when the causes are also transformed into positive ones, so that the end is achieved through propitious means. An example of this type of transformation occurred with Balaam. God could have let Balaam curse the people of Israel, and only later changed his curses to blessings. But instead, God "placed a hook in Balaam's mouth" – as the Midrash describes God's complete control over Balaam's powers of speech – so that only blessings came forth. Thus even the means – Balaam's prophecies – were favorable.

We pray that our dreams should be completely transformed for the good. Like Balaam's 'curses,' we want both the ends and the means to be auspicious and beneficial.

PINCHAS: ZEALOTRY FOR THE SAKE OF HEAVEN[122]

Pinchas' Lineage

When Pinchas saw a prince from the tribe of Shimon publicly cavorting with a Midianite princess, he took the law into his own hands. Using his spear, Pinchas killed them both. God praised his act of zealotry, rewarding him with the priesthood.

> Pinchas, the son of Elazar, the son of Aaron the *kohen*, was the one who zealously took up My cause among the Israelites and turned My anger away from them. (Num. 25:11)

Why does the Torah need to point out Pinchas' lineage here? This is particularly puzzling considering that the Torah just identified Pinchas a few verses earlier (25:7).

The Midrash (*Sanhedrin* 82b) explains that the tribal leaders mocked Pinchas: "His maternal grandfather [Jethro] fattened up calves for idolatrous sacrifices – and he had the audacity to murder a prince of Israel!" Therefore, the Torah publicized Pinchas' lineage through his father's side, Aaron the High Priest.

---

[122] Adapted from *Olat Re'iyah* vol. I, p. 494.

This Midrash requires clarification. Why was it so important to respond to these disparaging comments? Furthermore, what does it help if one of Pinchas' grandfathers was the high priest – his other grandfather was still a reformed idolater!

Pure Motives

Rav Kook explained that the Torah does not ordinarily approve of such acts of zealotry. They are sanctioned only if the zealot acted purely for the sake of Heaven.

Onlookers might have suspected that Pinchas harbored secondary motives. Perhaps he sought to demonstrate his faithfulness to Israel and its monotheistic faith, despite a grandfather who was a convert from paganism. Therefore, God testified that Pinchas acted as Aaron's grandson. What qualities characterized Aaron? The Sages wrote: "Be a disciple of Aaron, loving peace and pursuing peace, loving all people and drawing them near to the Torah" (*Avot* 1:12). Aaron, legendary for seeking the path of peace and reconciliation, would not have been suspect of ulterior motives. Pinchas' action, the Torah emphasizes, was worthy of his illustrious grandfather. He acted as befits the grandson of Aaron the High Priest, with selfless intentions and a pure heart.

PINCHAS: THE DAILY SHEEP OFFERING[123]

The central daily offering in the Temple service was the *Tamid*, an offering of two lambs. One lamb was offered just after daybreak, at the start of the day's service; the second lamb was offered in the afternoon, at its conclusion. The sheep were purchased using half-shekel coins collected from the entire Jewish people.

Why was a small sheep used for the *Tamid* offering, and not a more impressive offering? And why use only young animals, less than a year old?[124]

Bulls and Sheep

Some Temple offerings were brought from bulls, while others from sheep. A bull is usually a peaceful animal and a productive worker. But on occasion a bull can suddenly transform itself into a terrifying force of danger and destruction. For this reason, a bull is an appropriate offering for those seeking to atone for a life that

---

[123] Adapted from *Olat Re'iyah* vol. I, p. 130.

[124] Maimonides wrote that offerings are *chukim*, Divine statutes for which we do not know the reason. Yet that assertion did not deter scholars throughout the ages – including Maimonides himself – from suggesting possible reasons to explain various details of the Temple service.

has tragically fallen into a grave state of ruin and disaster.

Sheep, on the other hand, provide a suitable offering when the problem is not one of destructive behavior, but rather a general spiritual decline and indulgence in materialism. The peaceful but mundane sheep are a fitting metaphor for our daily struggle against the negative influence of involvement in worldly matters.

With regard to the Jewish people as a whole, one cannot speak of widespread corruption and moral decay. The *Tamid* offering, purchased with funds from the entire nation, does not atone for the extreme vices of evil individuals. Rather, it is meant to meet the nation's general spiritual needs: to uplift lives from the poverty of a materialistic existence and renew their aspirations for a life rich with meaning and holiness.

Yearlings

Why use sheep in their first year? Unlike older beasts, who are often difficult and ornery, these young sheep do not symbolize a life that is dominated by self-centered materialism. Since the intrinsic holiness of the Jewish people does not allow worldly influences to be etched deeply into the nation's soul, the *Tamid* offering is best represented by young, relatively innocuous animals.

MATOT: BEAUTEOUS EVIL[125]

The Offering of Midianite Jewelry

After the reprisal attack against Midian, the Israelite soldiers presented an unusual donation to the Tabernacle: gold jewelry seized from the Midianite women.

> We wish to bring an offering to God. Every man who found a gold article – an anklet, a bracelet, a ring, an earring, or a body ornament – to atone for our souls before God. (Num. 31:50)

Why did the soldiers bring this odd offering to the Tabernacle? The Talmud (*Shabbat* 64a) explains that they felt a need for atonement – not for improper actions – but for improper thoughts when they came in contact with the Midianite women.

Still, why not bring a more conventional offering? And why does the Torah list all of the various types of Midianite ornaments?

Some of the jewelry was of the normal variety, worn in full view, such as rings and bracelets. Other pieces, however, were of an intimate nature, worn underneath the clothes, like the *kumaz*, a

---

[125] Adapted from *Ein Eyah* vol. IV, p. 116.

suggestive body ornament. From the association that the Torah makes between ordinary jewelry and intimate ornaments, the Talmud derives the moral lesson that "to gaze at a woman's little finger [for enjoyment] is like staring at her undressed."

What is so terrible about enjoying a woman's natural aesthetic beauty?

The Snare of Superficial Beauty

On its own accord, beauty has intrinsic worth, and can make a positive impression on the soul. The soul gains a wonderful sense of expansiveness when it experiences aesthetic pleasures that are pure.

However, if the beauty is covering up that which is ethically repulsive, this attractiveness becomes a spiritual hazard. The external charm is but a snare, entrapping in its inner ugliness those caught in its net. In general, we only succumb to that which is morally repugnant when it is cloaked in a veneer of superficial beauty.

This was precisely the *casus belli* for the war against Midian. The young women of Moab and Midian enticed the men with their outer beauty, leading them to perform the vile idolatrous practices of Pe'or. The Midrash describes their method: "When [the Israelite man] was overcome by lust and asked her to submit to him, she pulled out a statue of Pe'or from her bosom and demanded: 'First, prostrate yourself before this!'" (*Sifrei* 25:1; Rashi on Num. 25:2)

This phenomenon encompasses an even greater pitfall. The simple act of staring at that which is prohibited undermines the soul's healthy sense of moral rectitude and purity. If we are attracted to that which is morally repugnant, we become desensitized to the ugliness of the sin. The superficial beauty not only conceals the inner sordidness, it diminishes our loathing for it.

Even if the soul has not been sufficiently corrupted to be actually ensnared in the net of immorality, its purity has nevertheless been tainted by an attraction to that which is forbidden. For this reason, the Israelite soldiers who fought against Midian required atonement. To make amends for their spiritual deterioration, they brought a particularly appropriate offering: gold jewelry, whose shiny and glittery exterior concealed its corrupt inner core. The officers donated jewelry that is worn openly, as well as ornaments worn intimately. They recognized that both types of jewelry share the potential to desensitize the soul and damage its integrity.

MASSEI: UNCHECKED VIOLENCE[126]

Regarding a society where murderers are able to evade punishment through bribery, the Torah admonishes:

> Do not defile the land in which you live and in which I live. (Num. 35:34)

In what way does allowing murderers go unpunished "defile the land"? Why does the Torah emphasize that this is the land where both the Jewish people and God dwell?

The Sages taught in *Shabbat* 33a:

> For the crime of bloodshed, the Temple is destroyed and the *Shechinah* departs from Israel. As it says, "Do not defile the land in which you live and in which I live." If you do defile it, you will not dwell in it, nor will I dwell in it.

Why is the appropriate punishment for legal corruption the destruction of the Temple, the loss of the *Shechinah*, and exile?

---

[126] Adapted from *Ein Eyah* vol. III, p. 188.

The Impact of Murder

Cleary, a society in which violence and bloodshed are rampant is not fulfilling its basic obligation to provide security for its citizens. But from an ethical-spiritual perspective, murder reflects a far more tragic phenomenon.

The Torah describes the Divine aspect of the human soul with the term "*tzelem Elokim*." What is this "image of God"? The Torah posits that the Godly qualities of goodness, of wanting to help others, of giving and nurturing, are inherent to the human soul. Those who have killed a human being have corrupted their souls to such an extent that they have completely negated their innate *tzelem Elokim*. Instead of promoting life, they bring about its loss and destruction.

Destruction of the Temple

The *Beit HaMikdash* was not built solely for the benefit of the Jewish people. When King Solomon dedicated the Temple, he announced that it was "also for the stranger who is not from Your people Israel, but will come from a distant country for the sake of Your Name" (I Kings 8:41). The Temple is meant to be a "house of prayer for all peoples" (Isaiah 56:7), a beacon projecting the Torah's message of ethical monotheism and enlightenment throughout the world.

However, in order to influence and better humanity, the ethical state of the Jewish people must be healthy and robust. When Israel has fallen to the lowest levels of cruelty and violence, what kind of moral example can the *Beit HaMikdash* provide to the world? How can the Temple service inspire other nations, when they see that the values it represents have not even succeeded in uplifting the Jewish people, repairing social injustice and eradicating bloodshed? Unable to serve its universal purpose, the Temple loses its raison d'être.

Loss of Divine Presence

This explains the connection between a corrupt society and the destruction of the *Beit HaMikdash*. What about the second consequence, the departure of the *Shechinah*?

We must first understand the significance of God's Presence in Israel. The national soul of the Jewish people aspires to goals far greater than social justice. Our objective is not merely to create an orderly society that provides safety and security for its members. What point is there in creating a self-centered, materialistic society, even if its citizens are safe from violence and instability?

This is where God's Presence comes in. The Jewish nation has an inner holiness that elevates the value of life. Through the *Shechinah*, the nation's soul aspires to the highest and loftiest good. It strives to live according to the most elevated, Godly values.

Spiritual goals are like building blocks, attained step by step. The nation must first acquire a basic moral level, the common mores appreciated by all peoples. Only then is it possible to aspire to higher levels of holiness. If the *Beit HaMikdash* is no longer standing due to a corrupt and immoral society, how can the soul of the nation attempt to elevate itself to attain its unique goals? In such a state, the *Shechinah* departs from Israel.

Exile from the Land

The third punishment for national corruption is exile. The presence of the Jewish people in *Eretz Yisrael* is tightly bound to its universal influence as a nation. Saintly individuals may certainly promote much holiness and enlightenment. But the impact of an entire nation, expressing holiness in all aspects of its national life, is of a far greater magnitude.

When the Jewish people cease to have a positive influence on other nations, as indicated by the destruction of the Temple and the departure of the *Shechinah*, then even their continued dwelling in the Land of Israel is called into question. "If you defile the land, you will not dwell in it and I will not dwell in it."

ספר דברים

THE BOOK OF

DEUTERONOMY

DEVARIM: MOSES SPEAKS![127]

The Merchant and the King

The Book of Deuteronomy is essentially a collection of Moses' farewell speeches, delivered to the Jewish people as they prepared to enter the Land of Israel. The eloquence, passion, and cadence of Moses' discourses are breathtaking. One can only wonder: is this the same man who claimed to be "heavy of mouth and heavy of tongue" (Ex. 4:10)?

The Sages were aware of this anomaly. The Midrash (*Devarim Rabbah* 1:7) offers the following parable to explain how eloquence is a relative matter:

> This is like a man selling purple cloth, who announced, "Purple cloth for sale!" Hearing his voice, the king peeked out and called the merchant over.
>
> "What are you selling?" asked the king.
>
> "Nothing, Your Highness."
>
> "But before I heard you call out, 'Purple cloth for sale,' and now you say, 'Nothing.' What changed?"
>
> "Oh no!" exclaimed the merchant. "I *am* selling

[127] Adapted from *Otzarot HaRe'iyah* vol. II, pp. 131-133. (Originally published in *Itur Sofrim*.)

purple cloth. But by your standards, it is nothing."

The same idea, the Midrash concludes, may be applied to Moses and his speaking abilities. When standing before God, Creator of the faculty of speech, Moses announced, "I am not a man of words" (Ex. 4:10). But when it came to speaking to the Jewish people, the Torah records: "These are the words that Moses spoke."

Who May Be a Prophet?

In order to properly understand Moses' claim that he possessed inferior oratory skills, we need to examine a basic question regarding the nature of prophets and prophecy.

In the *Mishneh Torah,* Maimonides describes the prerequisite character traits and intellectual qualifications to be a prophet. He then writes:

> One who has perfected himself in all of these traits and is in perfect health – when he enters the *pardeis* [i.e., when he studies esoteric wisdom] and is drawn to those lofty and abstract matters... immediately the prophetic spirit will come to him. (*Yesodei HaTorah* 7:2)

This description seems to indicate that prophecy is purely a function of one's moral and spiritual preparation. Once one has attained the necessary spiritual level, he automatically merits prophecy.

However, Maimonides later writes that those who strive to attain prophecy are called "the sons of prophets" (see 2 Kings 2:15). Despite their intense efforts, they are still not full-fledged prophets. "Even though they direct their minds, it is possible that the *Shechinah* will inspire them, and it is possible that it will not" (ibid. 7:5). This statement indicates that attaining prophecy is not dependent only upon one's initiative and efforts. Even those who have attained the appropriate spiritual level are not assured that they will receive prophecy.

How can we reconcile these two seemingly contradictory statements?

Natural or Supernatural?

Many aspects of the spiritual realm parallel the physical world. We find that the physical world is largely governed by set laws of nature and physics. Only on occasion does Divine providence intervene in the rule of nature. The same holds true for the hidden resources of the soul. There are set, general rules that govern their functions. But there are also situations that go beyond the natural faculties of the soul.

We may thus rephrase our question as follows: is prophecy a naturally occurring spiritual talent for those who prepare themselves appropriately? Or does it fall under the category of the supernatural, dependent upon God's will at that time, when He chooses to perfect the world by way of prophetic message?

Ruach HaKodesh and *Nevu'ah*

To resolve this dilemma, we must distinguish between two types of prophecy. The first is an inner revelation in one's thoughts, called *"ruach hakodesh."* This is naturally attained Divine knowledge, a result of the soul's nobility and its focus on lofty matters. This level of prophecy is a natural talent that God established within the soul.

There is, however, a second type of prophecy. This is *"nevu'ah,"* from the word *"niv,"* meaning "expression" or "utterance." *Nevu'ah* is the consummation of the prophetic experience; prophecy goes beyond thought and is concretized in letters and words. This form of prophecy is not a natural faculty of the soul. It reflects a miraculous connection between the physical and spiritual realms, a supernatural phenomenon of Divine Will commanding the prophet to relay a specific message to the world.

We may now resolve the apparent contradiction in Maimonides' writings. When he wrote that the prophet will automatically attain prophecy, Maimonides was referring to the prophetic insight of *ruach hakodesh*. From his description, it is clear that he is speaking about a prophecy experienced mentally: "His thoughts are constantly attuned to the holy. They are bound under God's Throne, to grasp those holy and pure images, perceiving God's wisdom [in all aspects of creation]."

When, on the other hand, Maimonides spoke of *nevu'ah*, he wrote that even though the prophet directs his mind, he will not necessarily merit prophetic communion with God. This form of prophecy is dependent upon God's Will, and not on the soul's natural talents.

Moses' Mistake

Now we can better understand Moses' claim that he was not "a man of words." Moses was certainly aware of his stature as a prophet. Maimonides teaches that a prophet "recognizes that he is no longer as he once was; but rather that he has been elevated above the level of other wise individuals." Moses was aware of his spiritual level – but only as one worthy of *ruach hakodesh,* of a prophetic mental state. He assumed that the greater level of *nevu'ah* would be similarly recognizable by one who merited it. Since Moses did not sense this level of prophecy within himself, he declared that he was not a "man of words" – i.e., one meriting prophecy expressed in speech.

Moses' reasoning, however, was flawed. The inner prophecy of thought is a natural talent of the soul and the result of the prophet's spiritual efforts; thus the prophet is aware that he merits *ruach hakodesh.* The external prophecy of *nevu'ah,* on the other hand, depends on God's Will, according to the dictates of Divine providence at that time. The first level is comparable to the laws of nature in the world, while the second is like supernatural miracles performed on special occasions. Thus *nevu'ah* does not reflect the inner qualities of the prophet's soul.

God's response to Moses is now clearer. "Who gave man a mouth? ... Who made him blind? Was it not I, the Lord?" (Ex. 4:11) The world has two sides, the natural and the supernatural. The mouth is part of the natural realm, whereas blindness is a special condition. Both, God told Moses, come from Me. Just as you attained the natural level of *ruach hakodesh,* so too, it is My will that you will be granted the supernatural level of *nevu'ah*.

The Prophetic Nature of *Devarim*

One final question: why is it that the Midrash only clarifies Moses' oratorical skills in the book of Deuteronomy? The answer to this question is to be found in the difference between the prophetic nature of Deuteronomy as opposed to the other books of Moses.

Regular *nevu'ah* occurs in this fashion: the prophet would first hear God's message, then the Divine Spirit would come over him, and he would relate what he had heard. The prophecy of Moses, however, was totally different. The *Shechinah* would "speak through his throat," even as he spoke to the people. Moses was merely a mouthpiece for the Divine Presence.

As a result, the first four books of the Pentateuch do not demonstrate Moses' oratory talents. The book of Deuteronomy, on the other hand, is a reflection of Moses' talents in the same way that the prophetic books of other prophets reflect their individual style of speech.

Were it not for Deuteronomy, we could have taken Moses' claim at face value and understood that he was literally "heavy of mouth and heavy of tongue." But after reading the eloquent discourses of *sefer Devarim*, we realize that Moses was in fact referring to his prophetic abilities. Moses meant that he was unworthy of verbal *nevu'ah*. With regard to ordinary speech, however, Moses was only "heavy of mouth" in comparison to the King of the universe.

DEVARIM: DI ZAHAV - TOO MUCH GOLD[128]

What is "Di Zahav"?

Deuteronomy opens with a detailed description of the location where Moses delivered his final speeches:

> These are the words that Moses spoke to all of Israel
> on the east bank of the Jordan River... near Paran,
> Tofel, Lavan, Chazeroth, and Di Zahav. (Deut. 1:1)

Why do we need to know the precise location of Moses' orations? The Sages explained that each of these names held a special meaning – and a veiled rebuke – for those listening. "Di Zahav," for example, was a reminder of the Sin of the Golden Calf ("*zahav*" meaning "gold").

According to one opinion, however, the name "Di Zahav" also indicated a justification for the behavior of the Jewish people:

> What is "Di Zahav"? This is what Moses told God:
> "Master of the World! It is because of all the silver
> and gold that You showered upon the Israelites –
> until they said, "*Dai!*" [Enough!] – that is what caused

---

128 Adapted from *Ein Eyah* vol. I, pp. 140-141.

them to make the Golden Calf."[129] (*Berachot* 32a)

Do you know anyone who had enough money and refused to accept more?

The Human Drive For More

The basis of serving God is our natural drive to continually advance and achieve. The goal of life is to be close to God, Whose perfection is boundless. Thus we must continually perfect ourselves in order to draw near to God. Of course, this aspiration can never be fully attained. We are never able to say, "Enough! I have achieved everything." Each accomplishment makes us aware of even greater challenges and goals.

In order to lead us on this path of constant growth, God planted within the human soul the incessant drive to always seek more. As Solomon noted: "The soul will never be sated" (Ecc. 6:7). This drive also compels us regarding material acquisitions: "One who loves silver never has his fill of silver" (Ecc. 5:9). Our drive for more is an indication that we can only attain our true goals through continual spiritual growth.

Limited Aspirations

When the Israelites sojourned in the wilderness, all of their physical needs were taken care of. They drew water from the well of Miriam, manna rained down from the sky, and their clothes

---

[129] The Midrash interprets the name Di Zahav as "*dai zahav*" – "enough gold."

never wore out. In this situation, they had little to gain by seeking additional possessions and wealth. It would just be more to carry. The soul's natural drive was artificially suppressed, so that when the Israelites were showered with more silver and gold than they could ever need, their response was, "Enough!"

This was Moses' defense for the Jewish people. Their unique existence in the wilderness, where all their needs were miraculously provided, stifled their soul's natural desire for more. Dependent upon gifts from Heaven, lacking challenges and goals, they became satisfied and indolent. And this impacted their spiritual aspirations.

Since their natural drive to advance was weakened, the Israelites turned to more easily attainable spiritual goals. And this is what led them to the Sin of the Golden Calf.

What is the root of idolatry? It is the psychological desire to cleave to something closer to us, something tangible and finite. It is the choice not to seek out the infinite and boundless, but to take the easier route, to be content worshipping a force which is easy to identify and relate to.

This aberrant form of spirituality suited a people with limited aspirations. This is what Moses told God: "Di Zahav – it is because of all the silver and gold that You showered upon the Israelites, until they said, 'Enough!' – that is what caused them to lower their sights and worship the Golden Calf."

VA'ETCHANAN: INTRODUCING PRAYER WITH PRAISE[130]

Moses' Prayer

The Torah records Moses' pleas to be allowed to enter into the Land of Israel:

> O God, Eternal! You have begun to show me Your greatness and power. What force is there in heaven or earth that can perform deeds and mighty acts as You can? Please, let me cross [the Jordan River] and see the good land.... (Deut. 3:24-25)

Rabbi Simlai analyzed Moses' prayer, breaking it up into two components:

1. **Praise** – "You have begun to show me Your greatness...."
2. **The actual request** – "Please let me cross...."

This, Rabbi Simlai explained, is a model for all prayers. One should begin by praising God, and only afterwards present one's requests.

We need to understand this model. Is it simply a matter of

---

[130] Adapted from *Ein Eyah* vol. I, p. 147 on *Berachot* 32a.

flattering God, just as one might 'butter up' a mortal king before making a request? Or is there a deeper significance to this protocol for prayer?

How does Prayer Work?

Rav Kook explained that the requirement to precede prayer with God's praise relates to the very foundations of prayer and its efficacy. Following this format prevents us from grossly misinterpreting the mechanics of prayer.

One might think that prayer is some sort of magic loophole built into the framework of Divine providence, and that by pleading our case it is possible to cause God to change His mind. The notion that we have the power to influence God's will, however, is untenable.

Rather, we should view prayer as a wonderful gift which enables us to refine ourselves. Prayer does not effect a change in God; prayer effects a change in us. It is only by virtue of the soul's moral and spiritual elevation that prayer has the power to annul harsh decrees. We cannot change the basic universal order manifested in a particular decree. But we can change ourselves. Then, as a result of our transformation, the decree is no longer relevant.

Thus it is advisable to introduce every prayer with praise of God. Such praise affirms God's eternal nature and ensures a correct understanding of the efficacy of prayer.

Even Moses

It is noteworthy that Rabbi Simlai's insight was gleaned from examining a prayer of Moses. One might consider himself above making such a mistake regarding the nature of prayer. Yet we find that even Moses, despite his unparalleled knowledge of spiritual matters, took care to introduce his request with praise of God. Certainly we should follow Moses' lead, thereby ensuring that we correctly grasp the true nature of prayer.

VA'ETCHANAN: WITH ALL YOUR SOUL[131]

Rabbi Akiva's Martyrdom

When the Romans decreed that teaching Torah is a crime punishable by death, Rabbi Akiva's response was not surprising. The great scholar, who had supported Bar Kochba in his revolt against Rome, gathered people together and gave public Torah lectures.

It was not long before Rabbi Akiva was charged and convicted. When the rabbi was brought out for public execution, it was the hour to recite the Shema. As the executioners flayed his skin with iron combs, Rabbi Akiva recited the Shema, concentrating on fulfilling its words: to love God "with all your heart, all your soul, and all your might."

The Talmud records Rabbi Akiva's final words before his death. His students asked him: "Our master! Even to this extent?"

The sage responded:

> All my life I have been troubled by this verse, "You shall love God... with all your soul." As I have explained its meaning: "all your soul" – even if they take your life. I have always wondered: will I ever

---

[131] Adapted from *Ein Eyah* vol. II, pp. 344-345 on *Berachot* 61b.

have the privilege of fulfilling this mitzvah? And now that the opportunity has finally arrived – shall I not seize it?

This exchange between Rabbi Akiva and his students requires clarification. What is the meaning of their question, "Even to this extent?"

The Purpose of Shema

One might think that the daily recitation of Shema is a preparatory act. Each day we accept upon ourselves the yoke of Heaven, and prepare ourselves to love God, even at the cost of our lives. This daily declaration ensures that we will have the necessary reserves of courage and commitment should there arise a need for the ultimate sacrifice of martyrdom.

This is why his students were surprised. Their teacher had already withstood the test. He had accepted martyrdom with noble determination. Even the cruelest instruments of torture had failed to deter him. What need, then, was there for Rabbi Akiva to recite this final Shema? Why prepare for that which he was now fulfilling?

Rabbi Akiva, however, understood the intrinsic value of the Shema. This declaration of love for God and acceptance of His rule is not just a tool to train the spirit. Each recitation of the Shema is in itself a wonderful act. Each time we declare God's unity, our souls acquire greater holiness and closeness to God. The Shema is not just a means to prepare oneself; its very recitation refines and elevates the soul.

Until his final declaration of the Shema, Rabbi Akiva had recited the Shema with the thought that he was willing to sacrifice his life – "with all your soul" – for love of God. His entire life, he had wondered whether he would be able to fulfill the mitzvah of the Shema in its most extreme, most demanding, form. "Will I ever have the privilege of fulfilling this mitzvah to its utmost?" At the hands of the Romans, he accepted the reign of Heaven while sacrificing his life – not just as a mental vision, but in real life.

His Soul Departed With *Echad*

The Talmud relates that as Rabbi Akiva concentrated on the final word of the Shema, his soul departed.

Rabbi Akiva breathed his last with the word *"Echad"* – "God is one." A master of Jewish law, the scholar was able to infer legal rulings from the smallest markings in the Torah's text (*Menachot* 29b). In the final analysis, however, all of the detailed laws and myriad interpretations that he had propounded during his lifetime were all part of a single harmonious system. Everything Rabbi Akiva had taught shared the same underlying theme: how to live life according to the supreme principle of God's oneness. It was thus fitting that his final word should be *"Echad."*

EIKEV: FOUR BLESSINGS AFTER EATING[132]

When you eat and are sated, you must bless the Lord
your God for the good land that He has given you.
(Deut. 8:10)

The Torah does not specify the exact text of *Birkat Hamazon*,
the blessing recited after eating a meal. The Talmud, however,
informs us that it comprises four blessings, authored over a period
of a thousand years:

1. Moses composed the first blessing, "הַזָּן" ("the One
   Who provides sustenance for the entire world"), when
   the manna fell in the desert.
2. Joshua composed the second blessing, "עַל הָאָרֶץ" ("For
   the Land"), when the Jewish people entered the Land
   of Israel.
3. David and Solomon composed the third blessing, "בּוֹנֵה
   יְרוּשָׁלָיִם" ("the One Who rebuilds Jerusalem"). David,
   who established Jerusalem as his capital, wrote, "Your
   people Israel and Your city Jerusalem." And Solomon,
   who built the Temple, added, "The great and holy
   Temple."

---

[132] Adapted from *Ein Eyah* vol. II, p. 218 on *Berachot* 48b.

4. The Sages of Yavneh[133] composed the final blessing, "וְהַמֵּטִיב הַטּוֹב" ("The good King and Benefactor"), to commemorate the miracle that occurred with the dead of the city of Beitar. These Jews were killed by the Romans during the failed Bar Kochba revolt of 135 C.E. For months, the Roman authorities refused to let them be buried, but miraculously, their bodies did not rot.

The Order of the Blessings

Is there a pattern to the order of these four blessings? Rav Kook explained that the blessings follow a clear progression: from the needs of the individual to those of the nation; and from our physical needs to our spiritual aspirations.[134]

The very acting of eating contains a certain spiritual danger. Over-indulgence in gastronomic pleasures can lower one's goals to the pursuit of sensual gratification and physical enjoyment. The Torah therefore provided a remedy – a special prayer to be recited after the meal. *Birkat Hamazon* is "a ladder resting on the ground yet reaching the Heavens," a spiritual act that enables us to raise ourselves from petty, self-absorbed materialism to lofty spiritual aspirations.

In order to attain this higher awareness, we must climb the

---

[133] Rabban Yochanan ben Zakai transferred the Sanhedrin from Jerusalem to Yavneh after Jerusalem's destruction at the hand of the Romans in 70 C.E.

[134] A similar progression may be found in the requests of the *Amidah* prayer.

'ladder' step by step:

1. The first rung of the ladder relates to our own personal physical welfare.
2. On the next rung, we express our concern for the physical welfare of the nation.
3. On the third rung, we focus on the spiritual well-being of the nation.
4. Lastly, we aspire to be a "light unto the nations," a holy people who influence and uplift all who were created in God's image.

This progression is accurately reflected in the blessings of *Birkat Hamazon*. First, we recite the blessing of "Who sustains the world," composed when the manna fell. This prayer corresponds to the physical needs of each individual, just as the manna-bread sustained each Israelite in the barren desert. The manna also provided loftier benefits, as it spiritually uplifted all who witnessed this miracle. But its primary function was to provide for each individual's physical needs.

The second level – concern for the physical welfare of the entire nation – is the subject of the second blessing, "For the Land." When Joshua led the people into their own land, the Land of Israel, he set the stage for the establishment of a nation with all of the usual national assets: security and defense, self-government, agriculture, economy, natural resources, and so on.

Concern for the spiritual well-being of the Jewish people is the theme of the third blessing, which deals with the spiritual center of the Jewish people: Jerusalem. King David composed the first part, "For Your people Israel and Your city Jerusalem," expressing our prayers for the spiritual state and unity of the Jewish people.

King Solomon added, "For the great holy Temple." This reflects the highest goal: the spiritual elevation of all humanity. When dedicating the Temple, Solomon prayed that this holy building – "a house of prayer for all nations" – would ensure "that all the peoples of the world will know that God is the Lord, there is no other" (I Kings 8:60).

In this way, *Birkat Hamazon* bestows profound spiritual value to our private meals – a prayer that guides us, step by step, to a holier world.

The Promise of Beitar

One might become discouraged, however, when faced with the bitter reality of the exile and the current state of the Jewish people. Therefore, the rabbis of Yavneh, following the destruction of the Temple and the failed Bar Kochba revolt, composed the final blessing, "The good King and Benefactor."

With the fall of the great city of Beitar, the last hopes for Jewish independence were crushed for thousands of years. Nonetheless, the Sages saw tremendous significance in the fact that the dead did not decompose, and were eventually given a proper burial. This was a Heavenly sign that even if the nation of Israel appears to be lifeless, struck down by the sword of our enemies, we nonetheless retain our spiritual essence, like an inner fire smoldering imperceptibly inside a black piece of coal, cool to the touch. We are confident that we will yet attain our highest aspirations, despite the many years we may have to wait. Just as those who sleep in the dust will return to life in the appointed hour, so too, the Jewish people will rise to national greatness in the end of days.

EIKEV: ANIMALS SERVED FIRST![135]

The Torah promises that if we observe the mitzvot and sincerely love God, we will enjoy timely rain and bountiful crops:

> I will give plants in your field for your animals; and
> you will eat and be satiated. (Deut. 11:15)

Rav Abba Aricha, the celebrated third-century scholar, called attention to the order of the verse: first the animals eat, and only then the people. He learned from here that one should not eat before first placing food before one's animals.

Why is this? Should not people eat first, since they are more important? Are not humans "the crown of creation"?

Rav Kook explained that this Talmudic rule of etiquette contains several moral lessons:

- Given our central place in the universe, we have a responsibility to look after all creatures.
- Our food (and in the case of the farmer, also his livelihood) is supplied by cows, chickens, and so on. We should feed these animals first as an expression of the fundamental gratitude we should feel toward these

---

[135] Adapted from *Ein Eyah* vol. II, p. 180, on *Berachot* 40a.

creatures which provide us with our basic needs.

- If we lack food for a short time, we may comfort ourselves with spiritual or intellectual pursuits. This is an integral aspect of the human soul, which is not sustained "by bread alone." Animals, however, have no such alternate outlets when they are pained by hunger. Therefore, it is logical to deal with the animal's hunger first.

- In purely physical aspects, animals are superior to humans. Is there a human being who is stronger than a bear, faster than a horse, more agile than a cat? Our superiority over animals lies exclusively in the spiritual realms: in our intelligence and our higher aspirations. Therefore, when it comes to physical sustenance, animals take precedence to humans, and by right are served first.

RE'EIH: UPROOTING IDOLATRY IN THE LAND OF ISRAEL[136]

As a condition for inheriting the Land of Israel, the Torah demands that all forms of idolatry be destroyed:

> You shall utterly destroy all the places where the nations whom you are driving out worship their gods.... You must tear down their altars, break up their sacred pillars, burn their Asheirah trees, and chop down the statues of their gods. You must obliterate their names from that place. (Deut. 12:2-3)

The Torah stresses that this obligation to destroy idolatrous artifacts is primarily binding in the Land of Israel. As the Sages commented,

> "You must obliterate their names from that place" –
> in the Land of Israel you are commanded to pursue idolatry [until it is totally eradicated], but not outside the Land. (*Sifri*; see Maimonides, Laws of Idolatry 7:2)

Idolatry is clearly the antithesis of Judaism's message of

---

[136] Adapted from *Orot HaKodesh* vol. II, pp. 423-424.

monotheism. The imperative to fight idolatry should not be limited to a particular location. So why does the Torah confine the eradication of idolatry to the Land of Israel?

Opposing Worldviews

The conflict between monotheism and idolatry is a contest between two fundamentally opposing worldviews. Idolatry sees the world as divided and fragmented, a place where competing gods/forces of nature clash and struggle with one another. In this bleak worldview, the material outweighs the spiritual, and life is reduced to the pursuit of physical wants.

Monotheism, on the other hand, teaches that the world has an underlying unity. As one's sense of the universe's inner harmony deepens, one's longing for the spiritual grows stronger. Higher aspirations take on greater significance; the world advances and is progressively enlightened.

The Land of Israel and Monotheism

The Sages wrote that "The air of the Land of Israel makes one wise" (*Baba Batra* 158b). *Eretz Yisrael* is bound to the spiritual life of Israel, the Torah; and the essence of the Torah's wisdom is the inner truth of a united reality. The special atmosphere of the Land of Israel instills greater awareness of the world's unified foundation. For this reason, obliteration of idolatry is especially important in the Land of Israel.

Outside the Land of Israel, the harmonious vision of a unified world cannot be fully revealed. There, a fragmented worldview reigns, emphasizing division and isolation. A grim sense of existential estrangement pervades all aspects of life. Any attempt to reveal the hidden unity of the world is hindered by the "impurity of the lands of the nations." The lands outside of Israel suffer from the foul odor of idolatry. The Sages wrote that Jews living outside the Land are "idol-worshippers in purity" (*Avodah Zarah* 8a). In other words, they are unintentionally influenced by the cultural environment of the foreign countries in which they live.

This distinction is also manifest in the difference between the Torah of *Eretz Yisrael* and the Torah of the exile. The Torah outside the Land excels in detailed arguments and the fine dialectics of *pilpul*. Its qualities reflect the general sense of divisiveness felt there.[137] The Torah of the Land of Israel, on the other hand, is illuminated by a lofty wisdom which connects the details to their governing moral principles. "There is no Torah like the Torah of the Land of Israel" (*Breishit Rabbah* 16:7).

Only by residing in the Land of Israel can one be truly free from the influence of idolatry. The Torah explicitly links living in the Land and monotheistic faith: "I took you out from the Land of Egypt in order to give you the Land of Canaan, to be your God" (Lev. 25:38).

---

[137] "R. Oshaia taught: '*No'am*' refers to the scholars of *Eretz Yisrael*, who treat each other graciously [*manimim*] when engaged in halachic debates. '*Chovlim*' refers to the scholars of Babylon, who attack [*mechablim*] each other when debating halachic issues" (*Sanhedrin* 24a).

RE'EIH: SEARCHING FOR THE TEMPLE SITE[138]

Surprisingly, the Torah never spells out exactly where the Temple is to be built. Rather we are instructed to build the *Beit HaMikdash* "in the place that God will choose":

> Only to the place that the Eternal your God will choose from all your tribes to set His Name – there you shall seek His dwelling place, and go there. (Deut. 12:5)

Where is this place "that God will choose"? What does it mean that we should "seek out His dwelling place"?

The Hidden Location

The Sages explained that the Torah is commanding us, under the guidance of a prophet, to discover where the *Beit HaMikdash* should be built. King David undertook the search for this holy site with the help of the prophet Samuel.

Why didn't the Torah explicitly state the location where to build the Temple? Moses certainly knew that the *Akeidah* took

[138] Adapted from *Shemu'ot HaRe'iyah* (*Beha'alotecha*), quoted in *Peninei HaRe'iyah*, pp. 273-274, 350-351; *Shemonah Kevatzim* I:745.

place on Mount Moriah in Jerusalem, and he knew that Abraham had prophesied that this would be the site of the *Beit HaMikdash*.[139]

Maimonides (*Guide to the Perplexed* III: 45) suggested that Moses wisely chose not to mention Jerusalem explicitly. Had he done so, the non-Jewish nations would have realized Jerusalem's paramount importance to the Jewish people and would have fought fiercely to prevent it from falling into Israel's hands.

Even worse, knowledge of Jerusalem's significance could have led to infighting among the tribes. Each tribe would want the *Beit HaMikdash* to be located in its territory. The result could have been an ugly conflict, similar to Korach's rebellion against Aaron's appointment to the position of High Priest. Maimonides reasoned that this is why the Torah commands that a king be appointed before building the *Beit HaMikdash*. This way the Temple's location would be determined by a strong central government, thus avoiding inter-tribal conflict and rivalry.

"Between His Shoulders"

In any case, David did not know where the *Beit HaMikdash* was to be built. According to the Talmud (*Zevachim* 54b), his initial choice fell on Ein Eitam, a spring located to the south of Jerusalem. Ein Eitam appeared to be an obvious choice since it is the highest point in the entire region. This corresponds to the Torah's

---

[139] After the *Akeidah*, "Abraham named that place, 'God will see'; as it is said to this day: 'On the mountain, God will be seen'" (Gen. 22:14). Rashi explains: "God will choose and see for Himself this place, to cause His Divine Presence to dwell there and for sacrifices to be offered here."

description that "You shall rise and *ascend* to the place that the Eternal your God will choose" (Deut.17:8).

However, David subsequently considered a second verse that alludes to the Temple's location. At the end of his life, Moses described the place of God's Divine Presence as "dwelling between his shoulders" (Deut. 33:12). What does this mean?

This allegory suggests that the Temple's location was not meant to be at the highest point, but a little below it, just as the shoulders are below the head. Accordingly, David decided that Jerusalem, located at a lower altitude than Ein Eitam, was the site where the *Beit HaMikdash* was meant to be built.

Doeg, head of the High Court, disagreed with David. He supported the original choice of Ein Eitam as the place to build the Temple. The Sages noted that Doeg's jealousy of David was due to the latter's success in discovering the Temple's true location.

The story of David's search for the site of the *Beit HaMikdash* is alluded to in one of David's "Songs of Ascent." Psalm 132 opens with a plea: "Remember David for all his trouble" (Ps. 132:1). What was this trying labor that David felt was a special merit, a significant life achievement for which he wanted to be remembered?

The psalm continues by recounting David's relentless efforts to locate the place of the Temple. David vowed:

> I will not enter the tent of my house, nor will I go up
> to the bed that was spread for me. I will not give sleep
> to my eyes, nor rest to my eyelids – until I find God's
> place, the dwellings of the Mighty One of Jacob. (Ps.

132: 3-5)

David and Doeg

What was the crux of the dispute between David and Doeg? Doeg reasoned that the most suitable site for the Temple is the highest point in Jerusalem, reflecting his belief that the spiritual greatness of the Temple should only be accessible to the select few, those who are able to truly grasp the purest levels of enlightenment – the *kohanim* and the spiritual elite.

David, on the other hand, understood that the Temple and its holiness need to be the inheritance of the entire people of Israel. The *kohanim* are not privy to special knowledge; they are merely agents who influence and uplift the people with the Temple's holiness. The entire nation of Israel is described as a "kingdom of priests" (Ex. 19:6).

The Waters of Ein Eitam

Even though Ein Eitam was never sanctified, it still retained a special connection to the *Beit HaMikdash*, as its springs supplied water for the *Beit HaMikdash*. The Talmud relates that on Yom Kippur, the High Priest would immerse himself in a *mikveh* on the roof of the *Beit HaParvah* chamber in the Temple complex. In order for the water to reach this roof, which was 23 cubits higher than the ground floor of the Temple courtyard, water was diverted from the Ein Eitam springs, which were also located at this altitude.

Rav Kook explained that there exists a special connection

between Ein Eitam and the High Priest's purification on Yom Kippur. While the *Beit HaMikdash* itself needs to be accessible to all, the purification of the High Priest must emanate from the highest possible source. Yom Kippur's unique purity and power of atonement originate in the loftiest realms, corresponding to the elevated springs of Ein Eitam.

SHOFTIM: THE HIGH COURT IN JERUSALEM[140]

The Jurisdiction of the Sanhedrin

What happens if a local court is unable to decide a case? In such situations, the Torah gives ultimate authority to the Sanhedrin, the High Court of 71 elders in Jerusalem:

> If you are unable to reach a decision in a case... then you should set out and ascend to the place that God will choose. You must approach the Levitical priest and the judge... and you must do as they tell you. You must keep the Torah as they interpret it for you, and follow the laws that they legislate for you. (Deut. 17:8-11)

In what areas did the High Court have jurisdiction? Was it only in legal/Halachic matters, or also in matters of faith?

In other words: does Judaism permit intellectual freedom in thought and beliefs, as long as one follows the codes of Halachic conduct? Or are there principles of faith which all must accept?

---

[140] Adapted from *Igrot HaRe'iyah* vol. I, pp. 123-124, letter 103 (*Tevet* 5668); *Orot*, pp. 89-90.

The Clarity of the Torah of *Eretz Yisrael*

The Babylonian and Jerusalem Talmuds appear to disagree over this issue. The Babylonian Talmud in *Sanhedrin* 87a states that the cases brought to the High Court were legal in nature. It explains that the term "*davar*" ("matter" or "case") mentioned in the verse refers to a Halachic dispute. The Jerusalem Talmud, on the other hand, holds that "*davar*" also includes Aggadah or non-legal disputes. What is the crux of this disagreement?

Rav Kook explained that this dispute is a result of the essential difference between the Torah of *Eretz Yisrael*, as represented by the Jerusalem Talmud, and the Torah from outside the Land of Israel, as represented by the Babylonian Talmud.

The different approaches of the two Talmuds originate in the limitation of prophecy to the Land of Israel.[141] The Torah of *Eretz Yisrael* benefits from prophetic influence, and this affects its style and fundamental nature.

Since the Torah of the Land of Israel is rooted in prophetic knowledge and insight, elaborate discussions are superfluous. The scholars of *Eretz Yisrael* arrive at legal decisions through an intuitive insight into the underlying principles. This explains the terse style of the Jerusalem Talmud, where subtle hints are often sufficient in order to reach the final Halachic decision.

The Babylonian Talmud, however, lacked this prophetic input. The Babylonian scholars engaged in intricate discussions, using complex legal reasoning to clarify the Halachah. Thus, unlike the expression commonly found in the Jerusalem Talmud, "*Ta chazi*" or "*Ta chami*" ("Come and see"), the Babylonian Talmud uses the

---

[141] See *Mo'ed Katan* 25a; *Kuzari* II:14.

expression *"Ta shema"* ("Come and hear"). *"Ta shema"* indicates a greater distance from the source, analogous to the difference between the clarity of that which is seen as opposed to that which is only heard.

Halachah and Aggadah

The difference between the two Talmuds is not limited to style. The author of *Chovot HaLevavot*[142] wrote in his introduction that matters of faith and belief, which are the foundations of Aggadic material, do not fall under the jurisdiction of the High Court. This, he explained, is because these teachings are not a matter of received traditions, but rather the fruit of our intellectual efforts.

This position, however, is not universal. Other scholars, such as Rav Hai Gaon,[143] held that also Aggadic teachings are binding.

The opinion of the *Chovot HaLevavot* is suitable to the Torah as it manifests itself outside the Land of Israel. There, without prophetic influence, beliefs are based solely on our powers of logic and reason. Since interpretation of Torah principles is a matter of intellectual effort, it is natural to distinguish between the detailed study of Halachah, which requires meticulous legal analysis, and the less rigorous study of Aggadah. For this reason the Babylonian Talmud distinguishes between Aggadah and Halachah, ruling that the prohibition of *"Lo Tasur"* (defying the rulings of the High Court) only applies to legal matters.

In *Eretz Yisrael*, however, where Torah is rooted in prophecy,

---

[142] Rabbi Bahya ibn Paquda, eleventh-century scholar and philosopher.
[143] The head of the Talmudic academy at Pumbedita in Babylonia (modern-day Iraq) (939-1038).

the legal and non-legal areas of Torah share a common foundation. Beliefs, just as much as practical deeds, are grounded in received tradition and prophetic inspiration. Therefore the Jerusalem Talmud rules that the High Court's authority also extends to Aggadah.

The *Kohen* and the Judge

This distinction allows us to understand the Torah's command, "You must approach the Levitical priest and the judge who will be at that time." Why mention both the *kohen* and the judge?

These two officials represent two forms of Torah authority. The *kohen* represents Torah that utilizes prophetic means in order to ascertain the Halachah. The *kohen's* Torah comes from his position as God's emissary: "From the *kohen's* lips they will guard knowledge... because he is an angel of the God of Hosts" (Malachi 2:7). This is particularly true of the High Priest, who required Divine inspiration in order to consult with the Urim and Thummim (*Yoma* 73).

The judge, on the other hand, represents Torah adjudicated according to logic and legal reasoning. By mentioning both the *kohen* and the judge, the Torah indicates that both approaches are valid, and both are binding. If the Torah had only mentioned the *kohen*, one might think that only Torah based on prophetic inspiration would retain this authority. And if the Torah had only mentioned the judge, one might have thought that there is no place for Divine inspiration in the Halachic process, as might be understood from the verse, "[The Torah] is not in Heaven" (Deut. 30:12).[144]

The Future Unity of Aggadah and Halachah

It is natural to differentiate between the expansive study of Aggadah and the technical mindset required for intricate Halachic analysis. In the depths of the soul, however, there lies an inner aspiration to unite these two areas.

With the illuminating light of the era of redemption, the differences between these two areas of Torah will become less clear-cut. The esoteric part of Torah will become more revealed, and the exoteric part of Torah will become more transcendent and closer to the mystical side. The Zohar expresses the special connection of the Torah of *Eretz Yisrael* to the Messianic Era by characterizing the Babylonian Talmud as the "*temurah*," the "substitute," while the Jerusalem Talmud is the "*geulah*" – the redemption itself (*Zohar Chadash*, Ruth).

---

[144] The Talmud in *Baba Metzia* 59b records a disagreement regarding the status of an oven made from coils of clay (*tanur akhnai*). Rabbi Eliezer supported his position with miracles and even a Heavenly Voice ("*Bat Kol*"). But the Sages still ruled against Rabbi Eliezer, insisting that decisions are reached by majority rule; miracles and Heavenly Voices are not part of the decision process, as "The Torah is not in Heaven."

SHOFTIM: THE WISDOM OF CIVIL LAW[145]

Three Types of Courts

The Torah commands that a system of courts and police be established in every town. The Torah's judicial system contains three levels of courts:

1. **Regular courts** of three judges who deal with matters of civil law – litigation and other monetary cases (in Hebrew, *dinei mamonot*).

2. **Higher courts** made up of 23 judges who hear cases relating to capital crimes (*dinei nefashot*). These courts were called "Minor Sanhedrins."

3. **A supreme court** consisting of 71 judges, called the "Great Sanhedrin." Located in the Temple complex in Jerusalem, this high court had two functions: (a) to clarify the law in new or unclear cases, and (b) to promulgate new decrees.

The Complexity of Civil Law

Acceptance to the bench of the Great Sanhedrin was certainly

---

[145] Adapted from *Ein Eyah* vol. II, p. 391.

most prestigious. All judges are required to be wise and humble, to love truth and hate bribery, to be well-liked and respected. Members of the Supreme Court were expected to be among the greatest scholars of the generation. They needed to be proficient in many of the sciences, such as medicine and astronomy.

We would similarly expect that membership in a Minor Sanhedrin court would demand a greater level of scholarship than participation in a humble three-member court. However, the Talmud indicates that cases of civil law require greater expertise and wisdom than the capital crimes that are judged in the Minor Sanhedrins.

> A student who has humbly accepted his teacher's rebuke on two occasions will be worthy to distinguish between civil law and laws of capital crimes.
>
> As Rabbi Ishmael taught: One who wishes to be wise should study civil law, for no other area of Torah study is as intricate; it is like a flowing wellspring. (*Berachot* 63b)

This Talmudic statement raises a number of questions. What sort of reward is this for a suffering student? And why is civil law more complex than other areas of Torah?

Civil versus Criminal Law

For some students, proficiency in their studies comes easily and quickly. Other students must struggle in order to master the material. The student who perseveres in his studies, despite blunders in class, will be compensated for his efforts. As a reward for his diligence and determination, he will not only grasp the particulars of the law, but will also gain insight into its underlying principles. This insight goes beyond the actual details, which are taught directly. It reflects a much more profound understanding of the subject matter.

Civil and capital crimes are both areas of law, yet they differ fundamentally in their objectives. The primary goal of civil law is to resolve monetary disputes between individuals and restore property to its rightful owner. It is only as a secondary goal that current or future benefits to society as a whole are taken into consideration. Capital crimes, on the other hand, are usually cases where there is nothing that can be rectified or returned. Here the primary goal is to protect society from future offenses.

Because of this fundamental difference, monetary law is intrinsically more complicated. Since the judge must decide between conflicting claims of ownership in all of the numerous situations of interpersonal relations, this type of law inherently deals with many more intricate details and complex issues. Study of civil law is therefore one of the most challenging areas of Torah study. True mastery of this subject requires a profound understanding of the underlying issues – an understanding that can be attained only by the most diligent and persevering students.

KI TEITZEI: WAGING WAR[146]

When you wage a war against your enemies, and God
will give you victory over them ... (Deut. 21:10)

War is perhaps the most tragic and horrific aspect of the human
condition. Our most fervent wish is for peace. Peace is the final
blessing of *Birkat Kohanim*. The closing statement of the Talmud
also extols the unsurpassed importance of peace: "The Holy One
found no vessel more capable of holding blessing for Israel than
peace" (*Oktzin* 3:12).

So why does Jewish law include such concepts as compulsory
and optional wars – *milchemet mitzvah* and *milchemet reshut*? Why do
we find that the greatest spiritual leaders of the Jewish people –
Abraham, Moses, Joshua, Samuel, King David, Rabbi Akiva – all
led their nation into battle?

In a letter penned in 1904, Rav Kook explained:

It would have been totally impossible, at a time when
all of the surrounding nations were truly wolves of the
night, that only the Jewish people would refrain from
waging war. The nations would have joined together
and destroyed the remnant of the people, God forbid.

---

[146] Adapted from *Igrot HaRe'iyah* vol. I, letter 89, p. 100; *Orot*, pp. 13, 15.

On the contrary, it was absolutely crucial to act without mercy in order to evoke fear in the wild savages.

We look forward to the day when the human race will advance to the state when war will become unnecessary. The Torah, however, does not attempt to proceed too quickly, before the world is ready.

> Nothing ruins the groundwork for perfecting human society as much as the influence of lofty ideas on masses who are not ready to accept them. Those who sought to advance humanity by imposing the Torah's ethical teachings before the world was ready for them completely misunderstood God's intention. The proof [that this approach is faulty] is apparent in the phenomenon of those who burnt their victims alive in auto-da-fé [during the Spanish Inquisition] under the banner of "Love your neighbor as yourself." This is because the Torah's lofty ideals require preparation. As the Sages cautioned: "The Torah is an elixir of life for those who follow it diligently... but the careless will stumble in it" (*Shabbat* 88b, based on Hosea 14:10).

The cruel conflicts that we witness are a result of ethical constraints that were artificially imposed upon the nations of the world. This created an unhealthy society suffering from severe distress. It induced destructive traits, mental imbalance, and deep-rooted anger. Festering resentment erupted into horrible acts of destruction and cruelty, with a brutal violence that exposed their still unrefined character.

Even for the Jewish people, regarding matters pertaining to the public and national arena, the Torah did not attempt to impose unrealistic saintliness. This would have led to an unnatural, forced piety. The Torah's objective is to establish an ethical awareness in the hearts of the people based on their own free will. That is why we find that the Torah is tolerant regarding certain war-related issues, such as the law allowing soldiers to take female captives (Deut. 21:10-14).

The Divine Purpose in War

Yet one may still ask: what is the purpose of war?

In his book *Orot*, Rav Kook sought to uncover God's purpose even in war. Great wars, he explained, have an important function in the world: they awaken yearnings for the Messianic Era. Solomon described the hour of redemption as "the time of the songbird (*zamir*)" (Song of Songs 2:12). It is a time to prune (*zamir*) and cut down the wicked.

But what about the many innocent lives lost in the destructive surge of violence? This phenomenon contains a measure of *mitat tzaddikim mechaperet*, a lofty atonement that comes from the death of the righteous. These souls elevate to the Source of life, and bring universal good and blessing to the world.

With the conclusion of a war, the world is renewed with a new spirit, and the footsteps of the Messianic Era can be heard. Thus the daily prayers make a connection between war and the light of redemption: "the Master of wars, Who sows kindness and brings forth salvation... You will shine a new light on Zion."

KI TEITZEI: AMALEK – CONSTRUCTIVE DESTRUCTION[147]

Remember what Amalek did to you on your way out of Egypt. When they encountered you on the way, and you were tired and exhausted, they cut off those lagging to your rear, and they did not fear God. Therefore... you must obliterate the memory of Amalek from under the heavens. (Deut. 25:17-8)

True Erasing

The Torah prohibits 39 categories of *melachah* – activities which are forbidden on the Sabbath. One is to erase writing. There are, however, different forms of erasing. Erasing merely to blot out what is written is a destructive act, and destructive acts are not forbidden on Shabbat by Torah law. *Melachah* is constructive activity, similar to God's creative acts when forming the universe.

So what form of erasing is prohibited on the Sabbath? *Mocheik al m'nat lichtov* – erasing with the intention of writing again. One's intention must be to clean the surface in order to write over the original letters. This type of erasing is a positive, constructive activity, and therefore is incompatible with the special rest of the

---

[147] Adapted from *Mo'adei HaRe'iyah,* pp. 241-242.

Sabbath day.

Restoring God's Name and Throne

Rav Kook explained that this principle may also be applied to the mitzvah of "erasing" Amalek. The mitzvah is not simply to obliterate Amalek so that there will no longer be any more Amalekites in the world. That would be a purely destructive act.

What then is the true mitzvah of destroying Amalek?

Amalek's goal was to eradicate the nation which bears God's Name in the world. Amalek could not tolerate the idea of a people with whom God made a special covenant, a people whose very existence implies ethical obligations and holy aspirations. The complete expression of the mitzvah to destroy Amalek is accomplished when we "erase in order to write." It is not enough to wage war against Amalek. The destruction of Amalek must have a productive goal. We must obliterate Amalek, and all that this evil nation represents, with the intention of "transforming the world into a kingdom of the Almighty."

As the Midrash explains:

> "God's Hand is raised on His throne: God shall be at war with Amalek for all generations." (Ex. 17:16)

> Why is the word for "throne" shortened, and even God's Name is abbreviated?[148] God swore that His

---

[148] The verse uses the word "כֵּס" instead of the more common word "כִּסֵּא" for "throne." And it uses the shorter, two-letter Name of God, as opposed to the regular four-letter Tetragrammaton.

Name and His Throne are not complete until
Amalek's name will be totally obliterated. (*Tanchuma
Ki Teitzei* 11; Rashi ad loc)

We are charged to replace Amalek with the holy letters of
God's complete Name. We must restore God's complete throne –
i.e., God's Presence in the world – through the special holiness of
the Jewish people, who transmit God's message to the world.

KI TAVO: TWO PATHS OF BIKKURIM[149]

Fresh and Dried Fruits

The mitzvah of bringing the first fruits (*Bikkurim*) to the Temple, the spiritual focal point of the nation, contains an important message for our own service of God. The *Bikkurim* offering demonstrates how each individual is able to connect his private activities – the fruits of his labors – to the nation's holiest aspirations.

The Mishnah explains how the first fruits were brought to the Temple:

> Those close to Jerusalem would bring fresh figs and grapes, while those further away would bring dried figs and raisins. (*Bikkurim* 3:3)

The Mishnah describes the *Bikkurim* offerings of two groups of people: those who lived near to Jerusalem and could bring fresh fruits; and those who lived further away, and had to be content with bringing an offering of dried fruit that could withstand the long journey.

---

[149] Adapted from *Ein Eyah* vol. II, p. 412.

Two Paths: Torah and Prophecy

These two situations – living in close proximity to Jerusalem and living some distance away – correspond to two spiritual paths the Jewish people have taken throughout history: the path of Torah and the path of prophecy, each with its own advantages and benefits.

The path of Torah is paved through the development of the Oral Law, as the nation applies Halachah to all aspects of life. The fruit of these legalistic efforts, however, may seem dry and uninspiring. This is particularly true when this path is compared to that of prophecy, which deals with Divine wisdom and lofty matters, and is closely connected to meditative prayer and the Torah's mystical teachings.

When the Jewish people lived in the Land of Israel and the *Shechinah* dwelled in their midst, their spiritual world centered primarily on prophetic enlightenment. We have been promised that the gift of prophecy will return to us – and on an even higher level – thus providing a lofty holiness that engages the heart and soul with knowledge of God. When we will be able to guard this gift, we will merit it once more – when we are back in our land, close to God's Presence, and protected from the misguided beliefs of foreign nations.

However, after we were banished from our beloved homeland, it became necessary to take the second path – a path capable of retaining its special character, despite exile and dispersion. This is the path of Torah, as the Sages wrote: "From the day the Temple was destroyed, the Holy One has only the four cubits of Halachah in His world" (*Berachot* 8a). The legal system of Halachah may appear to be dry and barren; but like the dried fruits of the *Bikkurim* offering, it contains hidden reserves of spiritual life and vitality. It is this path of Torah that preserved the Jewish people throughout the difficult challenges of a long and bitter exile.

Complementary Paths

The switch between the path of prophecy and the path of Torah took place during the Second Temple period, when prophecy ceased. In preparation for the exile that would follow, those spiritual forces of the nation that had previously focused on prophecy now concentrated their talents on the discipline of Halachah, developing and refining the study of Torah. These efforts enabled the Jewish people to survive as a separate nation in foreign lands, distinguished from other nations by an all-encompassing Halachic lifestyle.

These two paths are reflected in the paradigm of the *Bikkurim* offerings. Those close to the spiritual center prefer the delicious fresh fruits. However, the gifts from those living far away – dried figs and raisins that may appear to be shriveled and lifeless, but have the advantage of retaining their flavor despite the long journey – are also valued and beloved. Together, the two conduits of Torah and prophecy provide endurance and vitality for the nation's special service of God.

KI TAVO: THE FARMER'S DECLARATION[150]

Tax reporting in the Torah? In a way, yes....

Twice every seven years, in the fourth and seventh years of the Sabbatical cycle, the Jewish farmer must testify that he correctly distributed tithes from his crops. He makes the following declaration, preferably in the Temple itself:

> I have removed all the sacred portions from my house. I have given the appropriate ones to the Levite and to the orphan and widow.... I have not violated Your commandments, and have forgotten nothing. (Deut. 26:13)

What exactly is this declaration? The Mishnah explains as follows: "I have not violated Your commandments" – I have been punctilious in all the laws of *ma'aserot*, such as tithing each type of produce separately. "And have forgotten nothing" – this does not refer to forgetting the mitzvah, but its spiritual context: I did not forget to bless You and mention Your Name when tithing (*Ma'aser Sheini* 5:11).

What is special about tithing, that only this mitzvah requires such a declaration? Why must we testify that we were punctilious

---

[150] Adapted from *Ein Eyah* vol. II, pp. 406-407.

in all its minutiae, and remembered to praise God when distributing *ma'aser* to the Levite and the poor?

Meticulousness in Mitzvot

There are two aspects to every mitzvah. First, each mitzvah has its own unique function and purpose. In addition, all mitzvot are Divine commands, enabling us to connect to God. They elevate our emotions and character traits, as they resonate with the innermost soul.

How do we show that we are performing a mitzvah as a command from God? By carefully complying with all of its rules. Many mitzvot have a clear and obvious purpose. Were they simply a matter of good citizenship or societal obligations, we would perform them anyway – but without such meticulous observance. Punctilious attention to each detail demonstrates our awareness that we are fulfilling God's Will.

The mitzvah of tithing serves obvious purposes. Some of the produce goes to feeding the poor and needy (*ma'aser ani*), while the rest (*terumah* and *ma'aser rishon*) supports Torah study and Divine service by providing for the *kohanim* and Levites, the spiritual leaders of the nation. Especially with regard to mitzvot whose purpose seems obvious, it is important that we recognize that our intellectual powers cannot fully grasp all of their significance and beauty; nor can we truly appreciate the extent of their national and universal benefit throughout the generations.

For mitzvot with revealed reasons such as tithing, it is important to declare that we discharged them meticulously. We should look at mitzvot just as any other creation of God. The commandments have exact parameters, just as the laws of nature operate according to precise rules and processes.

The Privilege of Giving

Why is it so important that we praise God by reciting a blessing when performing the mitzvah of tithing?

An individual who supports others could mistakenly believe that he is the one providing assistance. He may harbor thoughts of his own greatness and importance, leading him to look down on those who receive his help. Such an attitude could undo any spiritual benefit gained from the charitable act. This danger is particularly serious with regard to the *kohanim*. It is not enough that the nation supports the *kohanim's* efforts to disseminate Torah. The *kohanim* and their spiritual activities need to be beloved and respected by the people. How sorry are those who measure success by the amount of glittering metal they manage to hoard!

In order to prevent this misconception – that those giving are superior to those receiving due to their greater financial means – the benefactors must truly understand that not only are they giving, they are also receiving an immense benefit. By supporting Torah study and the Temple service, they become partners in spiritual endeavors that uplift the entire world.

Therefore, they must not forget to bless God, and express their gratitude for the wonderful privilege to be part of this great enterprise.

KI TAVO: ACCEPT AND THEN ANALYZE[151]

How should we learn Torah – with an open heart, or with a critical eye?

Moses told the people, "Pay attention (הַסְכֵּת) and listen, Israel." (Deut. 27:9) Why does Torah use this unusual word, "הַסְכֵּת"?

One explanation proposed by the Talmud is that "הַסְכֵּת" is a composite word, formed from the words "הַס" ("be quiet," "hush") and "כַּתֵּת" ("to shatter"). When studying Torah, we should first be *quiet* and accepting, even if we fail to fully understand the reasoning. Only afterwards should we try to analyze and dissect what we have learned, raising whatever questions we have.

This follows the advice of Rava, the fourth-century Talmudic scholar, who counseled: "One should first study [Torah] and only afterwards scrutinize" (*Shabbat* 63b).

Why is it wrong to question and criticize from the outset?

Acquiring a Complete Picture

If we attempt to analyze a topic immediately after having learned it, the results of our inquiry will be of poor quality, reflecting superficial and incomplete knowledge. We must first gain an

---

[151] Adapted from *Ein Eyah* vol. II, p. 390.

overall understanding of the subject at hand and all relevant topics.

For this reason, the Sages advised that we train ourselves to listen carefully and acquire much knowledge before introducing our own opinions and views. If we have difficulty understanding certain matters, we should not be quick to criticize. Initially, we need the quiet patience of "הַס" to uncritically absorb the subject matter and the methodology of study.

After we have gained a complete picture of the subject, then we may participate in the intellectual battles of *milchamta shel Torah,* "the battle of Torah." Then we may "כַּתֵּת" – attack and critique that which we feel is illogical or unreasonable. But we should not be hasty to criticize before acquiring expertise in the subject. Tragic errors often result from rash students who were too quick to challenge and tear down.

Thus Rava taught, "First study, and afterwards scrutinize." We should first gain broad expertise before attempting to delve into in-depth investigations and suggest new interpretations. When Torah is initially approached with an open heart, the ensuing analysis with a critical eye will bring a blessing to all.

NITZAVIM: TESHUVAH FOR THE GENERATION OF REBIRTH[152]

For some time I have been struggling with an inner conflict, and a mighty force impels me to speak about *teshuvah* [penitence]. All my thoughts are focused on this topic. *Teshuvah* holds a primary place in Torah and in life. All the hopes of the individual and of society depend on it.

So begins Rav Kook's introduction to *Orot HaTeshuvah* ("Lights of Penitence"), perhaps his most popular work, first published in 1925. The compact book was beloved by its author, and Rav Kook himself would study its teachings during the month of Elul after morning prayers. One student reported hearing Rav Kook say: "I worked extensively on *Orot HaTeshuvah*. Whoever studies it properly will find light in every word." He also declared: "*Orot HaTeshuvah* should be studied endlessly."

What is so special about the book's outlook on *teshuvah*?

---

[152] Adapted from *Mo'adei HaRe'iyah*, pp. 52, 55. *Celebration of the Soul*, pp. 26, 28-29.

Teshuvah – Returning to Life

Orot HaTeshuvah illuminates the concepts of sin, punishment, and penitence. It explains that sin primarily harms the one who sinned, as it cuts him off from the roots of his very being, from the light of his soul. This estrangement is sin's worst punishment. *Teshuvah*, on the other hand, redeems the sinner from this darkness. It rejuvenates him, restoring his previous state of life and joy.

The word *teshuvah* literally means "return." It is not an escape from the world. On the contrary, it is "precisely through genuine, pure *teshuvah* that we return to the world and to life" (*Orot HaTeshuvah* 14:30).

Already in his introduction, Rav Kook described *teshuvah* as an underlying force that influences all aspects of life, not only the realm of the sacred: "*Teshuvah* holds a primary place in Torah and in life." Thus one who frees himself from unhealthy habits – this is also a type of *teshuvah*.

Additionally, Rav Kook posited that this powerful force is not limited to the failings and triumphs of the individual. It also applies to failures and successes of the nation and the entire universe: "All hopes of the individual and society as a whole depend on it."

National and Spiritual Revival

Rav Kook firmly believed that a secular national revival, the entire program of rebuilding the Land and the nation, could not succeed without a parallel revival in holiness, with lofty manifestations of this holiness expressed in both personal and public spheres.

But what path would lead the generation of rebirth to the gates of *teshuvah*? The routine approach is doomed to failure. One cannot reach out to the idealistic youth of such a generation, brimming with life, vigor, and creativity, with a severe demeanor and punctilious demands of small, everyday deeds – demands that they consider to be a sign of weakness and a feeble spirit.

No, the generation must be awakened via an optimistic spirit of greatness and courage. "*Teshuvah* comes not to embitter life," Rav Kook taught, "but to make it pleasant" (ibid. 15:6). "*Teshuvah* is essentially a return to [our] origins, to the source of supernal life and existence in their wholeness" (ibid. 12:8).

In an article printed in *HaYesod* in 1934, he explained:

> *Teshuvah* is the great key to redemption. Many things inhibit *teshuvah*, but the major obstacle, particularly to collective *teshuvah*, is the misconception of *teshuvah* as atrophy of the soul, as the enfeebling and debilitation of life. This false image also impairs the *teshuvah* of the individual. But more than anything, it hinders collective *teshuvah*, the *teshuvah* of the nation.

> We must disclose the secret that the genuine *teshuvah* of the entire nation of Israel is a mighty, powerful vision that provides reserves of might and strength, imbuing all of our spiritual and pragmatic values with a lofty spirit of vigorous, surging creative energy from the power of the Rock of Israel. This living *teshuvah* flows not from isolated, fragmented souls, but from the treasury of the nation's collective soul, *Knesset*

Yisrael.... In this way, the united soul of Israel is prepared to return to its former strength, as in days of old.

HA'AZINU: THE DIVERSITY OF ISRAEL[153]

An anecdote relates how a certain Jew was stranded for many years on a deserted island. When he was finally rescued, he boasted of his many accomplishments on the island, including the construction of two synagogues.

"Very impressive," responded his rescuers. "But why two synagogues?"

"This is the synagogue that I attend," explained the man, pointing at one structure. "The other one is the synagogue I refuse to step foot in."

The joke would not be humorous if it did not contain a kernel of truth. The Jewish people often seem to be 'blessed' with an overabundance of infighting. Why is there so much division and conflict?

The Borders of the Nations

The song of *Ha'azinu* compares the heritage of Israel to that of the other nations of the world:

> When the Most High gave the nations their inheritance... He set up the borders of the nations,

---

[153] Adapted from *Orot* p. 169, paragraph 6; *Midbar Shur*, pp. 110-115.

corresponding to the number of Israel's children.
(Deut. 32:8)

What are these "borders of the nations"? And in what way do
they correspond to the "number" of Jewish people?

Every nation is blessed with unique national traits. Each nation
possesses special talents and makes a unique contribution to the
world. This specialty may lie in the arts, sciences, organizational
ability, and so on. The verse refers to these areas of specialization
as "borders."

All of the talents that can be found among the nations of the
world also exist in the "number"– that is, in the diversity – of the
Jewish people. Historically, we have seen that Jews were always at
the forefront of a remarkably diverse range of professions and
disciplines.

Seventy Souls

The Midrash describes the diversity of Israel by comparing the
size of Jacob's family who went down to Egypt – seventy souls –
with the seventy nations of the world. This number represents the
seventy archetypical souls, each with its own unique characteristics
and talents. When God commanded Moses to organize leaders to
govern the people, He told Moses to gather seventy elders (Num.
11:16). With these leaders, Moses brought together the people's
diverse range of outlooks and natural gifts.

The multi-talented diversity of the Jewish people, however, has
a downside; it makes them more prone to internal friction and
conflict. Each talent strives to express itself fully, often at the

expense of other talents. The Sages noted that "The greater the person, greater his evil inclination" (*Sukkah* 52a). This insight is true not only for the individual, but also for the nation. When a nation is blessed with great talents, it has a greater potential for internal strife.

The Floating Palace

The Midrash uses a striking image as a metaphor for the Jewish people. It compares the nation to a palace constructed on top of many boats. As long as the boats are tied together, the Midrash notes, the palace will remain secure.

It is natural for each boat to try to make its own separate way in the sea. It is only the palace on top that keeps the fleet of boats together and ensures that they sail together in the same direction.

What is this palace? It is the force that guards against internal strife and unifies the Jewish people – the Torah itself. In its highest state, the Torah encompasses all areas of knowledge. The seventy elders, representing the full range of souls, gathered together to unite the people under one flag, "to perfect the world under the reign of God" (from the *Aleinu* prayer).

Diverse disciplines are harmoniously united when they can emphasize their contribution to the common good, as developed and refined under the guidance of the Torah. Then the diversity of the Jewish people becomes a blessing, as the nation is united via the root of its inner being – the Torah.

VEZOT HABERACHAH: A TORAH OF FIRE[154]

God came from Sinai... He brought them a Law of
fire from His right hand. (Deut. 33:2)

Why did Moses, in his final blessing before his death, refer to
the Torah as "*Eish Dat,*" a "Law of fire"? And what does it mean
that the Torah came from God's "right hand"?

The Spiritual Realm

The right hand is ordinarily the stronger one. The metaphor of
God using "His right hand" to transmit the Torah is meant to
indicate that the true power and foundation of the universe lies,
not in the physical world, but in its spiritual side. While the
relative importance of the spiritual reality may appear
counterintuitive, this may be better understood when one
considers, by way of analogy, the relative strength of human
intellect and spirit over brute physical force. (For example, a
human being is capable of capturing a beast far more powerful
than him.) The Torah is rooted in the more powerful realm of the
spiritual – God's "right hand."

---

[154] Adapted from *Ein Eyah* vol. II, pp. 347, 335.

The Clarity of Moses' Prophecy

In addition, these poetic metaphors of *Eish Dat* and God's "right hand" are meant to convey the unique clarity of Moses' prophecy. The Sages wrote that Moses' prophetic visions were more precise than those of any other prophet. Moses saw through an *aspaklaria me'irah*, a "clear lens."

Prophecy is ordinarily attained through a combination of the faculties of intellect and imagination. In addition to intellectual insight, prophets need images in order to properly grasp and later transmit their prophetic messages.

Moses' prophecy, on the other hand, was based solely on intellect. His prophecy was perceived through a "clear lens," without the murky vision of the imagination (*Guide to the Perplexed* II: 36). For this reason, the Torah of Moses is called *Eish Dat*, a "Law of fire." His prophecy came from pure intellect, like a blazing fire that purges all impurities.

Ezekiel described his prophetic experience as "God's hand was upon me" (37:1). Unlike Moses, Ezekiel did not speak of the *right* hand. In fact, he specifically meant the *left* hand. Ezekiel needed to utilize his powers of imagination – the feebler, less distinct left side – in order to understand his visions.

The Torah of Moses, on the other hand, was based on the more powerful right side. It flowed solely from the strength and clarity of Moses' cognitive powers. This unique Torah was thus a "Law of fire from His right hand."

BIBLIOGRAPHY

Ein Ayah – commentary on Talmudic Midrashim, arranged according to the book *Ein Ya'akov*. Rav Kook began writing on tractate *Berachot* while serving as rabbi in Zaumel. He wanted to publish *Ein Ayah* while in Jaffa in 1906, but he lacked sufficient funds for the undertaking. He continued to add material over the years, penning his final entry (two-thirds the way through tractate *Shabbat*) in Jerusalem in 1934 (he passed away the following year). As in his other early work, *Midbar Shur* (which was similarly delayed before being printed), this commentary reflected his fervent belief that our generation needs to deepen its understanding of the Torah's philosophical principles. Rav Tzvi Yehudah Kook made use of some of these commentaries in *Olat Re'iyah*. Published by HaMachon al shem HaRav Tzvi Yehudah Kook (Jerusalem 1995).

Igrot HaRe'iyah – three-volume collection of letters written by Rav Kook between the years 1886 and 1919. First published in 1923. Published by Mossad HaRav Kook, Jerusalem, 1962. A fourth volume for the years 1920–1925 was published by HaMachon al shem HaRav Tzvi Yehudah Kook (Jerusalem 1984).

Midbar Shur – sermons written by Rav Kook while serving as rabbi in Zaumel and Boisk in 1894–1896. One of Rav Kook's first writings, but mysteriously lost. Finally printed by HaMachon al shem HaRav Tzvi Yehudah Kook (Jerusalem 1999).

Mo'adei HaRe'iyah – a blend of stories and writings of Rav Kook about the holidays by Rabbi Moshe Tzvi Neriah. Published by Moriah (Jerusalem 1982).

Mussar Avicha – ethical tract on awe of Heaven and Divine service. First printed by Rabbi Tzvi Yehudah Kook in 1946, but it was written some fifty years previous. Published by Mossad HaRav Kook (Jerusalem 1979).

Olat Re'iyah – two-volume commentary on the prayer book. Rav Kook began this project while in London during WWI, and continued after his return to Jerusalem. However, he only wrote as far as midway through the introductory psalms (*Pesukei deZimra*) of the morning prayers. Rabbi Tzvi Yehudah Kook completed the work by collecting appropriate texts from various unpublished writings, and printed it in 1939, several years after his father's death. Published by Mossad HaRav Kook (Jerusalem 1983).

Orot – collection of essays, many analyzing Israel's national rebirth. The book was arranged by Rabbi Tzvi Yehudah Kook, and first published in 1920. Despite rabbinical controversy concerning certain passages in the book, Rabbi Tzvi Yehudah taught that this work is, in comparison to Rav Kook's other writings, his "Holy of Holies." Published by Mossad HaRav Kook (Jerusalem 1982).

Orot HaKodesh – expositions on Divine service, prophecy, the spiritual experience, etc., collected and organized from Rav Kook's diaries (see below, *Shemonah Kevatzim*) by his student, Rabbi David Cohen (known as "the Nazir"). The Nazir spent twelve years preparing the four-volume work, considered by many to be Rav Kook's magnum opus. Published by Mossad HaRav Kook (Jerusalem 1985).

Otzerot HaRe'iyah – five volumes of writings collected from various sources, together with a number of indexes and summaries of Rav Kook's writings, by Rabbi Moshe Yechiel Tzuriel. Published by Yeshivat HaHesder Rishon LeTzion (2002).

Shemuot HaRe'iyah – based on Rav Kook's *Se'udah Shelishit* (third Sabbath meal) discourses in Jerusalem, which weaved together Halachah, Midrash, Jewish philosophy, and Kabbalah. After the Sabbath, Rabbi Kalman Eliezer Frankel would write down from memory summary notes of these long, intricate discourses. Edited and arranged by Rabbi H. Yeshayau Hadari, some were printed by the Dept. of Torah Education and Culture in the Diaspora (Jerusalem 1994).

Shemonah Kevatzim – the "eight notebooks," Rav Kook's spiritual diaries, from 1904, when he became rabbi of Jaffa, until his return to Jerusalem in 1919 after being trapped in Switzerland and England during the First World War. These eight volumes served as the raw material from which *Orot HaKodesh* was compiled (as well as much of *Orot*, *Orot HaTeshuvah* from chapter 4, and *Orot HaTorah*). Published in Jerusalem, 2004.

GLOSSARY OF HEBREW TERMS

Aggadah – non-legal, homiletic Talmudic texts.

Avot – the Patriarchs (Abraham, Isaac, and Jacob).

Akeidah – the Binding of Isaac.

Beit HaMikdash – the Temple in Jerusalem.

brachah (pl. *berachot*) – blessing

brit milah – the mitzvah of circumcision.

Eretz Yisrael – the Land of Israel.

Halachah – Jewish law.

kohen (pl. *kohanim*) – a priest, descended from Aaron.

korban (pl. *korbanot*) – Temple offerings.

Matan Torah – the Revelation of the Torah at Sinai.

mikveh – ritual bath.

mitzvah (pl. *mitzvot*) – commandments of the Torah.

parashah – section of the Torah read in Sabbath service.

Shechinah – God's Divine Presence in the world.

Shema – declaration of faith in one God, from Deut. chapter 6.

tzaddik (pl. *tzaddikim*) – a righteous, pious individual.

tzedakah – charity

RABBI ABRAHAM ISAAC KOOK (1865-1935)

The celebrated first Chief Rabbi of pre-state Israel, Rav Kook is recognized as being among the most important Jewish thinkers of all times. His writings reflect the mystic's search for underlying unity in all aspects of life and the world, and his unique personality similarly united a rare combination of talents and gifts. Rav Kook was a prominent rabbinical authority and active public leader, but at the same time, a deeply religious mystic. He was both Talmudic scholar and poet, original thinker and saintly tzaddik.

RABBI CHANAN MORRISON

Rabbi Morrison graduated with a B.A. in Mathematics from Yeshiva University (New York). He studied for several years at Yeshivat Mercaz HaRav, the Jerusalem yeshiva founded by Rav Kook in 1924. He was ordained after completing rabbinical studies in the Ohr Torah Stone (Efrat) and Midrash Sephardi (Jerusalem) rabbinical seminaries. Rabbi Morrison taught Jewish studies for several years in Harrisburg, PA, before returning to Israel.

Rabbi Morrison is frequently featured on the Torah section of the Israel National News website, and his work can be read on his own website at http://ravkooktorah.org. He has published two books on the writings of Rav Kook: *Gold from the Land of Israel* (Urim, 2006), and *Silver from the Land of Israel* (Urim, 2010).

Praise for *Gold from the Land of Israel*

In these succinct and clearly-written essays, Rabbi Morrison has succeeded in expounding on major themes from Rav Kook's thought. Those who are not familiar with the Rav's teachings will be exposed to the profound ideas and remarkable scope of his writings.
–Rabbi Yehoshua Magnes, Rosh Yeshiva, Mercaz HaRav

Rabbi Morrison has done a remarkable job presenting Rav Kook's teachings in a clear, approachable fashion. I highly recommend this book for anyone seeking a good introduction to the inspiring wisdom of this preeminent scholar.
–Rabbi David Samson